Integrating Work and Family

CHALLENGES AND CHOICES
FOR A CHANGING WORLD

EDITED BY
Saroj Parasuraman and
Jeffrey H. Greenhaus

QUORUM BOOKS
Westport, Connecticut • London

Library of Congress Cataloging-in-Publication Data

Integrating work and family : challenges and choices for a changing
  world / edited by Saroj Parasuraman and Jeffrey H. Greenhaus.
      p.   cm.
    Includes bibliographical references and index.
    ISBN 1–56720–038–9 (alk. paper)
    1. Work and family.   I. Parasuraman, Saroj.   II. Greenhaus,
  Jeffrey H.
    HD4904.25.I58   1997
    646.7'8—dc20   96–43932

British Library Cataloguing in Publication Data is available.

Library of Congress Catalog Card Number: 96–43932
ISBN: 1–56720–038–9

First published in 1997

Quorum Books, 88 Post Road West, Westport, CT 06881
An imprint of Greenwood Publishing Group, Inc.

Printed in the United States of America

The paper used in this book complies with the
Permanent Paper Standard issued by the National
Information Standards Organization (Z39.48–1984).

10 9 8 7 6 5 4 3

Contents

Figures and Tables

Preface

Researchers and practitioners in a variety of social science disciplines have become vitally concerned about the widespread experience of work-family problems by men and women in contemporary society. The pervasiveness and complexity of work-family conflict have contributed to the emergence of work-family concerns as a prominent social issue of the 1990's. In response to these concerns, a wide array of new human resource specialties has emerged, such as work/family and diversity consultants, direct service providers, and service brokers in what has come to be known as the "Work/Life" field. Yet there is limited dialog among these groups of people and constituencies interested in gaining a better understanding about the issues involved. There is also little critical appraisal of what solutions work, what solutions don't work, and why.

The publication of this book is the culmination of our long-standing desire to foster informed dialog and debate among the various constituencies that share an interest in, or have responsibility for implementing, well-thought-out and enduring solutions to the work/life dilemmas of employees, families, and employers. The decision to bring out this volume was inspired by the enormous success of the Fifth International Stein Conference on "Work, Family, and Community in the 21st Century: Issues, Challenges, and Agenda for Change," sponsored by the Louis and Bessie Stein Foundation and held in Philadelphia in November 1994. Organized by the College of Business and Administration at Drexel University, the conference featured leaders from government and industry, as well as work-family experts and researchers from universities and think tanks, who are in the vanguard of research and practice on work-family issues.

The favorable reactions to the conference as a whole, the enthusiasm and energy generated by the presentations, and our desire to continue the dialog by sharing with a broader audience varied perspectives on work-family issues prompted us to prepare this book. *Integrating Work and Family: Challenges and Choices for a Changing World* addresses the challenges of achieving work-family balance in the context of the ongoing transformation of the world of work and family. Of the 21 chapters in the book, slightly over half are substantially revised versions of the initial presentation made at the 1994 Stein Conference. They were revised extensively to expand both the theoretical and empirical underpinnings of the chapter. We also expanded the coverage of topics by adding several new chapters to provide a more complete treatment of some issues (e.g., work-family issues from an international perspective), and/or add a perspective not included in the conference program (e.g., ethnically and culturally diverse workforces).

The book is aimed at three audiences. The first group to whom this book is directed includes educators and researchers in management, organizational behavior, women's studies, and the sociology of work who are interested in gaining additional insights into work-family issues. Individuals involved in teaching courses on careers, women and men in management, diversity, organizational change, family studies, and work and organizations of the future should find the book useful as a specialty text. A second major audience for the book is consulting psychologists and social workers interested in helping their clients understand and manage work-family concerns more effectively. The third group includes human resource professionals and executives in public and private sector organizations, training and development personnel, work-family and diversity consultants, and other decision makers responsible for crafting or implementing policies and programs designed to promote work-family integration. This audience also includes women and men in business and other organizations who are interested in enhancing their own understanding of work-family issues in order to achieve a better balance between work and family, and to facilitate more effective management of the work-family concerns of their subordinates.

ACKNOWLEDGMENTS

This book has come to fruition with the support, encouragement, tangible help, and facilitation of a number of people at various stages of the project. We would like to express our deep appreciation and sincere thanks to these individuals for the many different ways in which they contributed to the preparation of *Integrating Work and Family*. Since the idea of publishing this book originated at the 1994 Stein Conference, we would first like to thank Dr. Kenneth N. Geller, Assistant Vice President and Director, Office of University Resources and Services (OURS) at Drexel University, for departing from tradition and selecting work, family, and community as the theme for the 1994 Stein Conference, and for asking us to cochair the event and organize the conference. We are grateful to the Louis and Bessie Stein Foundation for sponsoring and providing financial support for the conference. We would also like to express our appreciation for the enthusiastic presence of members of the Stein family. Very special thanks go to Marie Schebb and Kim Keegan of OURS for their excellent administrative support and facilitation of communications with participants before, during, and after the conference.

The supportiveness and encouragement of Arthur H. Baer, former Dean of the College of Business and Administration at Drexel, are acknowledged with sincere thanks. We also acknowledge the ongoing support of Dr. Milton Silver and Dr. Bay Arinze, former and current heads of the Management Department, respectively. Several graduate students gave generously of their time and energy to activities related to the conference and the preparation of the book. We are appreciative of the contributions of Rita Bernert, Ken Jacobs, Mark Kramer, and Yasmin Purohit in tape-recording the presentations at the conference. We thank Lisa DiStefano, Barrie Litzky, June Morris, and Romila Singh for taking on the arduous task of transcribing the tapes into hard copy. Thanks also go to David Yost, Assistant Director of Nesbitt College's Design and Imaging Studio at Drexel University, for his outstanding assistance in preparing some of the graphics. We would like to give a special vote of thanks and our sincere appreciation to Shanna Weaver for her expertise in converting the final version of the chapters into a common format and word-processing style. Her sense of responsibility, attention to detail, and cheerful attitude made it a pleasure to work with her.

We would finally like to express our deep appreciation to the many experts who have contributed chapters to this volume. Their cooperation and responsiveness to our comments and suggestions greatly facilitated the editorial process and the timely completion of the finished manuscript. We hope that readers will find *Integrating Work and Family* to be informative, helpful, and provocative.

PART I

Issues and Challenges in Managing Work-Family Linkages

CHAPTER 1

The Changing World of Work and Family

*Saroj Parasuraman
and Jeffrey H. Greenhaus*

The closing decades of the 20th century have witnessed unprecedented changes in work and family—the two preeminent arenas in which men and women in contemporary society play out their lives and seek to satisfy important human needs. The unfolding changes in the composition of the workforce together with the growing proportion of workers in nontraditional family forms have focused heightened attention on the conflicts faced by employed men and women in balancing the competing demands and responsibilities of work and family roles. In a recent study of the changing workforce, the Families and Work Institute reported that work-life balance was ranked among the most important factors considered by individuals in accepting a new position.[1] Indeed the growing concern about work-family problems and their adverse consequences for employees, families, and employers have led to the emergence of work-family integration as a prominent social issue of the 1990's.[2]

This chapter provides an overview of the major economic, legal, and social forces impacting employees, families, employers, and the interrelationships among them as a backdrop for the examination of the conflicts and challenges faced by men and women in pursuing productive careers in conjunction with satisfying family lives. We then examine current approaches to managing work-family needs of employees, and review critically the use and effectiveness of various corporate initiatives and "family-friendly" programs designed to support men and women in their efforts to integrate work and family roles. The chapter concludes with a description of the purpose and scope of the book.

NATURE OF THE WORK-FAMILY PROBLEM

The problem of balancing work and family arises from work-family conflict, which reflects a mutual incompatibility between the demands of the work role and the demands of the family role. The most prevalent type or form of work-family conflict occurs when the *time* demands of one role make it difficult or impossible to participate fully in the other. Schedule conflicts and work-role overload are examples of this form of work-family conflict. Work-family conflict may also involve some form of interference between one role and another. This may occur when symptoms of psychological *strain* (e.g., anxiety, fatigue, irritability) generated by the demands of the work or family role intrude or "spill over" into the other role, making it difficult to fulfill the responsibilities of that role. A third type of work-family conflict arises when the *behaviors* that are expected or appropriate in the family role (expressiveness, emotional sensitivity) are inappropriate or dysfunctional when used in the work role.[3]

These types of work-family conflict can produce difficulties for employees and their families, for employers, and for society as a whole. Excessive interference of work with family can have adverse effects on individuals' marital relationships and quality of family life. Chronic interference of family with work responsibilities can jeopardize employees' career progress, and thereby reduce their satisfaction with their work lives. From an employer's perspective, severe work-family conflicts can interfere with employees' concentration on their jobs, increase absenteeism, and in extreme cases, lead to voluntary turnover.[4] Thus, the widespread experience of work-family conflict creates multiple problems that affect different stakeholders in different ways.

WHOSE PROBLEM IS IT?

This is not just a rhetorical question. One's beliefs about who "owns" the problem are likely to influence one's attributions or beliefs about who has, or should bear, responsibility for helping individuals and families manage work-family conflict. This in turn is a function of the lens through which one is looking at the "problem." It can be argued that the decision to pursue a career and also have a family is based on individual choice. Hence, the conflict is viewed as the outcome of the employee's inability to handle multiple roles and prevent his or her family life from intruding into the work role. Therefore, the responsibility for managing the tensions arising at the intersection of work and family is thought to lie with the individual and his or her family.

This line of reasoning is consistent with the dominant cultural values of individualism and minimal employer or governmental intrusion into individuals' private lives. However, it fails to recognize the reality that most people (including women) work out of economic necessity, to support themselves and their children and other dependents.[5] Therefore, not seeking employment is not a viable option for men or women. Family-role demands do not diminish materially for employed women, who generally shoulder the lion's share of the responsibility for home maintenance and child rearing. Yet single-earner men typically have pursued active and productive careers together with marriage and children without extensive conflict, a situation made possible by the gendered division of roles and the (unpaid) services of nonemployed wives. The application of the individual responsibility argument in this situation would lead to the conclusion that work-family problems belong primarily to married women with children, who therefore have to choose between a career and a family—a very heavy price to pay for nearly half of the total U.S. workforce. Although clearly indefensible from legal, political, ethical, and human perspectives, such a conclusion is unwarranted from a pragmatic point of view as well. Business, industry, and the economy as a whole would collapse if women with children were to withdraw from the workforce. Moreover, the argument suggests the need for women to make trade-offs with regard to work and family that men have not had to make.

Neither perspective described here is really tenable given the new realities of work and family. The decline in the proportion of households with full-time homemakers and the increasing proportion of workers with responsibilities for family care as well as their jobs indicate a heightened potential for employed women *and* men to experience work-family conflicts and related problems in balancing the responsibilities of work and family roles. Due to the time pressures and role overload experienced by women in dual-earner relationships, their partners are facing increased pressures to assume a larger share of the responsibilities for home maintenance and child rearing.

Recent research indicates that substantial numbers of men are vulnerable to experiencing conflict arising from the intersection of work and family roles. The findings of the National Study of the Changing Workforce by the Families and Work Institute revealed that 40% of employed parents experienced work-family conflict at least some of the time; 38% of employed mothers and 19% of employed fathers reported feeling nervous and stressed often or very often within a three-month period.[6] In a large survey of working adults conducted by the *New York Times*, 83% of working mothers and 72% of working fathers reported that they experienced conflict between the demands of their jobs and the desire to see more of their families.[7] These findings indicate that both women and men are troubled by the conflicting demands of their work and family roles, and seek to achieve a better balance between them.

The work-family problems experienced by employees, if not managed effectively, can adversely affect their quality of work life, family satisfaction, and the quality of life overall. Clearly, employers and the larger community are also affected by these problems. Thus, all of these constituents have a stake in their solution. The responsibility for developing and implementing effective ways of managing work-family conflicts is therefore a shared one. We now turn to an examination of the environmental factors that have contributed to the prevalence and complexity of work-family problems experienced by an increasingly diverse workforce.

ENVIRONMENTAL INFLUENCES ON WORK AND FAMILY

The workforce of today is radically different from that of 20 years ago due to changes affecting both the supply and demand sides of labor. The single most important change is the phenomenal increase in women's workforce participation, especially that of married women with children. Spurred initially by equal employment opportunity legislation, affirmative action, and the women's movement, the growth in women's workforce participation has been sustained by increased education, their desire for personal fulfillment, economic necessity, the high cost of living, and the high rate of divorce.[8]

As new forms of family structure have emerged, the traditional single-earner family consisting of a breadwinner husband, a homemaker wife, and children has declined to minority status and now describes only 10% of working households. In contrast, the proportion of families with no adult at home to provide care and child rearing has grown by leaps and bounds. Dual-earner families (the modal family form) and single-parent households are rapidly increasing. Increased immigration of Asians and other ethnic and culturally diverse minorities, has also contributed to the radical change in the demographic profile of the workforce. The most significant changes and trends in terms of their implications for work-family issues are highlighted here.

- Between 1970 and 1994, women's workforce participation increased twice as fast as that of men.
- Women comprised 46% of the total workforce in 1994, up from 38% in 1970.
- Of mothers with children under age 6, 62% are employed.
- Of mothers with children age 6–17, 75% are employed.
- Nearly half (40%) of all workers are members of dual-earner families.
- Single-parent families comprise 23% of the workforce and are the fastest growing segment.
- Women, people of color, and immigrants are projected to comprise 75% of the net additions to the workforce by the year 2000.[9]
- An estimated 15% of adult men and women bear responsibility for the care of aging parents or other elderly relatives, and the proportion is increasing.[10]

These changes in the demographic characteristics and lifestyles of the workforce are occurring at a time when businesses are also in a state of flux. Global competitive pressures have forced many companies to downsize their workforce and streamline their operations. Workforce reductions and the large-scale elimination of jobs have increased the workload of the survivors, while the reduction in the number of levels of management has reduced opportunities for advancement. Competitive pressures have also directed the attention of employers outwardly toward their markets, prompting them to be more responsive to customer needs and provide timely, high-quality service. The emphasis on superior customer service and satisfaction, together with reduced staffing levels, has created additional work-role pressures for employees. The increased use of telecommunications technology in business—fax machines, voice mail, cellular phones, computers, and computer networks—has further eroded the boundaries between work and other life roles, and made it possible for employees to be accessible to their employers across time and space. At the same time, the trend toward greater use of contingent workers has generated career uncertainties, fear of layoffs, and stress. Consequently, the psychological contract between employees and employers has been broken.

Thus, we have witnessed in recent years a collision course between employees, who are subject to increasing work-family pressures, and employers, who are preoccupied with profitability and survival in a highly competitive world. Both employees and employers are feeling the stress.

KEY ISSUES

What are the implications of these changes for work-family relationships? What are the specific issues for which employees need support and assistance?

Child and Elder Care

The analysis of changes in the demographic characteristics and family structure of the workforce reveals that a majority of families do not have a full-time parent or care provider in the home. The large proportion of employed mothers with preschool children, dual-earner couples, and single-parent families has created a huge demand for child care facilities and services. Employed parents with children make use of a variety of arrangements for the care of preschool and older children while they are at work. The finding that women who worked in companies with employer supports for child care were more likely to return to their jobs after childbirth demonstrates the benefits of such support for both employees and employers.[11]

In addition to the quality and affordability of the care provided, a central concern is the dependability of the child care arrangements. A recent study shows that despite backup arrangements, nearly one-third of the parents reported breakdowns in the child care arrangements over a three-month period. Parents who encounter fewer breakdowns in their child care arrangements experience less stress, cope more effectively, and tend to be more satisfied with their life in general. The study also reported that employed mothers miss an average of four days a year to deal with child-related concerns, such as caring for a sick child.[12] The difficulties experienced by employees in finding dependable and quality child care at an affordable cost have generated intense pressures on employers to support employees' needs in caring for their children and other dependents.

Employees' needs for family support include, not only the availability of adequate child care at affordable rates, but also assistance in caring for elderly parents or relatives. Currently, an estimated 15% of adult men and women bear responsibility for the care of aging parents or other elderly relatives.[13] The demands on employees for adult dependent care are expected to increase significantly with the impending growth in the population of elderly Americans.

Parental and Family Leave

The demands and pressures of the family role sometimes necessitate taking time off from work for such purposes as taking care of a sick child at home or caring for one's spouse or parent after surgery, as well as for childbirth or to care for a terminally ill parent. The inability to take limited leaves from work to meet such family responsibilities and needs often forces employees to quit their jobs altogether. Moreover, those who are unable to take enough time off, or who return to work earlier than desired, experience stress, fatigue, and strain, which can have adverse effects on their job performance. The Family and Medical Leave Act (FMLA) of 1993 represents a first step toward mandating the universal provision of leave with some assurance of returning to one's job to enable employees to deal with a host of personal and family health needs.

CURRENT APPROACHES TO MANAGING WORK-FAMILY CONCERNS

Although initially work-family concerns were either ignored or dismissed as a "woman's problem," the sheer numbers of parents in the workforce and rising pressures for employer support gradually prompted many Fortune 500 companies and other large organizations to implement a variety of "family-friendly" programs. The programs include child care resource and referral, parental or family leave, flexible work arrangements, spouse relocation assistance, alternative career tracks, and job sharing.[14] Competitive pressures to recruit and retain the most talented men and women also served as a catalyst for employers to begin to offer assistance to employees in balancing their work and family responsibilities.[15]

There is considerable variation in the types of programs and services offered, the comprehensiveness of the support, and the inclusiveness of the programs and services available. For example, with regard to child care, the assistance ranges from the provision of child care resource and referral services to employer-sponsored or subsidized on-site day care. Many of the programs are ad hoc or piecemeal efforts, unintegrated with other human resource policies and practices. Some programs are targeted primarily to managerial and professional staff. Large numbers of nonexempt employees in large and small organizations are not covered by any work/life benefits. Some highly publicized work-family initiatives are available to only a very select group of high-performance/high-potential professionals on a case-by-case basis at the administrative discretion of the manager. Not only is this elitist, it makes work-family support a reward for superior performance.

The extent to which the programs and services are utilized and effective also differs. Some programs are little used due to employees' lack of knowledge of their availability. Due to informational lags and the bewildering array of programs offered, many individuals lack the knowledge or the inclination to scout out all of the latest benefits that are available and are relevant to them. Some programs are perceived as stereotypically gender-linked and therefore are not availed of by men for fear of adverse effects on their career advancement prospects. For example, a new father may not avail himself of the parental leave program, or if he does take time off from work, he may disguise the reasons for it. Additional research is needed to determine the reasons underlying the limited usage of different types of work-family programs and facilities. This would facilitate the development of appropriate measures to motivate wider usage of available benefits.

Theoretical models of work-family role dynamics have identified three approaches to managing work-family conflict. These include strategies designed to: (1) modify the situation through restructuring or role renegotiation; (2) modify the meaning of the situation through personal role reorientation; and (3) manage symptoms of strain through such activities as transcendental meditation, recreation, and physical exercise.[16] This threefold classification of coping strategies can be applied to individual as well as organizational approaches to managing the work-family interface. It also parallels key elements of Friedman and Galinsky's three-stage model of the development of work-family programs.[17]

In examining organizationally initiated work-family programs from these perspectives, it appears that few involve any major restructuring or challenge existing assumptions, norms, and beliefs underlying organizational policies and procedures. The central objective in many of the interventions seems to be to ensure employees' attendance at work and to minimize the intrusion of family concerns into the work domain.

Despite the proliferation of corporate work-family programs, the goal of achieving balance between work and family role demands seems to be elusive. Although some of the work-family initiatives are creative and innovative, overall they reflect a closed-system approach to dealing with the problems. For example, the current unequal gender distribution of family responsibilities seems to be treated as a given in most discussions of work-family issues. Solutions to the work-family dilemma typically do not challenge the status quo or recommend any changes in the domestic division of labor between men and women. The current eight-hour workday and 40-hour workweek have remained unchanged for about 50 years. In devising meaningful solutions to the schedule incompatibilities between work and family, questioning the functionality of the standard workweek might pave the way for the exploration of bold new approaches to restructure work to be more supportive of the needs of employees to marry, form families, and have children. Employers could reduce their expectations of employees' time commitment to work for limited periods of time in order to facilitate family life. This could be compensated for by an increased investment of time and energy to the job prior to the arrival of children.

It is ironic that despite the publicly espoused importance of the family and family values as the core of the social fabric in the United States, direct government support or government-mandated private sector support that addresses work-family issues is minimal. Even more telling is the lack of a formal policy statement with regard to families that reflects the ideology underlying the government's limited role in the family arena. In the absence of a national policy on families, the work family agenda in the United States has been rudderless. The failure to articulate the spheres of responsibility of individuals, employers, and local communities for the welfare of the family has created a void, which has been only partially filled by employer initiatives. However, the corporate sector cannot shoulder the entire burden of responsibility, and other constituencies need to be brought in to enlarge the societal base of support for the family and its needs.

As the number and complexity of work-family issues continues to increase, there are many challenges still to be addressed. This book was written specifically to discuss and debate these problems, and to offer solutions that go beyond surface issues and deal with the root causes. The aims and scope of the book are described in the next section.

THE AIMS AND SCOPE OF THIS BOOK

Integrating Work and Family: Challenges and Choices for a Changing World responds to the challenges of achieving work-family balance in the context of the sweeping changes that are transforming the worlds of work and family. It adopts a stakeholder perspective for examining, analyzing, and understanding the increasing complexity of work-family interrelationships. A distinguishing characteristic of the book is its view of work-family tensions as a multifaceted social issue, as well as its examination of the nature and consequences of such conflict from the perspective of individuals, employers, and other stakeholders, including work-family consultants, counseling professionals, and other service providers. The book casts a wider net in its examination of work-family issues as they relate, not only to managerial and professional employees, but also to other vulnerable groups such as nonexempt employees and ethnic minorities. The book's strength lies in its integration of theory and practice within each of the major topic areas. Consistent with the stakeholder perspective, it calls for shared responsibility and collaborative approaches to developing creative solutions for managing the complex interface between work and family by individuals, their employers, other social institutions, the community, and government.

STRUCTURE AND CONTENT OF THE BOOK

The book consists of 21 chapters, which are organized thematically under the following five parts:

I. Issues and Challenges in Managing Work-Family Linkages

II. Looking at Work-Family Issues through Different Lenses

III. Legal and Cultural Perspectives on Work-Family Relationships

IV. Work-Family Initiatives and Career Development: Problems and Promise

V. Moving Ahead: New Directions for the Work-Family Agenda

Part I presents a broad overview of the environmental factors impacting work and family by identifying the critical issues and challenges faced by individuals, families, and employers in managing the complex interdependencies between work and family roles. In Chapter 1, Parasuraman and Greenhaus provide an overview of the environmental forces impacting work and family; identify the key issues and challenges faced by employees, families, and employers in balancing work and family; and critically review the effectiveness of family-responsive initiatives and programs by employers. In Chapter 2, Wohl presents a panoramic view of work-family issues and discusses the dynamic tensions among workers, workplace, family, and community against the backdrop of rapid advances in technology and changes in the structure of families, values, and lifestyles.

Part II, which examines the issues through "different lenses," includes six chapters, each providing a different perspective of work-family issues from the vantage point of a specific stakeholder. In Chapter 3, Christensen proposes a model for a comprehensive and strategic approach to work/life initiatives in the corporate setting and outlines the basic operating principles for implementing the strategy. In Chapter 4, Phillips examines the role of the work-family consultant in serving five constituencies: the employer; employee; local, community-based resource clearinghouses; the service provider; and the children and dependent elders to whom the services are geared. The chapter describes the role of the consultant as an information and knowledge resource on the basis of which organizations and people can make informed decisions.

In Chapter 5, Miller presents a senior manager's personal experiences in balancing her roles as employee, wife, mother, and community member. The chapter discusses the rewards and costs of both marriage partners pursuing professional careers, and the mechanisms and supports used in juggling roles and simultaneously maintaining a satisfactory family life, managing parental responsibilities, and finding time together as a couple. O'Hare presents the perspective of a counseling psychologist in Chapter 6, focusing on the themes around which work-family problems are reported by clients in dual-earner relationships. The chapter reviews different approaches to counseling dual-career couples, and discusses their utility and effectiveness. In Chapter 7, Kropf traces the evolution of research on work-family dynamics and emphasizes the need for new research designed to inform practitioners on what works, what doesn't work, and why. Gutek rounds out this section in Chapter 8 with a unique perspective that focuses on employees as consumers and the increased demands on employees' available time for shopping. She suggests the need to be innovative in providing services of value to busy employees and families at times and locations that are most convenient to them.

Part III examines cultural and legal perspectives on work-family issues, focusing particularly on the role of culture and values in shaping ideology, policies, and practices concerning work and family and the interrelationships among them. Chapter 9, by Lewis, explores the nature of work-family concerns and organizational responses across different national and cultural contexts, particularly the United States and the countries of the European Economic Community (EEC). The international theme is explored further in Chapter 10 with Komarraju's analysis of the role of cultural factors, family structures, and social norms as they influence work-family relationships in India. In Chapter 11, Klein looks at work-family issues from a diversity perspective. She discusses the need for sensitivity to cultural and other differences of ethnically diverse workers, and the need to tailor work-family programs to address their unique circumstances and needs. Chapter 12, by Drake, reviews the provisions of federal and state employment laws and examines their role in facilitating the balancing of work and family life. The chapter presents a critical analysis of the extent of protection that the Family Medical and Leave Act of 1993 really provides to employees, and the costs of this act and other laws to employers.

Part IV examines the impact of career development programs on employees and their families. The section also discusses the effectiveness of alternative career tracks, differential usage of work-family benefits by women and men, and the roles employers and employees can play in legitimizing alternative career paths. In Chapter 13, Riley and McCloskey examine telecommuting and flexible work arrangements as approaches to addressing the work-family needs of employees, using the experiences of a high-tech company as a case study. In Chapter 14, Brett reviews the effects of relocation on career advancement and argues for changes in the opportunity structure of careers to enable men and women with strong family values and career interests to pursue "protean" careers. Connor, Hooks, and McGuire explore the barriers to utilization of alternative career tracks in public accounting firms in Chapter 15 and discuss ways of legitimizing such alternative tracks. Chapter 16, by Powell, delves into the reasons for the gender differences observed in the use of work-family programs offered by organizations and proposes ways of motivating men and women to utilize available company supports that can help them to balance work and family life.

Part V examines cultural barriers to achieving a more effective integration of work and family and discusses the appropriate role of key stakeholders in addressing work-family problems. Emphasizing the need for comprehensive work-family programs with shared responsibility among the stakeholders, this section points to the need for systemic changes, and creative approaches in developing innovative ways of addressing work-family issues, so that both men and women can pursue meaningful careers concurrently with high-quality family and personal lives.

In Chapter 17, Bankert and Lobel present an experiential methodology for visioning the future and developing new approaches to dealing with the critical issues identified. In Chapter 18, Friedman and Johnson use their four-stage model to evaluate corporate work-family initiatives and conclude that only a handful of companies are in the final stage, which involves a redefinition of the nature of work and changes in assumptions about employee motivation and organizational success. Chapter 19, by Bailyn, examines the cultural barriers that contribute to the difficulties experienced by employees in attempting to integrate work and family life. The barriers stem from unquestioned assumptions underlying the way work is organized, evaluated, and rewarded. The chapter emphasizes that the business case for work-family issues must change, as must the specific responses that companies offer.

In Chapter 20, Googins identifies the community as a third, and much overlooked, partner with employers and employees in developing more effective responses to work and family dilemmas. The need to broaden both the conceptual framework from work and family to a work-family-community prism and the development of partnerships between workplaces and community are discussed. In the concluding chapter (Chapter 21), Greenhaus and Parasuraman integrate the conclusions that emerge from the stakeholder analysis of the issues, as well as the cultural, legal, and career development perspectives on work-family linkages. Calling on the need for government to play a more active role in framing the issues, the authors emphasize the importance of collaborative relationships based on the identification of shared values in devising bold new approaches to achieving a balanced and healthy work and family life for men and women alike.

NOTES

1. E. Galinsky, T. Bond, & D.E. Friedman, *National Study of the Changing Workforce* (New York: Families and Work Institute, 1993).

2. M.A. Ferber, B. D'Farrell, & L.R. Allen (eds.), *Work and Family: Policies for a Changing Work Force* (Washington, DC: National Academy of Sciences, 1991); D.E. Friedman & E. Galinsky, "Work and Family Issues: A Legitimate Business Concern," in S. Zedeck (ed.), *Work, Families, and Organizations* (San Francisco: Jossey-Bass, 1992), pp. 168–207.

3. J.H. Greenhaus & N.J. Beutell, "Sources of Conflict between Work and Family Roles," *Academy of Management Review* 10 (1985): 76–88.

4. J.H. Greenhaus & G.A. Callanan, *Career Management*, 2nd ed. (Fort Worth, TX: Dryden Press, 1994); J.H. Greenhaus & S. Parasuraman, "A Work-Nonwork Interactive Perspective of Stress and Its Consequences," *Journal of Organizational Behavior Management* 8 (1986): 37–60.

5. G.N. Powell, *Women and Men in Management*, 2nd ed. (Newbury Park, CA: Sage, 1993).

6. Galinsky et al., *National Study of the Changing Workforce.*

7. E. Galinsky, A.A. Johnson, & D.E. Friedman, *The Work-Life Business Case: An Outline of a Work in Progress* (New York: Families and Work Institute, 1993).

8. Ferber et al., *Work and Family.*

9. B.K. Googins, R.B. Hudson, & M. Pitt-Catsouphes, *Strategic Responses: Corporate Involvement in Family and Community Issues* (Boston: Boston University Center on Work and Family, 1995); S.A. Lobel, *Work/Life and Diversity: Perspectives of Workplace Responses* (Boston: Boston University Center on Work and Family, 1996).

10. A.E. Scharlach, *The Family Medical and Leave Act of 1933: Analysis and Appraisal* (Boston: Boston University Center on Work and Family and U.S. Bureau of Labor Statistics, 1995).

11. Scharlach, *The Family Medical and Leave Act of 1933.*

12. Ibid.

13. Friedman & Galinsky, "Work and Family Issues."

14. Ibid.

15. Googins et al., *Strategic Responses.*

16. Greenhaus & Parasuraman, "A Work-Nonwork Interactive Perspective of Stress."

17. Friedman & Galinsky, "Work and Family Issues."

CHAPTER 2

A Panoramic View of Work and Family

Faith Wohl

The new century is now less than a handful of years away. Sometimes it seems that the closer we get, the more we feel apprehension rather than anticipation, for the world appears literally to be shaking itself loose from its foundation.

Around us, the sturdy institutions that serve as the infrastructure for our lives are crumbling, but not with age or disuse. Rather, they are imploding with the pressure of change, the upheaval of new ideas, and the disruptions of restless, rootless people. Ethnic conflicts daily reshape the map of the world; social issues and scandals rock Congress, clergy, and monarchy alike; an uproar over lifestyles raises questions about the shape and meaning of families. Seemingly permanent walls and borders collapse, and new ones are built. Treaties are carefully forged and then broken within hours. And here at home, public opinion polls reveal puzzling inconsistencies and widening fractures among us.

It is not surprising that as the 20th century draws to a close in all its messy confusion, we who ride this trembling earth are finding it hard to keep our balance. If we believe the futurists, the only thing predictable in this context of change is that tomorrow will be totally unpredictable; the new world order will be global chaos and the pace and intensity of market competition will continue to accelerate. Some have even speculated that as national borders become increasingly fragile, the true conflicts that lie ahead will be between major cultures, transcending the constraints of maps and crossing political boundaries.

It is often said that answers to questions about the future may well lie in history. Surely some of them do. And yet, we need to be cautious in the lessons and parallels we draw, for so many things have changed forever that we may take out best guidance from Lewis Carroll's Alice who, during her experiences in Wonderland, said: "I could tell you my adventures beginning from this morning, but it's no use going back to yesterday, because I was a different person then.'' To the extent that we are different people living in a different time, we may only be able to draw on experiences of the recent past and the turbulent present to imagine what may be needed in a future that will be different from both.

Things are moving so quickly that we are often just like Alice—lost in the world beyond the looking glass, unable to find our way home and equally unable to fathom what lies ahead. We are trying, in fact, to function in a world where the rules seem made by real-life versions of the Mad Hatter and the Red Queen, with fundamental changes rocking the economy, the community, and the home. These play out each day in our increasingly chaotic lives—across kitchen tables, across desks and manufacturing lines, across all of the ordinary divisions of class, race, gender, and economic status.

The aim of this chapter is to provide a panoramic view of work-family concerns, achievements, critical issues, and challenges. The book in which this chapter appears explores that topic through many separate lenses. In an important sense, the ''panorama'' will emerge organically as the reader joins together, in a complete and comprehensive image, the separate views expressed by the writers whose chapters follow. My role is to sketch an initial picture with a broad brush, to lay out the totality without the details, the color, the intensity, or the complexity that will come from seeing how the scene looks through various eyes focused through very different lenses.

At the start, I want to point out that not only the lens you apply can change the view—so can the vantage point from which it is seen. A broad landscape, for example, looks quite different if seen from the mountaintop above than it does from the valley floor. Climate can also affect the view by imposing clouds and fog that obscure grandeur and beauty. Perspective and atmosphere can, and do, affect what we see. Thus, it is important to establish at the start of this book the context in which the views are captured—for that affects the completeness and clarity, not only of the panorama that emerges, but of the individual images as well. And we must also remind ourselves that if the earth is indeed trembling beneath our feet, as I allege, that too can affect the view through even the best binoculars, if they are held in shaky hands.

SCHEDULES, ROLES, AND VALUES: NEW QUESTIONS

As we study work and family through our separate lenses, we might well conclude that the view right now is obscured by conceptual fog, for many questions cloud our perspective. Significantly, they are different questions than those that were asked several years ago.

I thought Ellen Goodman, columnist for the *Boston Globe*, clarified those earlier best in a dinner speech I heard her give in the late 1980's. She said that when she first started writing about work and family, she thought the issue was about conflicts of *schedules*—the schedules at work, at the child care center, at school, at the pediatrician's office, at home—all of which seemed to be in conflict. At that point, we were preoccupied with time and making it more elastic, trying to squeeze more into every day, so that we could truly "have it all."

But then, she said, she came to see the field as centered in a conflict of *roles*. In fact, the issue revolved around the different needs and expectations made of us in our varying roles as parent, employee, citizen, and wife or husband. Somehow, in the frantic 1980's, those roles were going head-to-head. If we had learned to squeeze everything into the day by forgoing sleep, running the laundry at midnight, and exercising before dawn, those were, at best, only quantitative solutions. Role juggling required something more. It demanded qualitative adjustments. It was not just a question of whether we could cram it all in, but whether we could do it well—be good parents, loving spouses, committed workers and involved citizens, all at the same time.

Finally, said Goodman, she decided that the true conflict was not about quantity or quality, not about time or roles at all, or at least not these alone. She concluded that it was about a conflict of *values*—that there was something inherently different and conflicting about the values we applied at home and in our neighborhoods with those we used at work, and that this was the cause of the angst of the times. And of course, the conflict turned out to be about all of these—about schedules, roles, and values as they were reflected in the changing nature of the relationships between and among the many parts of our lives and the dynamic tensions among them.

There was a sense in Ellen Goodman's thoughtful reflections that there was at least clarity about what was expected and understood about the compartments into which we apportioned our energy and our time every day, but that we had only to learn how to balance and integrate them more effectively in a changing world. Today, however, I think we can see that there are profound questions about the parts themselves:

• We are no longer able to answer with certainty, for example, the question, "What is the workplace?" when workers are only loosely connected with laptops, fax machines, and teleconferencing across the globe, through world time zones, and in cyberspace. In a world in which a producer of copies advertises itself as "the branch office for the new American workplace" (which, the company claims, can be on the beach, in the kitchen, or wherever you wish to define it), we might well ask, "What (or, at least, where) is the workplace?" Wherever the workplace is located, it is demanding more and more from the worker, as companies respond to greater competitive pressure by producing more with fewer people. Wherever or whatever it is, the workplace has become a harsher, tougher, less paternalistic place—and one that is significantly less secure.

• We are no longer able to answer with precision and ease, the question, "What—or who—is the worker?" In this time of downsizing, contingent forces, and outsourcing, the very definition of employee seems increasingly elusive. Who is that person, what can be expected from her or him, and what do employees as a group expect from their employer? What we know is that, above all, workers want quality of life at work and at home, more than they prize anything else, including traditional forms of compensation and benefits. This may be somewhat at odds, or in conflict, with what the workplace expects and demands, with the employer's focus on customer satisfaction and on the economics of the "lean" and, often, the "mean."

- We may soon not be able to answer the question of "What is a job?" What role, if any, will jobs play in our fast-changing economy? Has the time for jobs as the central organizing mechanism for work really passed? Are jobs truly, as one business writer recently proclaimed, "social artifacts"?[1]

- And finally, I suspect we can no longer answer the many questions that follow from the most fundamental question of all—"What constitutes a family?"—as we continue to witness the emergence of new and different models for our closest and most intimate relationships. As we have learned to live with the blended family, the single-parent family, the dual-earner family, the gay family, and the dysfunctional family, the word *family* has come to cover so many varieties of arrangements that it has become nearly useless as a descriptor.

As we think about these questions, it should be clear that we are living during a fundamental rearrangement and vast transformation of both our economy and our society. As these brush against one another, the effect is not unlike the outcome of the shifting of the globe's tectonic plates—what results feels a lot like an earthquake. When the shaking stops and the dust clouds settle, the landscape will reveal itself to have been inevitably rearranged.

WORK, FAMILY, COMMUNITY: NEW CONTRACTS

With families in transition and businesses in retrenchment, what America needs is a new contract that redefines the critical agreements among work, family, and community: a contract that acknowledges the realities and needs of the 1990's and the first decade of the coming century, establishes and protects underlying values, and permits and supports the raising of children and the restoration of community.

Integrating work and family is thus ultimately an ethical issue that suggests the need for a new social balance in which work assumes its more rightful place within our lives—rather than demanding that we rearrange our lives around it.

In fact, all of our new questions about workers, workplace, family, and community—contribute to the changing nature of this social contract. In just the past few years, the very idea of a social contract has evolved rapidly from one that already could no longer promise or imply a guarantee of long-term or lifetime employment to one that raises real questions as to whether jobs as we know them will continue to exist at all. That is an enormous and unsettling change, which is often described as involving a new focus on "employability" instead of "employment."

When we conducted research among employees at DuPont in 1992 about their perceptions of a changing social contract, they were quick to clarify that they did not expect, or want, a lifetime guarantee of employment. But they also articulated, in thoughtful and compelling ways, their need for stability of employment so that they could plan—and not disrupt—the important events of family life. And they also made it clear that they expected the company to be well managed so as to attain that stability.

In contrast, author William Bridges, in his book *JobShift*, startled many by asserting that as a way of organizing work, the job itself, and not merely the long-term commitment to employment, is a "social artifact that has outlived its usefulness." "That much sought after, much maligned social entity, a job, is vanishing like a species that has outlived its evolutionary time. . . . Jobs in a fast moving economy are rigid solutions to an elastic problem."[2]

If this turns out to be true, what complexity does it add to our questions about workplace, family, and community? How does it change the relationships among them? What changes will it require in society as a whole if the job, with all that it currently has connected to it—everything from health care to child care— becomes even more tenuous? Where are the social policies and programs in the United States that can support family life if jobs can't—or won't—do so? What happens when irregular work takes the place of predictable employment for larger and larger numbers of people?

I have a real concern that our glib replacement of the idea of employment with employability may well ignore the less visible aspects of the social contract that employers have traditionally had with their employees. For in this nation, in contrast to most of the rest of the world, it is the workplace that offers what is provided by comprehensive public policies in other advanced nations. This is particularly true when you consider policies in support of families and children. If the social contract offered by the world of work changes rapidly or vanishes, a new social contract may have to come from the state, and currently there seems to be little political appetite or public will to have that happen.

WORKERS, MANAGERS, INSTITUTIONS: NEW PRIORITIES

While there is much we don't know as we look ahead, a few things are clearly changing. Both anecdotal and research-based evidence demonstrate that people are reconnecting to their personal lives, either by choice or by abrupt termination of their employment. A value is being reestablished for family. These new connections, which are totally personal and extremely intimate, can be an instrument for breaking the hold that the theory and practice of scientific management have long had on our major institutions—whether government or private enterprise.

At the same time, we know that the external world continues to impose the painful pressures of a fickle global marketplace. And while we seem currently to be in a time of rising corporate profits, these may be illusory or temporary at best. The combination of the two factors—new demands from within and without—put scientific management, with its rationality, rigid bureaucracy, and cold logic, on a collision course with the future. New management strategies are needed to stress rapid response to customer needs, flexibility, teamwork, risk taking, and the full development of the individual. In that environment of change, we find employees questioning, in unprecedented ways, their role, their purpose, and their treatment. And they are raising questions, particularly in such values-based arenas as diversity and family.

This new workforce has made it clear that its members have compelling needs, which they refuse to leave at home (since no one is there to take care of them), thus bringing to work, in their lunch pails and briefcases, family issues and concerns. They are also making it clear that they have changed priorities about the place that work has in their lives.

What employees are now saying is that the greatest work and family benefit is a job to depend on. A social contract with employers that can be maintained over time. A predictable standard of living. The continued existence of a vibrant middle class. A better quality of life, both at work and at home. These were not issues on the work and family agenda when it was initially formulated in the mid-1980's because they seemed already in place, fixed and immovable. They were the bedrock, the foundation on which other needs could be positioned—but we have to rethink that belief as we look ahead.

Thus, the last ten years have brought to public and private employers everywhere what Steve Priest of the Center for Ethics and Corporate Responsibility described in 1993 as the "number one ethical issue for corporations: a difficulty in performing at a high level at work, while maintaining a strong commitment to one's family at the same time."[3] Note that he not only described this as an ethical issue but that he spoke in qualitative terms—not of having it all, nor fitting it all in, but of experiencing the two central relationships in one's life at a high level of accomplishment. That's the dilemma, both moral and practical, that confronts us. That's the dilemma that created the work and family discipline. That, in fact, is the dilemma central to many of our personal lives.

And a difficult dilemma it is, as those of us who have experienced it or watched it unfold will quickly attest. While there are many things we can do to mute its effect on both workplace and home, I am not going to promise that we in the work-family field can fully resolve the radical shifts in American society that are at issue. We can modify time schedules, improve child care, and make family leave a legal right—in fact, we have already done all those things. But even as one of the most ardent advocates with the work-family portfolio, I won't stand up and declare victory, even when all companies have such programs in place—and we are a long way from that state of affairs.

I agree with the premise that we are talking about a dilemma of ethics, not one of time or place. The solution represents and reflects the need for a reassessment of personal and societal values. It probably requires a fundamental restructuring of roles and responsibilities—government and business, employer and community, husband and wife, parents and children. It won't bend to quick fixes or short-term innovations. In fact, we are catching up only slowly to some of what will be needed if people are to avoid being torn between two of the most important aspects of their lives—as they try to live a high-speed life in a slow-growth world.

Not surprisingly, we change agents in the work and family field have been promising a lot as we knocked down the corporate cultural artifacts of another era, predicting recruitment advantages, retention improvements, higher productivity, lower absenteeism, improved quality, and greater employee commitment. Year by year, as we made a place for ourselves in the array of human resource programs, we've found the right way to link our work with the current management imperative to prove that what we are trying to do is important and useful.

This was more than just a process of restlessly searching for the right message. It involved taking new images of the needs of the workplace and attempting to fit them together into the panoramic view that we've been trying to see. In fact, we were able to do this because the work-and-family issue is a means to help in all those arenas, which are all linked to the same root. In each case, the process requires tapping into the spirit and the heart of employees to build a new attachment with their workplace—new loyalty, commitment, and empowerment—in order to accomplish the desired ends.

THE COMMON GOOD: A NEW DEDICATION

As I look ahead to the milestone that faces us in the year 2000, it strikes me that what we need to dedicate ourselves to is achieving a restoration of the spirit of American enterprise in this country by reconnecting people to one another and to their lives outside of work. In other words, I see the essential nature of our work as captured in the role of community builder.

We who share different roles in the work and family profession can have a unique influence on repairing the sense of community and the mutual obligation to the common good that have been lost—in the excesses of the 1980's and the decade's focus on self; in the economic ravages of the early 1990's and the resulting pain and dislocation; and in the sterility of many business environments, which have turned from obligation and responsibility to a harsh survival ethic.

The source of spirit lies in the humanity of our employees—not their existence as points of data or full-time equivalents, their dollar cost, or even their role as consumers of expensive benefits. It is the spirit of people that must be released if we are to again be able to tap into their reservoir of energy and will—which must happen if American businesses are to grow and succeed for the long term.

Our field encompasses the two institutions most central to the most lives—the work people do and the relationships they enjoy. That implies much more than employment policies and programs. It demands not only repair within the walls of our employment institutions but that we join in the solutions needed by the communities in which we live.

Simply said, this issue matters. I believe it is at the heart of a central conflict of our time. That is the key challenge inherent in the subject of this book and the conference on which it is based. It involves the sense of community—the concept of common good—which we cannot yet see. We are still at the stage of looking through our separate lenses and not linking our insights or our efforts to the larger reality—the panoramic view.

I said earlier that we need to be cautious when predicting the future with lessons from the past. History tells us that as a nation, our inner strength always came from shared values set down by the unique circumstances of our early years and the extraordinary gifts of those who created the United States—values for individual freedom, commitment, and the rights and obligations of people. Those values shaped a remarkable spiritual heritage, which can guide us well as we grapple with the huge challenge of redefining the common ground on which we can come together, instead of fragmenting and fighting.

Ultimately, it is the spiritual strength of individuals and institutions that provides the necessary armor in which to engage a chaotic world—in this case, to reinvent work, renew family life, and reawaken our historic sense of community. That may be our only road map to the best lookout point from which to see the panorama that spreads before us, into the final years of this century and on past the millennium to the promise of the future.

I have to believe that the common good exists in relation to the needs of children. Work, family, and community must come together to do a better job for the next generation, and the one after that. While we individually tear ourselves apart over the dilemma—which to choose, work or family?—our children watch, and many of them suffer from what they see. It is for them that we must find the intelligent, caring, sensible solutions that improve the relationships among corporate, family, and social health. That is where a new contract can be forged. They are all linked, and right now they are floundering together. I believe that, instead, they can each contribute to positive progress for all.

It is for our children and grandchildren that we must apply increased determination and renewed spirit to work, family, and community. If we do so, the 21st century will be, as it should, a better time for all.

NOTES

1. William Bridges, *JobShift* (Reading, MA: Addison-Wesley, 1994), p. viii.
2. Ibid., p. 2.
3. Steve Priest, remarks made at conference "The Family, the Corporation and the Common Good," Chicago, April 22–24, 1993.

PART II

Looking at Work-Family Issues through Different Lenses

CHAPTER 3

Toward a Comprehensive Work/Life Strategy

Perry M. Christensen

Many companies have begun to address the work/life dilemma with a wide variety of initiatives. Few companies, however, fully adopt a work/life perspective as a management strategy to the full advantage of the company and their employees. In order to understand why companies fall short, we first need to understand the barriers and challenges that confront the issue within the corporate setting. Second, we will outline the basic operating principles of implementing work/life initiatives within a corporate setting and describe a model for a comprehensive and strategic approach to implementation. Unless corporations begin to address all components of the model, they risk falling short of attaining a strategic approach that provides multiple benefits for the company. Finally, I will suggest some new ways to view the work/life issue within an evolving corporate framework.

Case 1

A former audit manager at Ernst & Young described customer relations there as follows: "When clients say jump, we have to say, 'How high?' You can't say, 'I'd like to jump six feet today, but I can only jump three because of my kids.' They'll just go next door and find someone else."[1] Increasingly, a "customer focus," designed to meet customer needs quickly and flexibly, creates conflicts for employees as they try to manage their personal interests and family priorities to their satisfaction.

Case 2

Over the years, this trend has been called "layoffs," "downsizing," "right sizing," "career transitions," "outplacement," and "delayering." More recently, it has been referred to (cynically) as "organization ventilation" or "smart bombing." Regardless of terminology, John's coworker experienced it firsthand: he was laid off. The workload didn't diminish; in fact, the work was consolidated into John's responsibilities. Now there was more travel, more pressure, and the looming threat of job loss. His boss, who was equally threatened, could only shrug his shoulders and say, "Well John, you're lucky to have a job." Then, as if to add some humor, he informed John that "a job is the new status symbol of the '90's."

Case 3

A flattened organizational structure, such as is in place in many companies, requires a greater need to integrate across various functional areas. To achieve integration, Michelle's work continued to grow to include numerous task forces, cross-functional teams, and ad hoc assignments. The new work was assigned on top of her existing responsibilities. Michelle, however, was a single parent. She did not have a boss who understood her needs for flexibility. Combined with pressure outside of work, Michelle began experiencing debilitating feelings of inadequacy, at work and as a parent—feelings that adversely affected her performance on the job and in her family.

We all have experienced similar stories. As the controller for one of the world's largest privately held companies recently told me, "Either you are overworked or out of work." Within today's globally competitive environment, employees are increasingly faced with the pressures to meet customer needs—flexibly, quickly, creatively, and within reasonable costs. These pressures to perform are fueled by the looming threat of job elimination. The results: employees feel increasingly less in control of their jobs and future.

RAPIDLY CHANGING WORK ENVIRONMENT

In order to remain competitive within the global marketplace, companies are focusing on five areas:

- *Customer focus.* Companies are beginning to erase time zones and country barriers as the needs of global customers dictate an unrelenting attention to work.

- *Flexibility.* Fluid work processes demand a constant investment of human sweat equity, as a never-ending series of reengineered processes squeeze out the last dollar of productivity and value-added investment.

- *Innovation.* Customers demand an infinite number of product variations that change with the seasons and evolving market forces.

- *Speed of delivery.* Companies realize that shaving slivers of time increases profits. As a result, information flow, market assessment, creation of marketing opportunities, and product delivery have all accelerated.

- *Cost containment.* Companies are consolidating resources, focusing on value-added products and services, and increasing the productivity of employees, capital, and equipment.

BARRIERS AND CHALLENGES TO A STRATEGIC WORK/ LIFE APPROACH

The competitive forces within the changing business environment have created or reinforced numerous barriers to addressing the work/life dilemma.

Management Practices and Assumptions

Face Time Mentality. Dysfunctional and archaic managerial styles create some of the most insurmountable barriers to work/life balance. One style to which many supervisors still subscribe is the "line of sight" management technique, which equates employee commitment and contribution with physical presence. A friend who is a compensation consultant for a well-known firm described to me how she had to catch the 5:18 train home each day to attend to her family needs. At work, she was nicknamed "union" for using union hours. At home, after the children were in bed she worked another two to three hours, unknown to her supervisor. Frequently, employees reinforce the barrier by adhering to the "parking lot syndrome" (leaving work only after the boss has gone).

Equality versus Fairness. From the beginning of the industrialized period, work had to be systematized and standardized in order to be performed with a conveyer belt, assembly line, or standard operating procedure. Firms have tended to treat employees in the same way. Equality has meant "sameness"—treating everyone the same, with the same rules and standardized procedures. The nature of work has changed, and the variety and variability of people, the "intellectual capital" of business, has evolved. Yet it is still difficult to break out of the enduring mentality of treating people the same. The managerial task has evolved from an approach that emphasizes equality across all employees within the workforce to one that emphasizes fairness to each individual in the workplace.

Work and Family as a Women's Issue. Organizations that label work and family as a women's issue place an additional strain upon, and barrier for, fathers. As noted in *Time* magazine, "Employers that have been slow to accommodate the needs of mothers in their midst are often even more unforgiving of fathers. It is a powerful taboo that prevents men from acknowledging their commitment to their children at work."[2]

Dependency Creation. In a recent article in *Across the Board*, the author asked the question: "The resulting massif of corporate benefits and programs, however, raises real concerns over the typical downsides of a welfare state. Our empowerment efforts, in fact, create a dependency effect. If an employee's entire health support and child support system is sponsored by the corporation, what happens, should he be laid off?"[3] Are our work and family initiatives viewed by management and employees as a way of controlling choices or as a way to offer choices? Do our programs create dependency on the company or independence? Should the potential dependency of employees limit the creation for them of further choice and flexibility?

Entitlement Philosophy. Some managers feel that flexibility with work/life issues will only lead to a feeling of entitlement. Flexibility will not enhance productivity, but will create precedent-setting and "unsettling" costs of offering these benefits to employees. This approach is an extension of society's culture of consumption, where "more" is not only better, it is the only acceptable direction.

Limited Systems Thinking. Within the corporate structure, we have tried to create a sterile and stable environment, where the imposition of outside influences is threatening and in conflict with business priorities. As a result, we work in an organization "despite" a family and a personal life. However, while a focus on business priorities is critical, there is a natural and inseparable influence on work from other aspects of an employee's life. A systems approach prevails in work and personal life.

Our attempts to create an artificial separation of work and nonwork is analogous to the formation of government in the early history of the United States. The freedoms enjoyed in the United States were originally established based upon a simple separation of powers. One of these was a separation of church and state, which was viewed as a solution to the problems that drove some of the early settlers to seek freedom in this country. The separation of church and state, while conceptually appealing to the framers' sense of freedom, was never really possible, nor desirable. The values and belief system of the early settlers had a direct influence upon the type of government and legislative system that was established. This value foundation ultimately led to a state and federal government based upon the beliefs and values of the majority of the people, which continues to serve as the foundation for today's government.

Within all natural systems, including organizations, there is a balance and influence among and between the parts. For example, an ear infection can affect not only hearing, but balance, temperature, and pain senses. A broken arm affects not only the skeletal system, but also the nervous, circulatory, muscular, and skin systems. And while many people espouse a separation of work and life priorities, in practice, these artificial and unnatural separations are counterproductive.

No Value in the Family Experience. This lack of systems thinking extends to how managers may view the family experience. Freedom for women and men to invest in their family is seen by many as making a choice to detour from a career direction. Few managers view the choice as merely switching to a parallel road that heads in the same direction. Some managers also lack a vision of seeing the value of the family or personal experience in maintaining the stability and effectiveness of the organization. However, as Peter Senge emphasized, we cannot build an effective organization "on the foundation of broken homes and strained personal relationships."[4]

Success in the family and with personal relationships is very much a training ground for being a successful manager, just as being a successful manager is also good preparation for these relationships. We value the depth and insight that an international career can provide an employee. We acknowledge the breadth of experience gained by working in a variety of functions. We respect the contribution and involvement of a coworker's community leadership. And yet we do not value and, worse, sometimes even trivialize, the depth, perspective, and skill gained as a result of managing a family and personal interests.

Resistance from Human Resources

Work and life initiatives historically have resided within the human resources function. However, in recent years, the human resources function, as well as other staff groups, has come under tighter cost control. Functions within human resources are being outsourced and otherwise pressured to become leaner, control costs, and justify their business contribution and existence. These trends are necessary to ensure the viability of the business. In addition, human resources is revitalizing efforts to strengthen the "bottom line" and become a business partner with line management. As a result, human resources is often the first area to eliminate work/life initiatives if the return on investment is not immediate and measurable or the initiatives are viewed as a needless "social service."

Programs versus Practices

Over the years, attention to work/life programs has grown. Many companies have made significant progress through the creation of programs to address work/life needs. This attention has been enhanced by the visible contribution of publications such as *Working Mother* magazine and its list of "Best Companies to Work for Working Mothers." Unfortunately, company programs are frequently glitter without substance or accolades without application. To the detriment of the work/life field, the attention on programs has sounded the clarion call that "all is well" in corporate America, when in reality the bell is sometimes made of tin—it looks impressive to the public eye but is hollow-sounding to the employees, who know the reality only too well. The glaring gap between programs and actual practices has served to desensitize corporate leaders to the real problem of implementation.

BASIC PRINCIPLES

A comprehensive and strategic approach to work/life initiatives is based upon simple, core principles.

- *We like to be successful.* People like to be successful and make a contribution in *all* areas of their life that are important to them. When we are not successful, we feel discouraged. There is a mental toll for work that is unfinished or problems unresolved, or in cases where we have not been successful in an area that is a priority for us (whether that is work or family). However, we can't always be successful at everything that is important to us. The challenge is to keep our effort and results within an acceptable range in order to minimize the mental and emotional drain.

- *We are all unique.* Individuals have unique needs, skills, abilities, and contributions.

- *We thrive on independence and choice.* Raising children and managing employees have both been described as the equivalent of trying to herd cats. As much as we want them to go in a certain direction, they have their own minds and beliefs, and they like to manage themselves and their choices. Most of us thrive on such independence.

- *We excel at things we enjoy doing.* In order to capitalize on the energy of employees, companies need to match the unique strengths and interests of individuals to the real contributions they can make in the company.

- *We need to build trust.* As we move to a flatter, faster organization where we will have to rely on the coordination and cooperation of people over whom we have no direct organizational control, we will need to rely more on the individual to self-manage and to provide a free-will contribution. The underlying principle is trust. Trust will need to be at the heart of effective management in the future. We must trust that individuals like to be successful at work, and that they will do their best. If we've been successful in matching their unique strengths to the needs of the company, we should be able to trust them to make that contribution.

A MODEL FOR A COMPREHENSIVE STRATEGY

Overcoming the barriers and challenges inherent in the workplace requires more than a band-aid solution. Tackling the issue head-on, in an effort to preserve intellectual capital and enhance productivity, requires a shift in the work culture existent at most companies. These shifts can only succeed if the focus is on developing and implementing a comprehensive strategy to work and life initiatives, which must be based upon core principles. One such model, which is utilized at Merck, is shown in Figure 3.1.

The model depicts (1) the organizational systems (communications, policies, and reward systems), (2) the business strategy and senior management support that serve as the bridge between the organizational and individual levels, and (3) the role the manager and individual play in "what" work is done and how it is done. All three areas of the model interact and reinforce each other to form an integrated strategy to work/life issues.

Senior management, consequently, plays the pivotal role, in the formation of either a supportive work/life management culture or a dysfunctional culture. Through the development of a business strategy that is integrated with the work/life strategy, senior management "gives permission" and opens the door to supportive manager/employee relationships lower in the organization. In addition, senior management dictates how the organization systems and structure will reinforce the work/life culture, creates expectations for the managers' roles, and reinforces the working relationships throughout the organization.

Figure 3.1
A Strategic Approach to Work/Life Issues

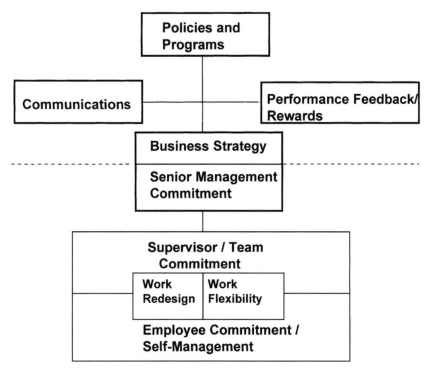

I would like to propose a "Standard of Excellence" for each area of the model. The standards should provide the yardstick against which we measure the effectiveness of company initiatives.

Policies and Programs

- The company provides a broad spectrum of policies and programs that address work/life issues. The breadth of programs should include policies that not only encourage people to come to work (e.g., sick child care, day care support, etc.), but also that strengthen the employees' abilities to contribute outside of work (e.g., community service policies, parenting skills seminars, etc.).
- Employees are involved in the development of these policies and programs.
- Policies and programs are communicated to employees through company media, human resources, and line management.
- Managers receive training on policies and programs.
- Utilization and business outcomes of policies and programs are widely communicated.
- Research and analysis are conducted to assess programs.

Senior Management Commitment

- Written commitment to work/life is a part of the formal mission/vision statement and is communicated widely.
- Commitment is communicated by the chief executive officer (CEO) and senior management in as many ways possible: in writing, in video, and in both casual and formal communications. More importantly, senior management should demonstrate commitment through visible personal actions that support work/life integration.
- Senior management's expectations of supervisors are clearly communicated.

Supervisor Support

According to several studies, employees who have more supportive supervisors are less stressed, experience less negative spillover from work to family, and feel more successful in balancing work and family life. Frequently, however, there is a gap between what senior management vocally support and what is actually practiced by supervisors and managers, who are generally pressured to show bottom-line results.

- Supervisors understand the business rationale of work/life initiatives.
- Supervisors are trained on policies and programs and on their latitude to implement.
- Supervisors know how work/life initiatives link to their specific business strategy and actively combine the two initiatives.
- Work/life initiatives are considered at management meetings on a regular basis.

Linkage to Business Strategies

- Human resources and line management work together to develop and link business strategies and work/life initiatives.
- Line management communicates the linkage to employees.

For example, many companies are beginning to integrate work/life issues with total quality management, diversity, quality of life, and management effectiveness initiatives.

Work Redesign and Work Flexibility

- Constantly challenge assumptions about how work is done and what work is done.
- Experiment with new ways to do work.
- Measure productivity and loyalty by accomplishment, not by how many hours a day an employee works.
- Employees are expected to take more responsibility for determining the work content, how and what work will be done, and the business outcomes.

At the heart of a strategic approach to work/life is the work itself. Unless a company can begin to address the work (both the content and process), it may not matter how many programs or policies are in place to support work/life integration. Addressing what work is done and how it can enhance manager and organizational effectiveness, this strategic approach can potentially utilize employees to identify inefficiencies in work processes, not in a manipulative way, but in a process that engages the heart and energy of employees to bring about needed change.

For example, many companies are attempting to reengineer work processes to eliminate low-value work and focus on critical, value-added work. At Merck Frosst, our Canadian subsidiary, we combined a reengineering effort with a work/life effort with surprising results. We knew that our sales representatives were extremely busy, due to the administrative components of their job as well as the actual sales function. We conducted focus groups with a large cross-section of the sales force. The focus groups, which were run by an outside consultant, focused on what could be done differently in their work in order to allow them to focus on important work as well as their family/personal responsibilities. The focus groups identified the increase in administrative work as a main culprit. Two sales task forces were established, and numerous changes were made to the administrative work. The most notable change occurred in the reporting procedures for sales representatives. To our surprise, over the years we had layered reporting requirements to the point where 27 reports were required from our sales representatives on a regular basis (weekly, monthly, or quarterly). The task force reengineered the administrative reports by eliminating, combining, or streamlining reports. In the end, only 11 reports were required on a regular basis. The effort was successful because we combined a work reengineering project with a work/life initiative. The end result was personally beneficial to the sales representatives (by freeing up more of their evening and weekend time with their personal interests) and beneficial to the company.

Reward Systems

- Supervisors receive employee feedback on how supportive they are of work and family initiatives.
- Employee feedback is linked to the reward system (e.g., merit, bonus). Nonmonetary and recognition mechanisms are utilized, particularly for creative solutions from innovative managers.

Employee Communications

- Supervisors are formally used to disseminate information. Formal vehicles for regular written communications exist, and program usage, success stories, industry trends, and business results are communicated.

- Employees from a wide range of levels provide regular feedback on current initiatives (e.g., surveys, focus groups, etc.).
- Employee committees and advocacy groups exist to evaluate current and proposed initiatives.

Self-Management

Given the nature of business many companies are constrained in the extent to which they can implement work/life initiatives. Many take the position of a CEO quoted in *Fortune* (''You can't bend so far to protect people's lifestyles that you cost them their jobs'').[5] A *Fortune* survey of 200 CEOs indicated that things will probably only get worse. In their survey, 80% said that they would have to push people harder in the 1990's in order to compete.[6] As Peter Senge noted, there is a constant drive and natural inclination to move toward imbalance.[7] We tend to focus on those areas where we have been successful. Moreover, this imbalance is not self-correcting.

A critical question is, ''In the absence of work and family policies, programs, senior management support, and reward systems, what can individuals do to still try to be successful in all the priorities of their lives?'' The majority of workers in this country do not benefit from company initiatives that support work and personal life. Others of us may find that the support we do have may ebb and flow. So a critical question becomes, ''How can we manage ourselves in a nonsupportive environment?''

Self-management skills become an additional factor for a comprehensive work and family strategy. This approach is also consistent with the increased emphasis on flatter organizations, which, by their nature, require increased self-management.

- Employees are encouraged to develop written mission and value statements.
- Employees receive material and training to effectively manage according to their values.
- Support groups are encouraged and used as additional resources for employees.
- Skill-based training is available on managing and maximizing time.

Self-management consists of three areas:

1. How we respond to, and manage, outside influences, including our response to our immediate supervisor, the organizational policies and programs, our family situation and constraints, and the nature of our work.
2. How we manage our use of time. Effectively managing our time includes establishing our priorities, adapting to spontaneous, unplanned events and balancing our achievements and relationships.

3. How we maximize our time, or "What can we do with what little time we have outside of work?"

FUTURE DIRECTIONS AND NEW PARADIGMS

In order to view work/life as a strategic component of management in the rapidly changing business environment, the issue needs to be repositioned in several ways.

Balance Redefined

The mere mention of work/family "balance" or "life balance" strikes fear into the hearts of many managers. Balance implies equal proportions of time and effort. Many managers do not feel comfortable unless they know that employees are giving their all toward the work objectives. This discomfort is escalated when dealing with a manager who equates "face time" on the job with accomplishment.

The concept of balance can be redefined with a sailboat metaphor. When winds push against the sail, the sailboat tips to one side and looks off-balance. Despite the precarious leaning of the sailboat, however, it is in perfect balance. As the wind increases, sometimes to gale force, the boat will lean even more precariously to the side. During these times of threatening winds, the sailboat can maintain equilibrium if three factors exist. First, the crew members need to be in close contact with each other and the boat. Crew members perform special functions and communicate constantly to ensure that if any unplanned problem arises, they can help each other and adjust to the circumstances. Balance, then, becomes a function of "connection"—with each other and the boat.

Second, during threatening winds, a boat can maintain balance if it has a keel of correct proportions: size, shape, and weight. The keel serves as the foundation of the boat. Unlike the anchor, which ensures stagnancy, the keel allows the boat to maneuver under difficult circumstances. Balance, then, is also a function of a solid foundation.

Third, some of us are "captains" on the sailboat and have responsibility for others. When the winds blow on the sail, we need to know and feel reassured that we have been effective in teaching responsibilities to our crew. We measure our success as captains, not by the time we have invested to influence the crew, but in how effective the crew is in sailing the boat—the crew must be knowledgeable, self-sufficient, able to adapt to changing circumstances, and ultimately, able themselves to perform the roles of teacher and captain. Balance is a function of how successful we view our efforts to be.

The parallels are hopefully clear in real life: balance in life is a connection with all of our priorities—a connection with all of the relationships that are important to us, development and reliance upon solid values and beliefs, and a sense of success in all of our priorities. Balance can ultimately bear fruit for the business with resilient employees who can weather the storms of life through connection with others and a reliance upon solid values.

Imbalance occurs when (1) time commitments at work and our entrapment into the "work success spiral" encourage us to "disconnect" from family and friends, (2) we fail to take the time to think out our values and priorities or to act on values we know we have, and (3) our attempts to maximize what little work time we do have seem to fall frustratingly short.

A New Social Contract

With the rapidly changing work environment, demands to provide fast, flexible, cost-effective, and customer-focused products are changing the demands placed on employees. Combined with trends in the downsizing of workforce and the outsourcing of services, employers openly emphasize that they can no longer assure long-term employment. As a result, the social contract of a stable, long-term relationship has dissolved in the solvent of worldwide competition.

Yet in today's uncertain business environment, a leader's task of mobilizing commitment toward a common vision is now more critical than ever. The work of the future will *require* a committed workforce—committed to making a free-will contribution to the company. Gone, however, is any mutual commitment of the company to the individual. Workers increasingly are finding employment in smaller firms, career movement between companies is accelerating, and competition for "the best" employee is intensifying. Until now, the only visible arsenal that companies have used to fight the "brain drain" has been in offering employees "employability"—the means to develop and learn additional skills. But for many, the attraction of employability as a means of tying the employee to the company is waning.

If we are to forge a new social contract—a renewed commitment—it must be based on the principles of trust, independence, and choice. For many of today's employees, commitment to the business comes as much from having opportunities for flexibility and freedom as it does from getting the chance to climb the corporate ladder. Companies that proactively address issues of work/ life balance *as a part of their business strategy* will be at an advantage in generating the kind of trust and employee commitment needed to compete effectively in the global marketplace. An integral part of the strategy is to require managers to manage holistically and to personally accept that work/life initiatives are an important part of a new social contract and renewed employee commitment. They may even be the most important part.

NOTES

1. *Wall Street Journal*, June 21, 1993, p. R6.
2. *Time*, June 28, 1993, p. 55.
3. *Across the Board*, July/August 1994, p. 21.

4. P.M. Senge, *The Fifth Discipline* (New York: Doubleday, 1990), p. 312.
5. *Fortune*, March 21, 1994, p. 64.
6. Ibid., p. 65.
7. Senge, *The Fifth Discipline*, p. 309.

CHAPTER 4

The Work-Family Issue from a Consultant's Perspective

Tyler Phillips

Corporations seeking to address the work-family concerns of their workforce often retain the services of a consultant to advise management, to offer a national or regional perspective on the trends in the work-life industry, and to provide supportive services to the corporation as it embarks on the process of crafting a work-life strategy that fits its goal and mission. A variety of work-life consultants are available. Some have a singular focus: they are able to provide assistance to the corporate management in developing an appropriate work-life response, but not able to provide any direct services to employees or to the community organizations that helps employees with work-life problems. Other consultants, like the Partnership Group, are full-service consulting companies, able to guide the corporation from the initial stages of assessing the needs of management and the employee population on through to policy development, actual delivery of supportive services to employees, and the development of new services and programs in the community where the employees live and work.

This chapter will discuss the variety of constituencies that need to be taken into account in the development of a comprehensive work-life strategy and the ways in which consultants may interact or assist in the process. Although it is based on the Partnership Group's experiences as a full-service consultant, it is acknowledged that some organizations may retain multiple consultants to address these issues and various constituencies. The important point, regardless of whether a single, full-service consultant or multiple consultants are involved, is that the needs of all constituents be integrated and taken into account as a whole before embarking on the design of a system to respond to the work-life needs of the employee population.

Typically, the work-family consultant has five separate, but related, constituencies to serve: (1) the employer; (2) the employee; (3) local, community-

Figure 4.1
The Work-Family Consultant's Constituencies

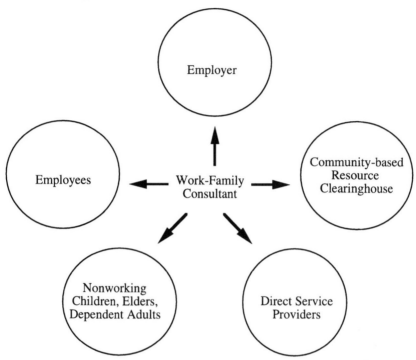

based resource clearinghouses; (4) direct service providers; and (5) the children, dependent adults, and elders to whom the services are geared. The role of the consultant is to understand the agenda of each of these five constituencies and the interrelationships between them; and to use this knowledge to help orchestrate the system so that it functions smoothly and to each constituency's advantage. (See Figure 4.1.) The consultant's role with each of these constituencies is described below.

THE EMPLOYER

The first constituent, the employer, typically engages the consultant to help develop or enhance work-life or work-family strategies and policies to better address issues raised by the organization's employees. When the consultant works with an employer, a four-phase process is typically used: (1) assessment, (2) planning, (3) implementation, and (4) measurement. A consultant may enter the process during any one of these phases.

In the assessment stage, the consultant works with the employer to help gain an understanding of the organization's position on what the Families and Work Institute has identified as a continuum of family and work programs and stages.[1]

Early-stage, or *stage one*, employers are typically in a reactive mode and have only limited knowledge about work-family issues. They may respond to employees who are raising issues by offering simple programs such as lunchtime seminars, flexible spending accounts, or adherence to the Family and Medical Leave Act. Through such actions, employers unwittingly become more involved with the large work-family agenda. These early-stage responses are usually programmatic, scattered, and reactionary. However, the work-family agenda becomes validated in the workplace during this process. Once the employer enters stage one and begins establishing work-family programs, it is inevitable that the organization will soon progress to stage two.

Whether the movement to stage two is accidental or part of a purposeful strategy championed by someone in human resources, the employer soon recognizes that it has several programs in the work-family arena—an employee assistance program, a wellness program, a flexible spending account, and so on. At this point the employer usually designates one individual as the focal person for all of the various work-family initiatives. In a large company, this position may be full time. In most organizations, it's assigned as an additional duty to someone in human resources. But by designating a focal person, the employer has evolved to *stage two*. Someone in the organization now has responsibility to evaluate how well the work-family programs are integrated.

The stage two employer begins to review its programs in an organized fashion and to evaluate their impact. The employer realizes that underlying these programs, policies, and practices form a basic set of core values about the organization's identity. This assessment leads the employer toward evolving into a stage three company.

Stage three employers recognize that the work-family programs are a part of the organization's culture—a set of values that define the way the organization operates. The major difference between stage three and stage two is that stage three is value driven. While companies may progress to stage two quickly, it often takes a long time to evolve to stage three because values take a longer time to change than behaviors.

Throughout the stage-by-stage evolution, the consultant's job is not to direct the employer, but to help the employer understand its position as an organization on the staged work-family continuum. This is accomplished through the use of assessment tools, like surveys and benchmarking, the evaluation of existing services, and the use of focus groups. Once the management and leadership of the organization understand what stage they are in, they can decide at what stage they would like to be as an organization. Management must also decide at what pace they wish to progress in order to realize their goals.

There are a number of tools the consultant and management can use to reach the desired work-family goal. Manager training, alternative work arrangements, consultation and referral services, and community support are examples of some of the work-family programs. Most work-family initiatives are implemented through policy changes, employee communication, and specific programs. The consultant will employ measurements to determine if these programs are working, if people are using them, if the people using them are satisfied, if the employer is receiving the outcomes it wants, and if the dollars invested by the employer are producing the expected return.

Program expectations may differ among people at various levels of the organization. The CEO may be much more interested in the organizational impact of the programs, while the benefits manager, at a lower level, may be more interested in the cost benefit. As a consultant, it is important to understand what method of evaluation is important to each layer of the organization.

Employer Trends

Currently, three trends are identifiable among employers. The first trend is a shift from a "family and work" agenda to a "people-friendly" environment. Some of this shift has been created by calls for parity by some employees without dependents, who view the movement toward "family-friendly" programs as discriminatory towards those without dependents. But perhaps more importantly, employers are beginning to recognize that employees have a variety of personal issues and responsibilities that spill over into working hours, and as a result, the focus on child care and elder care has expanded to include other "work-life" issues. These include problems related to home ownership and home repair, making major consumer purchases, dealing with pet care while traveling on business, handling personal financial issues, and finding lawyers and other professionals to help with various life issues. These problems affect all employees, whether or not they have dependents. In addition, all of these issues have an impact on workplace productivity if employees take time during working hours to address them. As a result, employers face a growing pressure to expand the work-life agenda beyond the narrow score of child and elder care.

The second trend is the increased use of performance measures to demonstrate cost benefits. Employers are no longer willing to spend money on programs or policies that they can't measure. Particularly in times of downsizing and cost cutting, they want to be certain that they are getting their money's worth. Therefore, consultants are increasingly being asked to demonstrate "payback" or return on investment for work-life programs. Such analyses look at the dollar value of increased productivity, reduced turnover, and reduced stress created by work-life programs. Although requests for payback analysis most often come from a stage two employer, where commitment to work-life issues is not yet a firm part of the organization's culture, in fact, the request to justify or measure performance for work-life programs may also come from another layer in the organization during budgeting or long-range planning processes.

The last trend is a result of employer downsizing. Many large companies are reducing their workforce substantially and will continue to do so. These employers use the period of change during downsizing to introduce quality, diversity, and work-family initiatives to support the survivors, who are now expected to produce more than they ever have before.

EMPLOYEES

The second constituency the consultant serves is the actual employee. In dealing with this constituency, the "consultant" in question is most often a case manager who works for the direct service arm of a full-service work-life consulting company. The employee struggles to balance his or her work life with his or her personal life. As the consultant/case manager relates to the employee, a separate four-step process is also used: (1) intake and assessment, (2) service plan development, (3) service delivery, and (4) follow-up and measurement.

At the beginning of this relationship, consultants often must help employees to define the scope of their problem. When employees call with a personal or family issue, the presenting problem is rarely the real issue. For example, there are times when an employee will call with a child care issue that turns out to be a problem with an elder who is watching the child. The consultant will solve the child care problem by resolving the elder care issue. Another example is when an employee calls with a housing issue, such as that of his or her mother buying a new house, when in reality it's a transportation problem. If the employee could only find his or her mother some interim transportation, the issue would be solved.

Employee issues are also tied directly to firsttime life events: the first time employees need child care; the first time they leave their child with a caregiver; the first time they have to decide whether their 4½-year-old is ready to start school this year; the first time their 9-year-old comes home and tells a dirty joke; the first time they buy a house; the first time they have to talk to their father about taking away his car keys. Many people are not prepared for these firsttime events, and the consultant can assist the employee in developing an effective plan and provide the resources and knowledge to help resolve the issue. When employees have some knowledge about an issue and know how they should act beforehand, the probability of success increases.

The consultant's role in taking the employee from intake to the development of a service plan is to help the employee set expectations. The service plan is a summary of what assistance the consultant will deliver to the employee. During service delivery, the consultant transfers the body of knowledge and set of behaviors needed to the employee so that he or she becomes equipped to resolve the issue. The consultant does this through education, research, and referrals. The consultant presents the employee with general information about the issue, whether a simple verbal explanation of terms or practices or written materials. Then, the consultant may provide the employee with, for example, the names of three nursing homes that all have vacancies, accept Medicare, and meet the family's requirements. The employee, in turn, would be expected to evaluate the referrals and decide which one of the three he or she wants to use.

Throughout the process there is continual follow-up and measurement. By working through the process with the employee, the consultant can help him or her over the hurdles and increase the level of success.

Employee Trends

Two important trends are occurring with the employee constituency. The first concerns the general aging of the workforce. The family and work industry has its roots in the delivery of child care services to employees, and although that may still be its dominant focus, the future will include a much heavier emphasis on the needs of employees' elderly dependents. In the manufacturing industries, where the average age of the workforce tends to be higher, an increased emphasis on the elder care issues of employees is already occurring. Consultants working in the work-life field need to be prepared to devote more attention to the elder care issues of the workforce and to have programs and services available to address them.

The second trend evident in the employee constituency is the increased use of new technology such as the Internet, CD-ROM, and E-mail. Employees have less time than ever, and consultants need to utilize every available means to communicate with them. Although services designed to help employees with work-life issues have historically been delivered via phone, fax, and mail, the future of employee communication and assistance may look very different. It is important for any consultant working with employees to investigate all options and look for ways to utilize the latest technologies to provide information, support, and access to referral information.

COMMUNITY CLEARINGHOUSES

The third constituency the consultant must address consists of community clearinghouses. Working with employers and employees, the consultant accesses such clearinghouses, which include any informed group, including local resource and referral agencies, area offices on aging, family service agencies, individual consultants, and junior colleges or community colleges that have detailed information about local care resources. The consultant relies on these networks and community resources for leads to direct service providers. In turn, the consultant provides them with information about changing technology and trends in the workplace.

An example of how this process works occurs when an employer wants to create a new, three-shift schedule. The consultant can inform local community organizations and work with them to provide resources to meet the increase in demand for services related to third-shift work, such as overnight child care.

Consultants also provide technical assistance to community organizations, which may include training and support for developing new resources within the community. Consultants can also improve the quality of services delivered by community organizations by providing feedback from customer satisfaction reports. The community organization is then able to determine where it stands in relation to similar organizations and improve its performance when necessary.

Community Clearinghouse Trends

There are two conflicting trends among community clearinghouses. Clearinghouses in some regions of the country are consolidating, while in other parts of the country, there's a decentralization or splintering taking place. A lot of this has to do with information and technology. When the technology changes, organizations have an opportunity to change their role. So, if an organization develops a computerized database for a larger geographical area, it may consolidate its efforts with other organizations. Or, if it is focusing on a more detailed, smaller area, it may decide to decentralize. A major part of the consultant's time is invested in building and maintaining the network. It is important for the consultant to understand the trends within a given area that affect a corporation's employees. If clearinghouses are consolidating, the consultant must focus on assuring that data at a local level will still be accurate and reliable in the larger database created by the consolidation effort.

If clearinghouses are splintering, the consultant must focus on developing relationships with the new entities being created and ensuring that the needs of employers and employees are understood by all parties involved. In addition, the consultant must continuously assess the role of new technology—including computer, Internet, and E-mail communication links—with community clearinghouses to assure that in a time when new organizations are being created, the most efficient means of communicating data about community resources is being utilized.

DIRECT SERVICE PROVIDERS

Direct service providers, the fourth constituency, are the agencies, organizations, and/or individuals that provide child care, health care, elder care, home care, or other direct services. Consultants provide referrals to them and may also provide them with training and technical assistance. They also facilitate networking among various providers, which increases the quality of available resources. Consultants assist the providers indirectly by educating employees who utilize their services. An educated consumer—for example, one who understands Medicare and how nursing homes operate—makes the whole process easier for the direct service provider.

Consultants play an important part in monitoring care providers. Employees are encouraged to call the consultant with any complaint. Elderly parents will be educated about health and safety standards and coached on how to express concerns to their caregivers. This takes the whole relationship of the provider and parent to a different level and is part of the process of monitoring compliance on the part of the direct service provider.

Direct Service Provider Trends

In a service-oriented economy, many new services are being invented all the time—both for profit and not for profit. We have seen growth in the nursing home industry and in alternative forms of child care centers in downtown areas (for example, emergency care programs); but many shortages continue to exist. In the child care arena, the shortages are usually tied to the economy. If the economy in a locale is strong, more people work and need care. However, there will be fewer people to provide care, so major shortages can occur due to increased demand. If the economy is soft, fewer people will be working and need care. However, there will be more people to provide care. In 1990, it was difficult to find a child care provider, and yet, four years later, in a very nice neighborhood in Boston, there was a banner around a tree that stated, ''I'll lodge your children in my house.'' Unfortunately, as soon as a shortage is addressed in one area, another appears somewhere else.

DEPENDENTS

The last constituency is made up of the children, dependent adults, and elders. The consultant's role here is to make sure that the dependent's perspective doesn't get lost by any of the other constituents since the dependents are not there to speak for themselves. Consultants have to make sure that in the zealousness of the other constituencies to address problems from their own perspective, inappropriate responses for dependents are not designed. A corporation that wants to address the problem of providing care for ill and mildly ill children may be encouraged to fund a sick bay in a hospital where children are cared for by nurses and other health care professionals. Alternately, the corporation may create a flexible work arrangement that makes it acceptable for the parent to go home and watch the child in a comfortable environment. Although the latter arrangement is slightly more difficult for the corporation to develop, it may be the best thing for the child. And, in the long run, a flexible work arrangement may create a more satisfied, and therefore more loyal, employee workforce. It is the consultant's role to advocate for the needs of dependent adults and children and to point out to the other constituencies the reasons why this focus often makes the best sense.

Dependent Trends

The trends among the dependent constituency are an expanded definition of the ''dependent,'' an expanded agenda of issues that dependent care programs must be able to address, and a greater geographic dispersion of dependents.

In the work and family industry, the term ''dependents'' historically referred to children and elderly relatives. However, corporations have begun to recognize that their employees frequently have responsibility for others who may not fit these rigid categories. Increasingly, the high divorce rate and problems with drug abuse have resulted in a large number of grandparents with custody of their grandchildren. Similarly, the AIDS epidemic has brought home to many corporations the fact that often, employees have responsibility to take care of their domestic partners. These and other social trends have resulted in an expanded notion of who can be considered an employee's ''dependents.''

As a result, the very issues that a dependent care program must be prepared to address have expanded. Grandparenting, custody issues, care options for dependent adults, and resources for people with AIDS are just a few examples. If the company's goal is to increase employee productivity and reduce employee stress by providing assistance with work-life issues, then it behooves the employer to define the scope of a dependent care program as broadly as possible. The consultant's role is to ''push the envelope,'' to help the corporation define its dependent care program broadly in order to be sure that the needs of all dependents are met and that the corporate goals are met as well.

The third trend among the dependent constituency is a greater tendency for geographic dispersion. This is most apparent in the elder care arena, where corporate restructuring and reengineering have resulted in wholesale employee transfers, consolidation and relocation of employees into corporate ''megacenters,'' and the resultant separation of families from the towns and cities where their elders are located. Even more serious is the increased proportion of American companies taking advantage of the global economy and developing operations overseas. For the consultant, this trend creates enormous challenges in program design and implementation. The increased incidence of long-distance elder caring, coupled with the rising average age of the elderly population, means that corporate elder care programs must become ever more creative in helping employees deal with serious elder care situations—hospitalization, nursing home placement, the diagnosis and management of dementia—from great distances. In addition, the increased numbers of corporate employees with dependents overseas have created a need for consultants to look for some integration between corporate expatriot programs and corporate work-life programs. More and more corporations are looking to create parity for their employees overseas by offering them work-life support as they help their dependents adjust to life in a new culture. Clearly, there is a role for the work-life consultant in helping corporate clients examine these issues and develop integrated programs that make sense for the dependents.

CONCLUSION

The consultant's major role is to understand the agenda of each of the constituencies and to facilitate working relationships among them. The consultant needs to educate these constituents, form networks with them, and help them recognize the other constituents' problems. Sometimes, this results in conflict. The needs of the employer to control costs, improve productivity, and contribute to the bottom line may sometimes seem to conflict with employees' needs for flexibility, support, and workplace empowerment. It is the consultant's role to help the employer sort out these conflicts and find compromises that contribute to solutions for all constituents. Although the consultant has five very different constituencies, only one of these constituencies (the employer) pays for the consultant's services. Yet without a careful consideration and balancing of the needs of all five constituencies, a work-life program will miss certain critical components. It is the consultant's role to play devil's advocate, to point out inconsistencies in program design, and to help the employer craft a program that meets the corporation's objectives while also meeting the needs of employees, dependents, community clearinghouses, and direct service providers.

The essential consultant's role is one of facilitating decision making. In the process, a fair amount of education is provided as employers struggle to understand their role vis-à-vis the other constituencies and to define their goals in setting up a work-life program.

As the work-life industry continuously changes, so will the role of the consultant. In some senses, corporations will have a greater need for consultant input as the definition of work-life expands and as the array of responses available to address work-life issues becomes more complex. Yet the need for consultants to address the five constituencies (outlined in this chapter) will not change. The challenge will be one of balancing conflicting agendas, helping with program implementation, measuring outcomes, and continuously recycling the process.

NOTE

1. E. Galinsky, D.E. Friedman, & C.A. Hernandez, *The Corporate Reference Guide to Work-Family Programs* (New York: Families and Work Institute, 1991).

CHAPTER 5

The Role of a Juggler

Susan Miller

VARYING PERSPECTIVES

No one challenges the fact that the rate and pace of change in our society have accelerated in the past few decades. Certainly, no small part of this societal evolution is the change we see in family lifestyles and workplace dynamics. In order to make the most of what I consider wonderful, but vexing, changes, we must rethink such topics as gender roles, and family and professional identity.

Most of this book is dedicated to addressing the work-family issues from the point of view of those responsible for developing and implementing policy. Let's call this a macro perspective. Key considerations on this level tend to focus on economic trade-offs and social, educational, and cultural ramifications.

This chapter approaches the issues from a totally opposite perspective, looking at the topic from the viewpoint of the individual personally involved with balancing work-family issues. At this micro level, the key considerations are actually quite similar in theory, but translated in an intensely personal way. Economic trade-offs suddenly are measured in terms of financial well-being, social and cultural ramifications center on marital status and family responsibilities, and educational issues become concerns for fulfilling professional aspirations.

So what does this micro-level view look like, and what can we learn from it? In short, the real benefit from intimately studying the issues of work and family is the appreciation that any policies on the subject must be able to be absorbed by every individual impacted—not always happily embraced, but at least understood.

I will share my own situation to bring the issues to life, to demonstrate how one person confronts the challenges of juggling multiple roles—how to be a successful professional woman in a dual-career marriage raising two young children. The purpose of sharing my experiences is not so much to establish a universal model that can easily be applied to others. Rather, it is to suggest just the opposite—that the decisions individuals make as they juggle the diverse responsibilities of work and family depend largely upon their circumstances. There are no textbooks or "how-to" books that can be followed blindly. Opinions and suggestions are many; their relevancy and applications must become personalized. Each of us must be somewhat of a trailblazer.

THE ACT OF JUGGLING

So what is it that I and many others in today's society must address in the work-family equation? To answer that question, let me first pose and answer another. Thinking back to childhood, who ever really answered with full honesty the seemingly simple question, "What do you want to be when you grow up?" I, for one, did not. I never realized that the response would have to be very complicated and require more than a single phrase answer. I never replied that I would grow up to be a juggler and supreme quick-change artist, donning the outfits of wife, mother, daughter, sister, friend, and business professional all at the same time. Yet each day, I am all of those things.

I am a juggler, as are many of my contemporaries. We constantly shift attention to a number of competing responsibilities. What makes the juggling act more an art than a science is that each juggler has a distinct set of balls to handle—based on both choice and circumstance. My approach to juggling will probably strike a familiar chord in many other professionals, if not in its entirety, in its theme of complexity and constant need for adaptation and change.

My husband and I are commuters living in the suburbs of New York City. We are raising two young children and establishing roots in the community. For us, dual careers are not a financial necessity; I enjoy working and am committed to my career. At the same time, I am totally committed to my two children, my husband, and the life we are forging together. We are fortunate in that health and elder care issues are not present. Certainly, that greatly reduces the potential dynamics of our lives.

Our choices to pursue dual careers and raise a family have created five primary balls that are most frequently tossed into the air. Let me briefly touch on each one:

- Parental responsibilities

- Professional success

- Basic household responsibilities

- Active community involvement

- Time for self and spouse

These balls are not all equally important; in fact, the relationships among them change over time as well. They all, however, need attention in my life. Further, as is the case in a real juggler's act, each time one ball gets tossed up into the air, it creates a "ripple effect" for the other balls, as if some invisible string connects them. And indeed, the linkage is just the reality of daily life.

With constant practice and a commitment to try new approaches, I have found it possible to achieve the balance necessary to keep every ball aligned and in motion.

Ball #1: Parental Responsibilities

As a parent, one must make difficult decisions about family and parenthood. The concept of a conventional household must be revisited—and with that re-visit, there must be a reassessment of the role of parent. Let me explain:

In dual-career families, when both parents work full-time outside of the home, the family structure must be redefined. My husband and I had to rethink whether our immediate involvement in the day-to-day activities of our children's lives mattered as much as their actual growth and development. We concluded that we did not have to be personally present at each milestone as long as we had established a nurturing environment in which such rites of childhood passage could occur. Whether it was a first word, first step, or the first goal in a soccer game, the accomplishment mattered more than our witnessing every event. That conclusion clearly has meant trade-offs and occasional moments of regret, but we focus on communicating our pride and satisfaction to keep our children happy.

While we did not have a family member conveniently located to participate in our home, we fortunately possess the means to have a full-time responsible adult in our home to fulfill a "parental" role in our absence. Like many, we have had to take the intensely personal topic of child rearing into a public arena; we had to introduce a stranger into the family fold and extend full parental privileges. In essence, we have created a triangular relationship.

What makes such a triangular relationship work is a willingness to share our core family values freely with another individual. Communication and decision making become an open affair, which is less private but ultimately stronger for the effort. Even with values being clearly articulated, we have to accept that with three adults supervising and setting rules, there are more opportunities for inconsistencies. But overall, it can definitely work.

To make this new structure work, parents must adjust the traditional deline-ations of the "mommy" and "daddy" roles. In place of strict gender-based responsibilities, my husband and I have had to apply a more flexible approach—one in which any parent (or even the adult caregiver) who is present takes on the task. Situations vary from family to family, of course, and the degree to which an individual is comfortable shifting roles ultimately determines how well this approach can work. For us, recognizing the limited number of hours in the day, identifying the myriad of competing responsibilities, and learning to slip in and out of multiple roles has proven to be the best possible solution.

Given that time is undoubtedly our most precious commodity, the seeming complexity of being flexible ends up to be a time saver. Our focus is on quality rather than quantity of time spent together as a family. But lest any reader think this is an easy—even guilt-free—action, I must also confess that my husband and I do each jealously guard a few special activities that we alone do with our children. For instance, unless I am out of town, I am the only one to oversee bedtime rituals and read bedtime stories. Conversely, Sunday breakfast is always prepared by my husband and the children; I merely show up to eat. (And the hidden benefit here is that we each carve out some quiet time for ourselves.)

There is another very positive consequence that emerges when one plays juggler. The acceptance of flexible parental roles creates a new vantage point from which to view child rearing. Importantly, the children themselves grow up accepting shifting roles and find it easy to appreciate diversity. Indeed, this is further reaffirmed when our children are with friends, for they see that children are raised in homes with a variety of family structures. Being raised without a single, traditional notion of family and without exposure only to gender stereotypes of parental roles, our children are growing up with a much more open-minded view of life.

Having said all of this, it would be naive to leave any reader with the thought that keeping family and professional concerns on an even keel is easy or even resolved just once. Life brings constant change, and circumstances require frequent "sanity checks" to take the pulse of everyone's mental health and well-being. After all, the juggler's trick is to respond to any changes in the breeze and to shift his or her weight accordingly to keep a balance. We have found that as long as our children are warm, affectionate, and happy at home and with friends, and as long as my husband and I still find our careers gratifying, then all is probably okay.

Ball #2: Sustaining Professional Success

I believe passionately that anyone can reach positive compromises between work and personal pursuits. The key is a commitment to confront both the issues and opportunities that are likely to arise openly, and then to have thoughtful discussions both at home and at the office. Frankly, it has been disheartening to me that so many of my friends—successful professionals in a myriad of careers—have not found the forum for open discussion at their place of work and have essentially "dropped out" of the mainstream workforce. What a boon this is creating for entrepreneurial ventures and enhanced support for volunteer organizations, but what a shame that so much talent is unutilized and failing to contribute to economic advancement in this country.

A series of personal decisions and, admittedly, some good fortune have allowed me to stay on-course with a career. That series of decisions had what I consider a "fortunate" base in that my professional interests revolve around marketing and business development careers. Choosing a career in the corporate world rather than in such fields as consulting and investment banking, where work schedules are hard to predict, facilitated every subsequent decision on career versus lifestyle.

For some, a professional interest will lie in a more demanding career arena. In those cases, what may prove most helpful is to tackle the notion of how to define career success. Standard industry measures do not typically account for compromises to accommodate personal responsibilities. Therefore, I recommend that any professional take on responsibility for defining success in his or her own career. For me, this has meant setting milestones for advancement on a timetable that I can accept and considering certain marketing positions over others.

Now I should add a word about good fortune, because I believe that everyone benefits from some luck along the way. I have been fortunate in that both my current and immediate past employer have been open-minded. I spent seven years at Avon Products, a company well known for its commitment to tackling work-family issues directly.

Four years ago, I left Avon to join Bloomingdale's. The change was not planned, but rather serendipitous. I was actually five months' pregnant and not in a job-search mode. My good fortune was in knowing Michael Gould, CEO of Bloomingdale's, and having already established a very strong level of mutual respect. He asked me to join his team, and upon hearing that I was pregnant, immediately added his congratulations. As he knew me, my work ethic, and my open communication style, there was no concern about the impact of a pregnancy on my segue into a new position. Following his lead, the organization adjusted to the situation and facilitated my maternity leave while hardly knowing me. And to this day, candid positions on trade-offs between work and family have been easily accommodated.

Communication and self-confidence have been the banners that I wave in the face of any professional contemplating the juggling act between work and family. Nonetheless, the pressures of a full-time job, compounded by the demands of a growing household, can seem daunting at times. At those times, I remind myself of the little things that I can control and that make my life a little easier. For instance, I have learned when and how to cut back and use time efficiently. For example, my position requires travel to all of our stores, but I can usually accomplish my trips in a single day if I plan them right.

Finally, I could not close this topic without acknowledging the extent to which technology makes my life easier. Computers, voice mail, fax machines, electronic mail, and even the occasional telecommuting routine have all freed up time for me. More accurately, they allow me to use time flexibly. Even something as seemingly innocuous as a car phone becomes a vital link to the office and makes the difference between leaving the office in time for dinner rather than just in time for a bedtime story.

That I have been able to negotiate so many commitments at once has required the active support of family members and business associates. But first and foremost, it has been driven by my belief in myself and confidence that I could make my disparate goals work together. There have been no rule books to follow, only my own instincts, enhanced by the input of valued friends and colleagues. And, whenever possible, I ignore the nagging questions of "if only" and "what if" in order to maintain my sanity. My career, my assessment of progress, my capacity to make decisions and accept the consequences of my decisions—all keep the juggling act in motion.

Ball #3: Household Chores

It is in the arena of basic household chores, those mundane but necessary tasks that keep a home running smoothly, that I have found technology and delegation to be my buzzwords. The recent boom in consumer-friendly technology, plus the explosion in the services sector, has made it much easier to keep juggling responsibilities. Letting go of traditional responsibilities and capitalizing on new conveniences really does pay off.

The resources available today are astounding and amazingly affordable; the trick is to learn how to use them most effectively, and to never consider them an indulgence but rather practical tools with time-saving benefits. Technology has a tremendous ability to make daily routines run more smoothly. On the more sophisticated end of the spectrum, opportunities exist to convert paper-based chores—bill-paying, financial management, budgeting—to on-line services via computer, fax, and telephone. For many, the flexibility and convenience of an electronic transaction far outweigh the slight expense such services may generate.

Even those on a smaller budget, or who consider themselves "low-tech" individuals, can reap benefits. A microwave oven, preprogrammable appliances, and even an instant hot-water spigot are commonplace in many kitchens. Timers for lights or a sprinkler system can alleviate worries about maintaining a well-kept, secure home.

The important rule in this arena is to remember that the accomplishment of the task matters more than who may actually have completed it or even how it was completed. In our household, such chores as supermarket shopping, trips to the dry cleaners, and errands around town can easily be handled by our caregiver while our children are in school or busy with playdates. Services as basic as housekeeping and lawn maintenance, coupled with the offers of free local delivery from the pharmacy or hardware store, also lift time-consuming tasks from our shoulders.

Eliminate tasks about which you feel no personal sense of accomplishment, and instead devote your newly freed-up time to pursuits you enjoy. Juggling household responsibilities will always demand some time and attention. But I see this as the one ball where responsibilities will get easier even as we add

more technical complexity to our lives. And another positive side effect of juggling this ball is that our children are growing up with an open-minded approach
to technology and its applications.

Ball #4: Active Community Involvement

Unlike the three balls already discussed, this is a ball put in motion purely
for its opportunity to yield personal well-being and create appreciation for all
one has. Giving back to the community taps into an altruistic sense of responsibility and can create a sense of emotional fulfillment that spills into other
aspects of one's life. Be it hands-on participation or largely a financial commitment, there is certainly psychic reward from doing something for the benefit
of others.

More than providing a private sense of well-being, this ball creates a ripple
for the other balls. For instance, my community activities in the Junior League
and the United Jewish Appeal not only help others in the community; I, too,
benefit. Participation as an officer of a volunteer organization requires that I
refine my interpersonal skills and work hard at building team consensus. There
is also opportunity to develop the art of persuasion and the ability to talk before
a public audience and think fast on my feet. I am more effective at my full-
time job as a result.

I also like to think that my involvement serves as a positive role model for
my two children. They need to learn to appreciate the many comforts they have
and respect the hard work necessary to maintain them. For now, my son and
daughter's donation to the local toy drive is more my doing than their own
initiative; one day, I hope the reverse will be true.

On an entirely different level, community involvement helps establish local
roots. This "connectedness" is valuable, not only to us, but, I imagine, to anyone who lives far from his or her family and hometown. As my children enter
the public school system, I am venturing more into local community decision
making. My involvement is my opportunity to provide input to the decisions
that affect my family life. This participation promotes an emotional bonding to
the community that builds relationships and a support system.

Finally, community involvement provides contact with other professionals
who are conducting their own juggling acts. Frankly, this is helpful and reas-
suring. Sharing experiences—the successes as well as the challenges—has generated new ideas, and even new solutions, for me and my husband.

Ball #5: Time for Self and Spouse

I have saved the best, or certainly the most challenging, ball for last. While
fulfilling the roles of parent, professional, and community volunteer are all important and gratifying, none of them can be fulfilled effectively unless the individual feels a sense of inner contentment. Nobody can function without a

modicum of personal space. Nor can a family function without strong spousal support ties. Both are vital for maintaining stable mental health and well-being.

In spite of the importance of this time, my experience has been that this is the ball most frequently dropped. It is dropped because it often seems like the most self-indulgent activity—that carving out some quiet personal time is a luxury busy people can ill afford. I cannot disagree more strongly. The ability to respect one's personal needs has been the foundation upon which my confidence to maintain a juggling act stands.

While I am emphatic that allocating some personal time is so critical, I have no strong feelings about how the time is actually spent. What matters only is that the activity or hobby generates a sense of happiness and offers some respite from the rest of daily living. The benefit to one's health that comes from physical exercise or sports is matched by the psychic rewards of having personal time. Sports, cultural pursuits, even pursuing do-it-yourself projects—any or all of them fill the bill.

Admittedly, with children, my personal outlets have become somewhat more humble; I can no longer jet off for a weekend to visit friends on the West Coast and handle the impact of a ''red-eye'' flight back. Nor do I want to spend several evenings a week away from home taking courses and/or attending seminars. But I have learned that my time spent curled up with a good book or listening to music while the rest of the family is happily occupied in another room helps keep me on an even keel.

Personal and family happiness also benefit from carving out time to spend as a couple. At the very least, my husband and I have learned that we must snatch every possible moment to talk—to catch up on assorted topics—and ensure that we remain in synch with one another. On the most basic level, our conversations serve to ensure that we make family decisions jointly and maintain consistency in the household. But on a much more profound level, our time together is key to our remaining strong, supportive partners. Social activities, even with other friends, provide emotional boosts.

Unlike any of the other balls in this juggling act, there is never an opportunity to delegate the responsibilities here. At home, our caregiver and technology both contribute to the smooth running of the household; in the workplace, effective partnerships with colleagues ensure that all tasks are completed in a timely and professional manner. The responsibility to oneself, however, rests solely on one's own shoulders. Again, this is the foundation upon which I build my entire life; having a sense of confidence and respect for its contribution to my well-being constantly reenergizes me.

CLOSING COMMENTS

The metaphor of juggling a handful of balls no doubt rings familiar to many professionals. The balls may comprise slightly different issues, but the fundamental principle remains intact: we all assume multiple roles and are constantly faced with the challenges of maintaining some sense of balance among the competing priorities.

I take heart in the fact that the topic of juggling work and family issues has garnered more attention in recent years and that more and more corporations are devoting their resources to understanding better the inherent conflicts and challenges that can arise and spill into the workplace. And I applaud all of the social agencies that have increased the flexibility and array of their services to accommodate the diversity of lifestyles and family situations in our country. But all of these efforts must focus on policy that can be implemented with a broad-based scope in order to achieve some level of economic feasibility.

The need remains for each professional to address the issues on his or her own, personal level. And only those who take the initiative to broach the topic— to seek an open and honest dialog both at home and in the workplace—will have an easy time juggling their lives. I have confidence that most organizations will be receptive to new possibilities. But they will not initiate them alone. Their focus is on protecting the overall interests of the total organization; each of us must take it upon ourselves to bring that macro view down to our micro level.

Companies can respond if presented with clear, carefully thought-out proposals to accommodate individual circumstances. Companies can accept a certain level of flexibility if an individual projects the confidence that the ultimate results will satisfy whatever business goals are ahead. What is most needed is: (1) open and honest communications, both at home and in the workplace; (2) an open-mindedness to hear, try, and accept new ideas; and (3) a flexibility to adapt to ever-changing circumstances. In the end, there is too much at stake for business and society to ignore these needs.

History provides no precedent for addressing these issues. Our greatest source of strength and success is our own passion to accept the challenges of a juggling act as an opportunity to stand behind our values and to live them with integrity.

CHAPTER 6

Managing Work-Family Tensions: A Counseling Perspective

Marianne O'Hare

The traditional image of the working dad and "stay-at-home" mom with children fits only 10% of U.S. families; the norm today is the dual-employed couple with children, representing 80% of U.S. families.[1] There are numerous economic and psychological benefits to the dual-employed family, which include a better standard of living; intellectual stimulation; increased personal satisfaction; valuing one another's abilities, talents, and ambitions; and freedom from traditional roles. Most women work to augment the family income, to support themselves or their families, and/or to attain personal fulfillment. Other benefits for women include a sense of self separate from spouse and children, greater intellectual companionship and contentment, and higher self-esteem.

For men and children, the dual-employed marriage can provide great satisfaction and fulfillment. Men can be free of total economic responsibility and family dependency and have an opportunity to parent and express their need to nurture and bond. Children benefit by having greater contact with both parents, less exposure to stereotypic sex-role behavior, positive role models, and the opportunity to develop independence.

The benefits of the dual-employed couple outweigh the costs, but conflicts, particularly around issues of equality, do exist.[2] Pressures of a dual-employed lifestyle include role overload and role conflict, normative dilemmas, sex-role and personal identity conflicts, and marital-role quality distress.

Much of the literature on dual-career couples focuses on the stresses and strains of either the couple or the wife[3] and on coping strategies.[4] However, several researchers have begun to explore various approaches to counseling the dual-career couple or those in a dual-employed relationship.[5] The purpose of this chapter is to describe some problematic issues that are frequently heard and addressed during counseling, and to identify themes that counselors should explore when working with dual-career/earner couples.

WORK-FAMILY ISSUES

According to Pleck, work/family issues have begun receiving increased attention, not because of the rise in the number of dual-career workers, but because of the increase in the larger group of dual-earner couples who affect social policy.[6] Counselors, therefore, should be mindful that not every working couple seen in counseling falls into the "dual-career" category. Gilbert defines the dual-career family as one in which both the woman and the man "pursued a lifelong career, relatively uninterrupted, and also established and developed a family life that often included children."[7] This lifestyle suggests an egalitarian relationship, differing from the view that women, regardless of employment status, have primary responsibility for the children and men have primary responsibility as provider.

In some cases, the dual-career couple's life may be more complicated and hectic than that of the dual-earner. The problems are, however, no more complex or severe. Dual-earner couples create greater social policy concern because, unlike dual-career couples, they have "less bargaining power with their employers, fewer economic resources to cope with their problems, and the economic consequences of the wife leaving the labor force are more severe for them."[8] It's important for counselors to be aware that the attitudes, behaviors, difficulties, and issues presented by dual-career and dual-earner couples can be very similar or very different. Frequently encountered work-family issues are discussed in the following sections.

Lifestyle Issues

Divorce, Remarriage, and the Blended Family. Many dual-career couples are not first-time married. In 1990, the divorce ratio was at an all-time high for both men and women, and the blended family is today's fastest growing group. Also, divorced women are the most likely to work full time.[9] Many remarried people have careers and children, and all the difficulties experienced by first-married dual-earner couples are compounded in remarried and blended families. Partners must not only adjust to their new spousal relationship, but many must take on the new role of stepparent. Power, boundary, and financial issues are among the major conflict areas.

Parent (Elder) Care. In the last 30 years, the number of people over age 65 has doubled; it is expected to double again by the year 2020.[10] Parent care presents numerous problems, and many couples, especially those who delayed having children, find themselves caring for their elderly parents at the same time that they are caring for young children. Nine out of ten women baby-boomers (the "sandwich generation") can expect to spend 17 or 18 years caring for children, older family members, or both while working outside the home.[11] This is also the first generation to be faced with having to care for two generations of older family members (typically, mothers and grandmothers). In addition to feeling stressed as the primary caregivers, women worry about who will care for the elderly without adequate programs providing quality long-term health care.[12]

The "Refilled" Nest. Today, 18 million young adults ages 18 to 34 are living with their parents.[13] Of those aged 24 to 34, many have returned to the home after divorce, difficult financial times, and/or loss of work. The majority of those between 18 and 24 have never been married and have never left the nest. As a result, many couples come for counseling either because they are returning home or because their children are returning home.

Relational Issues

Marital/Relationship Difficulties. Because dual-employed couples are frequently stressed, tired, and/or overwhelmed, time given to the relationship may suffer, especially if the couple has children and a high need for achievement.[14] Accompanying the need for achievement is the need for self-esteem-enhancing gratification in the form of "strokes" or appreciation for their efforts.[15] Often, these needs go unmet, leading to frustration and dissatisfaction with the relationship. Power struggles, feeling unsupported, or lack of mutual caring are common, particularly between very competitive partners.

Intimacy and Sex. Rice points out that conflicts in the area of intimacy are often masked by partners throwing themselves into the demands of work and family.[16] Couples may not find time for togetherness, and sexual relations may be infrequent and unsatisfactory. The notion of "spontaneity" is wonderful, but in reality, romance may have to be built into the relationship through scheduling and time management.

Personal Growth and Friendships. Frequently heard from one or both partners is, "I don't have time for myself or friends." In a study conducted by the Research Group on Women and Work (RGWW), 63% of the women respondents reported having little time for relationships outside marriage.[17] The RGWW study also indicated that, in terms of leisure time, married professional women had less than single professional women, and married, professional women with children had less than anyone, including single women with children. The study suggested that the presence of a husband actually decreased the amount of time a woman had for herself because of the increased domestic workload.

Partners frequently report feelings of guilt when they want time for themselves, they feel "selfish," because they "should not" leave the spouse and/or children. But stress, fatigue, and overwork contribute to a lowered immune system and emotional vulnerability, and men and women who put in excessive work and home hours jeopardize their physical and emotional health. Those who attempt to be super-persons become physically ill and burned out. Partners need to understand that having time for self or friends is an important way to cope, revitalize, and nurture oneself.

Education. More than 50% of the college students in the United States today are over age 25. By the year 2000, 50% of all college undergraduates will be older than 22.[18] And since 80% or more students are also employed, we might expect that one or both dual-career spouses attends college.

Often, women will interrupt their careers for childbearing and/or child rearing. Women who choose the "Mommy" track (taking time off from work to care for their children) pay a high price when reentering the job market. It is not atypical for such women to sacrifice career advancement and earning potential.

However, many women use the interruption as an opportunity for career change, starting their own businesses, or returning to school. In the RGWW study, women in relationships with a combined income of over $40,000 were more likely to return to education than those with lower incomes.[19]

Work-Related Issues

Role Overload, Conflict, and Coping Problems. Having both a career *and* a family, which is a "given" for men, is considered "trying to have it all" for women.[20] Most young people in our society grow up with the belief that they will one day be employed and have children. But girls, more than boys, give considerable thought to how to manage work and family life and how to integrate career with relationships and children. As adults, women, more than men, have to juggle it all.

In the RGWW study, 82% of the respondents experienced role overload as a definite problem, but most of the women reported that learning to live with the situation was their best coping method. In counseling, I see few women who easily "live" with the situation.

Workplace stress and work overload take a toll on the family, often in the form of anxiety, depression, psychosomatic complaints, or cardiovascular distress. Alcohol abuse is also associated with role overload, but in the RGWW study, only role deprivation was associated with alcohol abuse in women. It seemed that the busier a woman was, the less likely she was to drink.

Role conflict and coping with role conflict are well researched.[21] Conflict creates tension and stress, and, if left unresolved, leads to greater problems; it can also be an opportunity for growth and development. In addition, the number of roles a person has and role demands often intensify the conflict. Methods used by the individual to deal or cope with conflict will affect both the individual and the relationship. Hall and Hall categorized coping with role conflict into three types: confrontation and negotiation; a change of one's own attitudes and perceptions without consultation with others; and an attempt to satisfy all role demands.[22] Stoltz-Loike describes techniques of conflict resolution that a person can master, such as avoidance, accommodation, confrontation, compromise, and collaboration.[23] I find that another type of coping, escape (e.g. drinking, drugging, or exercise), can be used to distract oneself but does nothing to solve the conflict or problem.

Role conflict is frequently reported in counseling, and most women seem to try "doing it all," leading to stress, role overload, and burnout. Men, on the other hand, report either compartmentalizing their roles by separating the home situation from their work or prioritizing or reframing the situation without consulting their partners. Noncollaboration with one's partner usually results in misunderstanding and resentment.

Downsizing. During the last seven years, 85% of the Fortune 1,000 companies downsized, eliminating 6 million jobs, which is a loss of 3,000 jobs per day.[24] Intended to streamline operations and reduce labor costs, downsizing creates a number of psychological and behavioral problems for both survivors and those laid off. Rather than work harder, survivors become angry, cynical, disillusioned, depressed, and distrusting of management. Those laid off experience anger, anxiety, depression, and a concern about relocation (especially for families with young children).

Relocation. In our current "downsizing" climate, many couples are forced to relocate. Since the decision is usually based on income, couples generally locate to where the husband finds work. Relocation disrupts family life and routines and often creates adjustment problems.

Some couples opt for "commuter" marriages if one or the other spouse cannot find suitable employment or would rather not pass up career opportunities or advancement. Commuter and long-distance relationships are fertile ground for problems, but many young people whose identities are derived from their work will often maintain long-distance relationships rather than give up their employment. Some older couples rediscover autonomy, excitement, adventure, and romance in long-distance relationships, meeting on the weekends with renewed energy and heightened desire.

Finances. Which partner earns the most money does affect relationships. The average working wife contributes 40% of the family's annual income, and 80% of wives earn less than their husbands.[25] Those who earn as much or more than their husbands tend to keep that fact quiet. This may be because both men and women buy into the stereotypic notion that "real" men "should" earn more than their wives. Many relationships end in divorce when partners have a difficult time coping with the idea of the wife earning more than her spouse.

Gender/Role Issues

Child Care. The majority of parents, particularly mothers, cite child care as their most stressful issue. Over 60% of children under age 18 have working mothers and, of the married mothers, full-time working mothers are significantly more likely to utilize organized child care facilities than mothers with part-time jobs, who are likely to use family members and home care.[26] Many organizations have responded to the need for greater flexibility in the workplace by developing programs such as paternity leave, flexible hours, telecommuting, and child care services and centers. Still, women continue to have primary responsibility for the children and are more likely to take advantage of work/family options. This perpetuates a situation in which women do most of the care taking while men progress in their careers and have power over social policy and legislation.[27]

Gender-Role Stereotype Problems. Gilbert points out that traditional beliefs about women's relational nature and dependency pervade our society.[28] Men and women have been socialized to frame their experiences in stereotypic ways, believing that women prefer to live their lives through their husbands or their children. According to this view, a woman's role is to nurture and support her husband, and the man is entitled to expect her to play this role. Beliefs such as these can foster inequity and inflexibility in the relationship, the reinforcement and perpetuation of traditional roles, and feelings of guilt in women who enjoy independence and work involvement.

In addition, because of sex-role stereotypes, many men do not take women seriously. An exaggerated sense of self-importance and not recognizing women's need for independence may make it difficult for some men to listen to women or consider their ideas as having merit.[29]

Most couples in counseling believe that they hold no stereotypic ideas about the opposite sex or their partners. When these are uncovered however, couples, often surprised by the inconsistencies between avowed beliefs and reality, generally have a genuine desire to change. Showing no inclination toward change after recognizing the destructiveness in either partner's attitude or behavior can have disastrous effects on the relationship.

Household Responsibilities. Wives employed full time outside the home do 70% of the housework.[30] It's encouraging, however, that the number of men who more fully participate in child rearing and housework is steadily increasing. For example, it has been found that, as a woman's "net economic power" increases, so will a man's involvement in the household and parenting. Over 56% of the participants in the RGWW study reported that their husbands share significantly in household and parenting responsibilities, with women earning incomes in the $40,000 to $50,000 range reporting more equal sharing than those earning less.[31]

Gilbert indicates that there are three typical ways in which dual-career couples handle work and family roles.[32] In "role-sharing" relationships, both spouses are actively involved in household duties and parenting. In "traditional" families, parenting and household duties are the wife's responsibility in addition to her work role. And in "participant" dual-career families, parenting is shared by both parents, but household responsibilities are still primarily the wife's. In couples counseling, men often believe that they are "role sharing" but are actually in "participant" relationships, frequently creating friction between spouses.

COUNSELING THEMES

Currently, there is a growing body of literature on recommendations for counseling dual-career or dual-employed couples, and some researchers and psychologists have outlined workshops, frameworks for counseling, and strategies for change.[33] Three are particularly useful in describing what counselors do and might do to ameliorate the difficulties of dual-employed couples.[34]

In counseling, depending on whether the couples are dual-career or dual-earner, greater emphasis may be placed on some issues in the relationship more than others. However, most researchers and practitioners agree on the importance of exploring several themes, either independently or in combination.

Satisfaction and Fulfillment

The bottom line in the dual-earner relationship is how happy each partner is with his or her life situation. Do lifestyle benefits outweigh the costs? Does the struggle to integrate work and family roles increase each partner's sense of self-worth and the couple's positive feelings for each other?

Equity

Fairness may be the central issue in dual-earner relationships. Equity does not mean equality; that is, the relationship should "balance out," not by rigidly following a set of rules. Does the cost-benefit ratio result in satisfaction or distress? Can each partner anticipate that what she or he is doing in the present will have a future "payoff"?

Power

It can be assumed that both partners have power— that is, authority or influence in the relationship. What needs to be discerned is whether or not that power is recognized and how it is exercised. It is desirable for power to be equalized.

Dependency

Dependency (one's ability to rely on another) and interdependency (mutual reliance within the relationship) are healthy and adaptive. Does each partner feel that she or he has support and can depend on the other? Does each partner have the ability to be dependent at times and independent at other times?

Nurturance

Attention, affection, and the need to give and receive care are of vital importance if a relationship is to thrive. How do partners demonstrate their affection for each other? Does either partner feel emotionally drained from giving but not receiving?

Stress Management

Having to do with the ability to identify stressors and problem-solve, and related to role conflict and coping, stress management also has to do with the exploration of the personal, familial, and societal resources available, including hired help, relaxation and leisure time, and work schedules. How realistic are the partners in their expectations of one another? How able are they to anticipate difficulties and work together toward a desired goal?

Values Clarification

It can be expected that couples who do not share similar values (e.g., money, culture, religion, politics, education, ethics) will have difficulty. The more rigidly traditional the couple tends to be, the more likely the partners are to experience distress. Conversely, the more androgynous the couple, the greater will be the partners' adaptability and satisfaction.

Normative Dilemmas

When a couple's beliefs or social standards are sanctioned by society or those around them, a normative dilemma may be experienced. Dilemmas can encompass work policy, family, religious, moral, discipline, cultural, and other values. The importance of exploring these dilemmas is to help couples understand that some problems are not caused by the relationship or each other but by an outside referent that may influence their lives, and to assist couples in prioritizing, problem solving, and reducing stress.

Competition

Like power, competition is strongly related to equity in the relationship. Although competition need not be damaging, it can result in resentment and conflict if "having to win" means besting one's partner.

Decision Making

Also related to power, the style of a couple's decision making can result in marital satisfaction or distress. Who decides, and how is a decision made? Can the couple discuss and explore decisions to be made, the reaction of each partner, and the consequences? Is there a "quid pro quo," and is the exchange satisfactory?

Time Management

How does the couple utilize time? How would they like to spend the time? Does each partner agree on how the time should be spent? Again (related to equity), does one spouse feel as though she or he is being required to spend valuable time in ways she or he would rather not? In relation to coping, is the couple trying to do everything and/or please everybody?

Coping

Coping refers to the couple's way of dealing with interrole and intrarole conflict. What types of coping do the partners use? (Perhaps the partners are prioritizing and planning but not consulting with one another.)

Entitlement

When one partner believes that she or he has a right or inherent claim to something (for example, the other's nurturing or service), this special or superior belief can lead to serious problems. More often than not, entitlement is not acknowledged on a conscious level. Attention should be paid to how the relationship is structured. Does one partner expect that his or her needs will be met and disregard or minimize the needs of the other? How comfortable is each partner with his or her sex life and intimacy? Who asks to be thanked, and for what reasons?

Flexibility

A great source of stress, distress, and marital conflict is inflexibility. Partners who are able to bend are more likely to harbor fewer resentments and have a healthier lifestyle than those who rigidly adhere to certain "rules" or decisions.

Spousal Support and Support Networks

Relationships depend on the felt and actual encouragement and sensitivity received from one's partner. Support networks include one's partner, and friends, family, colleagues, and other resources in the community, which must be available in time of need. Help can be tangible, as in the form of money or baby-sitting, or intangible, such as a "shoulder to cry on." Having others to rely upon bolsters one's sense of stability and self-worth, is empowering, and creates a mutually caring environment.

COUNSELING DUAL-EMPLOYED COUPLES

Counseling dual-employed couples is similar to counseling any couple or individual, but there are also unique factors for counselors to consider. First, psychologists who work with dual-employed couples experiencing marital difficulties must check their impulse to make directives and decisions based on assumptions about the motivations of the partners and the effects on them of a dual-employed marriage.[35] For example, many of the couples with whom I work engage in role reversal. Many of the men are "Mr. Moms" and/or the primary caretakers of their children, and their wives are the "breadwinners." As the therapist, I must be aware of any biases and attitudes I may have toward a traditional family lifestyle, and I must also realize that both partners may or may not be career involved or ambitious and achievement oriented. Women (and some men) in these marriages may be working only to augment the family's finances or also seeking the intrinsic rewards a career or job has to offer.

Second, even with substantial social change, women continue to be linked more with the family and men more to the work system. Yet marital identity and marital role appear to be as salient for men in dual-employed relationships as for women. Both men and women experience their family roles as far more psychologically significant than their work roles, and their adjustment to family has a greater impact on their psychological well-being than their adjustment to work.[36] Studies indicate that the marital role is central to men's mental health and that "positive and negative marital experiences have similar influences on men's and women's mental health."[37] Many of my clients, for example, rely on each other and their family for happiness and support. And both men and women organize their schedules in order that the family may function as smoothly as possible. When partner support is not forthcoming, the relationship suffers greatly.

Third, it's important to note that some couples have decided to remain childless. Given the importance placed on children and families in our society, it's surprising that only 38% of our workforce has children under the age of 18.[38] Counselors must be cognizant of their own attitudes regarding childless families and be sensitive to childless employees, who may feel discriminated against in the workplace. Often I have had clients report that because a coworker must retrieve his or her child at a particular time, my client was asked to work overtime. As a result, the client may come in acting angry and resentful, complaining, and/or feeling guilty because of a belief that he or she "should" be less "selfish."

Fourth, counselors must be aware that dual-career couples tend to be cognitively oriented and verbal.[39] Counselors such as myself, who ascribe to a cognitive-behavioral orientation, quickly develop rapport with these couples and find this problem-solving approach to therapy to be advantageous. However, as Rice points out, we have to be careful not to overlook affective responses and not to reinforce verbosity which may be defensive.

Fifth, counselors should realize that not all cultures and societies think and behave as we do. Most of the dual-employed family research has been conducted in North America, thereby ignoring other cultural perspectives.[40] The need to remain current with the multicultural literature goes without saying. However, more often than not, I am educated by my clients with regard to their particular customs, beliefs, and behaviors. What I've discovered is that, culturally, attempts at balancing work-family roles can range from the more traditional to the most liberal.

Finally, although the literature may disproportionately focus on the effects of work on family, family also affects work, with each system having a significant impact on the other. With the exception of activity and location (and, in some cases, not even excepting location), there is no true separation of work life and family life. Company policies and expectations idiosyncratic to a particular job will influence the family's routine, leisure time, and security, but it is the family's ability to deal with pressure and be flexible and supportive that influences role performance.

Because of this interdependence, counselors should note the traditional values underlying American social policy and how they affect dual-employed families.[41] As the numbers of dual-employed families increase, social values and policies will change, hopefully addressing the needs of our workers and strengthening the reciprocal interaction of family, community, and the workplace. Counselors are in a position to influence both workers' and corporations' attitudes, enhancing the quality of their partnership, and, by extension, social values.[42]

NOTES

1. L.A. Gilbert, *Two Careers/One Family* (Newbury Park, CA: Sage, 1993).

2. Ibid.

3. E.S. Amatea & M.L. Fong, "The Impact of Role Stressors and Personal Resources on the Stress Experience of Professional Women," *Psychology of Women Quarterly* 15 (1991): 419–430.

4. F.S. Hall & D.T. Hall, *The Two Career Couple* (Reading, MA: Addison-Wesley, 1979).

5. Gilbert, *Two Careers/One Family*; J.M. O'Neil, D.M. Fishman, & M. Kinsella-Shaw, "Dual-Career Couples' Career Transitions and Normative Dilemmas: A Preliminary Model," *Counseling Psychologist* 15 (1987): 50–96; U. Sekaran, *Dual-Career Families* (San Francisco: Jossey-Bass, 1986); M. Stoltz-Loike, *Dual Career Couples: New Perspectives in Counseling* (Virginia: ACA, 1992); L.S. Walker, P. Rozee-Koker, & B.S. Wallston, "Social Policy and the Dual-Career Family: Bringing the Social Context into Counseling," *Counseling Psychologist* 15 (1987): 97–121.

6. J.H. Pleck, "Dual-Career Families: A Comment," *Counseling Psychologist* 15 (1987): 131–133.

7. Gilbert, *Two Careers/One Family*, p. 4.

8. Pleck, "Dual-Career Families," p. 132.

9. P. Ries & A.J. Stone, *The American Woman: 1992–93* (New York: W.W. Norton & Co., 1992).

10. Ibid.

11. Sekaran, *Dual-Career Families*.

12. Ries & Stone, *The American Woman*.

13. Ibid.

14. D.G. Rice, *Dual-Career Marriage: Conflict and Treatment* (New York: Free Press, 1979).

15. Ibid.

16. Ibid.

17. C.W. Konek & S.L. Kitch, *Women and Careers: Issues and Challenges* (Newbury Park, CA: Sage, 1994).

18. Ries & Stone, *The American Woman*.

19. Konek & Kitch, *Women and Careers*.

20. Gilbert, *Two Careers/One Family*.

21. N.J. Beutell & J. Greenhaus, "Integration of Home and Non-Home Roles: Women's Conflict and Coping Behavior," *Journal of Applied Psychology* 68 (1982): 43–48; Hall & Hall, *The Two Career Couple*; R.S. Lazarus & S. Folkman, *Stress, Appraisal, and Coping* (New York: Springer, 1984); Stoltz-Loike, *Dual Career Couples*.

22. Hall & Hall, *The Two Career Couple*.

23. Stoltz-Loike, *Dual Career Couples*.

24. G. Custer, "Downsizing Fallout May Be Widespread," *APA Monitor* 27 (October, 1994): 50–51.

25. Konek & Kitch, *Women and Careers*.

26. Gilbert, *Two Careers/One Family*.

27. Ibid.

28. Ibid.

29. Ibid.

30. Women's Action Coalition, *The Facts about Women* (New York: New Press, 1993).

31. Konek & Kitch, *Women and Careers*.

32. Gilbert, *Two Careers/One Family*.

33. Ibid.; O'Neil et al., "Dual-Career Couples' Career Transitions"; Rice, *Dual-Career Marriage*; Walker et al., "Social Policy and the Dual-Career Family."

34. Rice, *Dual-Career Marriage*; Sekaran, *Dual-Career Families*; Stoltz-Loike, *Dual Career Couples*.

35. Rice, *Dual-Career Marriage*.

36. J.H. Pleck, *Working Wives/Working Husbands* (Newbury Park, CA: Sage, 1985).

37. R.C. Barnett, R.T. Brennan, & S.W. Raudenbush, "Gender and the Relationship between Marital-Role Quality and Psychological Distress: A Study of Women and Men in Dual-Earner Couples," *Psychology of Women Quarterly* 18(1): 105–124.

38. L. Lafayette, "Fair Play for the Childless Worker," *New York Times*, October 16, 1994, Business section, p. 11.

39. Rice, *Dual-Career Marriage*.

40. S. Lewis, D.N. Izraeli, & H. Hootsmans, *Dual-Earner Families: International Perspectives* (London: Sage, 1992).

41. Walker et al., "Social Policy and the Dual-Career Family."

42. Stoltz-Loike, *Dual Career Couples*.

CHAPTER 7

A Research Perspective on Work-Family Issues

Marcia Brumit Kropf

Research that is useful to work-family practitioners must focus on building knowledge that informs their work. The work of work-family practitioners has changed and evolved over time and, as a result, research on work-family issues has changed dramatically over the last three decades.

Catalyst is a national not-for-profit organization, founded in 1962, which works with business and the professions to effect change for women through research, advisory services, and communication. The organization has a dual mission—to enable women in business and the professions to achieve their maximum potential and to help employers capitalize on the talents of their female employees. Catalyst's research on flexible work arrangements provides an excellent example of the ways in which research has changed to respond to the needs of practitioners.

CHANGES IN PRACTITIONERS' THINKING

The biggest changes in the work-family movement have to do with how practitioners think about the issues. There has been a shift in focus from the specific problem of care for the young children of working mothers to a much wider set of work-family responsibilities of all working people, regardless of age and gender. In the past, work-family conflicts were seen as an issue for women with young children. Current research studies, however, include as participants a wide range of men and women of all ages, who describe a variety of issues requiring their time and energy, such as the needs of school-aged children, care for elderly parents, and a commitment to personal development or community work.

There is a shift in focus from the assumption that family responsibilities must always accommodate a very demanding work life to the understanding that work and family responsibilities should be balanced. This shift grows out of the terrible pressure many people feel to spend long hours at work. As a result, research is moving from studying the impact of family responsibilities on work productivity to examining the impact of work expectations on family life.

There is a shift in focus from the design and delivery of very specific programmatic solutions to understanding the need for broader, integrated organizational changes. As the thinking about work-family issues has evolved, it has become more and more clear that specific programs targeted at specific employees are beneficial—but they are not enough. Broader, cultural change is needed so that employees who use specific programs are not marginalized or labeled, all employees feel their issues are being accommodated, and it really is possible for individuals to balance the multiple commitments in their lives. Work-family research, then, has begun to focus less on program effectiveness and more on organizational culture and change management.

There is a shift in focus from viewing family-friendly initiatives as benefits or favors to viewing them as support for specific business objectives. This shift accompanies the changes in the roles of women in the workplace over the last three decades. Work-family issues were first conceptualized as ways to help or support women who wanted to work. Now women are 46.7% of the labor force.[1] Most need to work to support themselves and their families. Women are among the valuable and experienced employees that organizations need to recruit and retain. With this change in thinking, research has begun to examine the links between the organization's business agenda and work-family issues.

These shifts in thinking have led to shifts in the questions researchers ask, the subjects they study, and the participants they include in their studies. Researchers have moved from thinking about questions like, ''What do working mothers need?'' or, ''How do you help business leaders become more aware of work-family issues?'' to, ''How do work-family issues impact business?'' and, ''How do you effectively implement programs?''

PREVIOUS RESEARCH ON FLEXIBILITY

In 1968, Catalyst published a study of part-time teachers.[2] The goal was to find ways to satisfy employment shortages by using educated women who were not working and who did not want to work full-time. The study involved a survey of 700 school systems to understand the attitudes and opinions of superintendents toward part-time work and case studies of actual programs in five communities. The purpose of the study was to raise the consciousness of educators and to provide possible models for part-time teaching programs. The study found that part-time teaching could be very effective. The assumptions, problems, and concerns raised by survey respondents with no experience with part-time work were not supported by the 300 respondents who employed part-time teachers. Nor were the anticipated problems found in the case studies. Nona

Porter, an organizer of one program, noted: "Many of our anticipated problems never arose."[3]

This study was followed by *Part-time Social Workers in Public Welfare*.[4] This study had the same goal and a similar purpose to the first and involved the development of a model program in Boston with 50 job sharers and an evaluation of the program two years later. The research began to link part-time work to a positive business value: the shorter workday was found to improve productivity and increase retention in a field with a high burn-out factor. Alice MacDonald, a part-time social worker and participant in the study, said: "Women want to work. But they want to be good wives and good mothers as well. The Catalyst Program was consciously designed to give us a chance to exercise all of our options as women."[5] This early research asked: "What are the attitudes of the leaders of organizations?" and "What does a model program look like?"

During the 1970's and early 1980's, Catalyst's research involved gathering information about specific programs and disseminating that information as widely as possible. An example from that period is the *Catalyst Report on Flextime*, which described the usefulness, significance, and potential of a specific program.[6] The research emphasis was changed, now asking the question: "What is the usefulness of these individual programs?"

In the mid-1980's, Catalyst began work on a major study of flexible work arrangements.[7] Catalyst's goal was to understand the programs developed by corporations and professional firms to retain high-performing management-level women. The purpose of this study was to examine the experiences of organizations implementing flexible work arrangements and the individuals using them. This study continued the shift in focus to organizations and involved an extensive review of the literature, and telephone interviews with 47 companies and firms, 78 employees, and 79 managers.

The study found a growing awareness of the benefits, for both employers and employees, of offering flexible work options. Most of the participants reported positive outcomes such as the retention of valued employees, especially women professionals returning from maternity leave; increased productivity and staffing flexibility; improved morale; and an advantage for recruiting female employees. The vice president and general counsel at a Midwestern corporation noted: "It takes a long time to get smart as a lawyer, and we want to keep smart people around."[8] This study asked the question: "What are the experiences of organizations and individuals around this issue?"

With *Flexible Work Arrangements II: Succeeding with Part-time Options*, Catalyst researchers decided to build upon the knowledge gained with the 1989 study.[9] The purpose was to compare the new findings to the 1989 study—to look at these programs across time and to learn more about how these arrangements might impact the careers of these who use them. Representatives from the companies included in the 1989 study were interviewed, along with representatives of additional companies and firms. In addition, 45 of the managers and professionals using flexible work arrangements (women interviewed in 1989) were located and interviewed again.

The study found that:

- the use of the arrangements was more widespread than in 1989,
- many of the organizations had formalized their policies,
- managers and supervisors continued to be resistant to these arrangements.

It also found that the primary users of the arrangements were women with children, who were very concerned about time with their children throughout their school and teenage years. They were using the arrangements for longer than expected—the average was just over five years. The women found that their careers slowed down, but felt that, compared to the alternative of leaving the workforce, the arrangement helped them to maintain career continuity. One woman noted:

The biggest one [benefit] is that I've been able to keep my career going in engineering. If I'd taken these five years off and chosen to stay home with my children . . . I'd be out of touch with all the things that are going on and obviously not able to come back at the level I was then or the one I'm at right now. It kept my career going.[10]

The research question evolved to: "What are the experiences of organizations and individuals over time?"

All of the research described so far, along with the work of other researchers, has helped to build a rich body of knowledge about the topic of flexible work arrangements. Catalyst research has moved from a focus on finding ways to encourage organizations to offer part-time alternatives to women with young children to a focus on how to retain valuable employees through the use of part-time programs.

BARRIERS TO FLEXIBILITY

All of this research, regardless of the focus, has helped to provide an understanding of the barriers that exist in organizations to the implementation and use of flexible work arrangements. These barriers can be summarized into six categories.

Policy Barriers

There are policy limitations. Many companies lack formal, written policy. This leaves managers and employees negotiating arrangements individually and informally, without guidance, and also communicates a lack of commitment. In companies where there is a policy, employees are often not aware that such policies exist. As a result, implementation is inconsistent, ad hoc, and dependent upon the sensitivity of individual managers.

Barriers Created by Work Definitions

There are limitations due to how work is defined. Work continues to be defined in terms of hours in the workplace. Success at work continues to be considered in terms of how much time employees spend at the workplace. These values create environments where employees are reluctant to request reduced hours or opportunities to work at home, even when their work could be accomplished successfully within an alternative arrangement.

Barriers Created by Information and Reporting Systems

The formal managerial and information systems within most organizations were designed to communicate and reinforce a definition of work based on hours spent in the office. These structures can serve as barriers. For example, many organizations use a head-count system, which counts each individual as one employee, regardless of the amount of time worked or the tasks accomplished, and therefore penalizes managers or department heads with employees who are working part-time or job sharing. Managers in those environments are generally unwilling to approve reduced work arrangements.

Managerial Barriers

There are limitations due to how people are managed. In traditional organizations, work is defined as occurring only in the workplace, and managers use ''line of sight'' to supervise employees, who are readily accessible during the traditional workday. In the 1993 study, for example, many of the women interviewed did not feel comfortable discussing their part-time arrangement with their managers, changing the specific arrangement, or raising issues such as the effect of a reduced work arrangement on career goals.[11] Communication critical to the effectiveness of alternative arrangements is thus hampered.

Cultural Barriers

There are cultural limitations. Organizational cultures reinforce traditional definitions of work. There are cultures where it is common practice to spend weekends in the office and schedule meetings early in the morning, in the evening, and on weekends. These behaviors reinforce the concept that only those who work long hours are loyal and committed employees. One woman reported that she was taken more seriously as a part-time consultant to her company than she had been as a part-time employee, even though her hours and her work remained the same.[12] Thus, arrangements created to retain valuable employees result in those employees feeling disengaged, underutilized, and not valued.

Barriers Created by Misunderstandings

There are limitations due to the gap between perceptions about alternative arrangements and the reality. Myths and stories circulate through organizations and are used as explanations for events. Often misconceptions are circulated, affect behaviors, and limit the use of flexible arrangements. For example, many managers report concern and nervousness about a formal policy because they believe such a policy will "open the floodgates," causing them to become inundated with requests. Research, however, has not found this to be the case.[13]

FUTURE RESEARCH

The concern of researchers and practitioners in the coming decade will be less on raising the consciousness of employers or on identifying and understanding the current barriers to effective implementation. Rather, the focus will be on overcoming the barriers described here and on the effective introduction and implementation of flexibility in the workplace as a mainstream concept. To do this, it is essential that there be an understanding of what works, and why.

Successful Strategies

Research is needed that focuses on identifying and evaluating successful strategies. Many employers who are beginning to consider alternative work definitions have no understanding of the practical issues involved in implementation. They have much to gain from the experience of those employers with a long history of offering alternative arrangements. Most organizations are learning about what works in isolation, on a trial-and-error basis. Sharing information about implementation strategies used by employers can enable a more widespread implementation of flexibility and eliminate the replication of mistakes.

A forthcoming Catalyst guidebook resulted from a project to gather information about concrete, hands-on, practical strategies used by organizations and managers who are experienced with this issue to implement and manage flexible work arrangements.[14] It isn't enough to identify managers and supervisors as barriers. Research is needed to answer the question: "What does management need to learn to do?"

Effective Implementation over Time

Research is needed to focus on the process involved in effective implementation as well as programs and initiatives. Currently, most available information is about specific programs or initiatives designed to overcome a specific problem: a one-day training program to raise the consciousness of managers, a communication process for sharing information about a policy, a decision to revise an organizational system for reporting productivity. There is little understanding, however, of the comprehensive process necessary to overcome the wide range of existing barriers and sustain alternatives over a long period.

Employers with a history of involvement with this issue describe the implementation process as continuous. The economic situation, the work constraints, the employees using alternative arrangements, and the needs of employees for these arrangements change over time. A program or initiative that is effective at one point in time for one individual may not be at another. It is critical, then, for researchers to look at the long-term process of implementing these initiatives. In addition, the benefits of these programs involve the retention of valuable employees and higher productivity in the workplace. These benefits cannot be fully understood or documented without studies covering longer periods of time.

Catalyst has begun a major study that involves studying, over a one-year period, four organizations in very different stages of implementation: two companies and two professional service firms.[15] The study includes focus groups, interviews, and surveys with a wide range of stakeholders: managers, clients, alumni, colleagues, human resources representatives, senior management, and employees who have an alternative arrangement.

A Vision for Success

Research is needed that helps to provide a definition of success. It is important to begin to really evaluate programs, not so much to justify them as to enhance and improve them. Both qualitative and quantitative measures of retention, productivity, reduced stress, and improved effectiveness of individual employees are needed. "How do we know when we've succeeded?" is thus an interesting question to consider.

CONCLUSION

The research on flexible work arrangements provides an example of changing research that is relevant to the directions for work-family research in general. Based on this understanding, new directions for future research include:

- the need to continually gather and disseminate information about what works.
- the need to understand the process—especially the educational process—involved in making the workplace family-friendly.
- the need to understand work-family programs and initiatives and their impact over time on all the stakeholders.
- the need to evaluate the success of these programs and initiatives.

In closing, it is important to acknowledge that work-family issues are critical ones for companies—and, therefore, for practitioners and researchers. In 1994, Catalyst conducted roundtables with young women in M.B.A. programs in a number of the major business schools. Some of these young women shared their concerns. One woman noted: "I find that I'm just not willing to put my personal life on hold just to have my professional life become better, and I expect to work for a corporation that understands how important that is for me."[16]

NOTES

1. U.S. Bureau of Labor Statistics, "Employed Persons by Occupation, Race, and Sex in Employment and Earnings," January 1996, p. 170.

2. Catalyst, *Part-time Teachers and How They Work: A Study of Five School Systems* (New York: Catalyst, 1968).

3. Ibid., p. 3.

4. Catalyst, *Part-time Social Workers in Public Welfare* (New York: Catalyst, 1971).

5. Ibid., p. 42.

6. Catalyst, *Catalyst Report on Flextime* (New York: Catalyst, 1978).

7. Catalyst, *Flexible Work Arrangements: Establishing Options for Managers and Professionals* (New York: Catalyst, 1989).

8. Ibid., p. 39.

9. Catalyst, *Flexible Work Arrangements II: Succeeding with Part-time Options* (New York: Catalyst, 1993).

10. Ibid., p. 36.

11. Ibid.

12. Ibid.

13. Catalyst, *Flexible Work Arrangements.*

14. Catalyst, *Making Work Flexible: Policy to Practice* (New York: Catalyst, 1996).

15. Catalyst, *The Reorganizing of Work: Effective Strategies for a Changing Workforce*, funded by the Alfred P. Sloan Foundation (New York: Catalyst, 1997).

16. Catalyst, *How Female MBA Students View Career Success, Work/Life Balance and Management Consulting* (New York: Catalyst, 1994), p. 12.

CHAPTER 8

Services and Work-and-Family Life

Barbara A. Gutek

Much of our discussion of work-and-family issues revolves around the major roles that we play and the extent to which fulfilling one role facilitates or hinders the fulfillment of other major roles. In particular, we focus on three roles: the work role, the spouse/partner role, and the parent role. In this chapter, I would like to encourage us to think about the consumer or customer role and how that role affects our lives as it evolves and becomes more time consuming.[1]

Researchers have done an excellent job of focusing on the demands of both work and the two family roles and the conflict that people often face when they try to discharge the obligations and duties of all three roles.[2] These studies and a variety of surveys bolster the view that many Americans feel they do not have enough time for their families or for themselves. In her very interesting book, *The Overworked American*, Juliet Schor both noted that Americans today are working more hours than they did in the recent past and provided some explanations for that situation.[3] In particular, she argued that whenever productivity is increased and some of the benefits of increased productivity go to workers, those benefits accrue in the form of higher wages, not increased leisure. She argued that people have acquired more goods (and larger houses to put them in), but that in the process, they have lost most of their leisure time.

Schor, an economist, focuses in particular on the expanding work role, suggesting that people work harder and longer for increased wages, which are later spent on goods and services. But she also contends that the increased wages are spent through increased consumption, suggesting that perhaps the customer or consumer role is expanding. While she does discuss how people spend their earned incomes, she does not focus particularly on the time and effort required to purchase those goods and services. In a book I recently completed, I note the growing use of technology in expanding the number and kinds of services that are available to businesses and families as well as the changing and growing customer role.[4] In writing this book, I came to believe that looking at the role of customer or consumer (in addition to the roles of parent and spouse/partner) will give us a fuller view of the work-and-family situation as it exists in the closing years of the 20th century in the United States. In this chapter, I hope to encourage researchers to address the customer role and changes in that role in their programs of research and to encourage practitioners to consider this in the development of their organization's work-and-family programs.

FAMILIES AND THE SERVICE ECONOMY

It is well known that the United States is now a service economy. The number, amount, and availability of services is impressive. The majority of people in the labor force are providers of goods or services; they include members of most of the professions as well as people who are usually called service workers. In all, over 70% of workers in the United States, Canada, and Britain work in services, as do over 50% of workers in Japan, Germany, France, and Italy.[5] Correspondingly, the money and time people spend acting as a customer have also increased. By one estimate, the average household expends 45% of its income on services, and when goods are added in, it is clear that buying goods and services involves a lot of a family's money and occupies a considerable amount of time.[6] Thus, the role of customer is as ubiquitous as the more widely studied roles of worker, parent, and spouse, and some indirect evidence supports the claim that it accounts for a significant amount of people's time. Americans spend three to four times as many hours a year shopping as their Western European counterparts. An even more astounding estimate is that the typical American spends about 9% of his or her non-working, non-sleeping time obtaining information about products; that is equivalent to about 950 hours per year per family, or four hours of information gathering for every $100 that is spent.[7] But time in the customer role is not limited to shopping or to gathering information about products people plan to buy, although these are major components of the customer role. Being a customer also includes time spent receiving medical and dental services; applying for a loan, a driver's license, or insurance; getting travel information and making reservations; registering for classes; standing in line at a fast-food restaurant; and finding an architect, nanny, plumber, or lawyer, to name just a few examples.[8]

In short, today, providing goods and services for one's family is done primarily by purchasing. Yet are not these goods and services intended to make life easier or more convenient for families? And isn't much of shopping considered an enjoyable activity? Indeed, being a customer—at least the shopping component—is often classified as a leisure activity. And by one account, shopping is the most popular weekday evening "out-of-the-home entertainment."[9] To that end, as of 1991, "four billion square feet of land [had] been converted into shopping centers, or about 16 square feet for every American man, woman, and child.''[10] Yet the customer role, like other roles one plays, is not always fun or entertaining. And in a world in which time is finite, an expanding customer role can cut into other roles. Unless one considers shopping or running errands together part of one's spouse or parent roles, buying goods and services can reduce the time one has for these roles. Particularly when people are putting more hours into their paid work and both parents are employed, any extra time required to purchase goods and services can cut into people's other relationships by reducing the time available for friendships or relationships with kin.[11]

SERVICE RELATIONSHIPS AND ENCOUNTERS

I have recently described the two fundamentally different types of service interaction involving different customer roles; I call them relationships and encounters.[12] In a service relationship, an individual customer seeks out a particular person who can provide needed goods or services. Each time that customer again needs the same goods or services, he or she returns to the same individual provider. If the customer is unhappy with the services rendered, he or she may find a new provider.

When a customer and provider first interact, they anticipate interacting again in the future, and their behavior reflects that anticipation. Thus, they are motivated to be courteous and polite and to behave in a role-appropriate manner. Over time, the customer and provider build up a shared history of interaction on which both parties can draw in their future interactions. As they become more familiar with each other, they can become more relaxed, and their behavior, while still "in role," need no longer be limited to very narrowly defined, role-appropriate conduct. The shared history of interaction that characterizes relationships allows both parties to accumulate information about each other that enhances future interactions. They can, for example, develop shortcuts in their interaction, and relationships typically can become more efficient and effective over time (i.e., the parties can accomplish more together once their relationship is established than they were able to do when the relationship began). Each can anticipate the other's wants and reactions.

Relationships seem like a natural or normal way to conduct transactions because they bear a surface semblance to other, more expressive relationships, involving kin, friends, and lovers. Like these other relationships, transaction relationships create bonds of attachment, trust, and commitment. Some customers will retain their hairdresser, stockbroker, physician, or baby-sitter if they change locations, even if this involves considerable effort on their part. Likewise, service providers will often accommodate the special needs of long-standing customers.

I contend that the delivery of services and goods has been undergoing a change from a reliance on delivery via relationships to delivery of more services via "encounters." Encounters, in contrast to relationships, consist of a single episode between the customer and provider. The customer does not expect to interact with the particular provider again; the next transaction will probably be with a different provider. Put another way, the customer's successive contacts over time involve different providers, but each provider is expected to be functionally equivalent. Thus, a customer should be able to complete a satisfactory service transaction with any of a number of interchangeable providers. Buying a hamburger at a fast-food restaurant is a classic encounter, but so is getting a driver's license, ordering airline tickets from an airlines reservation center, or going to the hospital emergency room or a health maintenance organizations (HMO) for medical care.

In an encounter, not only are providers assumed to be interchangeable, but the person may be eliminated altogether. Automated teller machines (ATMs) and the related automated check-in services at hotels and point-of-sale debit machines are becoming commonplace. So are the ubiquitous telephone encounters with machines; whether customers are trying to buy an airline ticket, question a charge on a credit card, or get an appointment with a physician, they are increasingly likely to encounter a machine telling them to punch a series of numbers, which may or may not culminate in access to a human being.

Encounters with people or machines constitute a social mechanism for delivering goods and services that is analogous to mass production in the manufacture of goods. Mass production increased the amount of goods produced, and mass production of service has, no doubt, increased the amount of services produced. Furthermore, encounters will not be limited to buying hamburgers or obtaining a driver's license; rather, services traditionally provided in relationships will steadily be organized so they can be delivered in encounters. Finding a way to structure interactions typically provided in relationships in an encounter format is an innovation often considered newsworthy. For example, the appearance of an organization offering brief, encounter-style back and shoulder massages merited news coverage ("They rub customers just the right way"). The New York-based "Great American Backrub" provides walk-in shoulder massages for $7.95 with the next available masseuse or masseur. (Other, similar organizations, such as the Seattle-based "Massage Bar," have also gotten a significant amount of news coverage.)[13]

I also see the encroachment of the mass-production delivery of services on the professions including medicine, stockbrokering, and the professorate. Medical patients, for example, increasingly have encounters with physicians in emergency rooms, HMOs, or clinics rather than in the office of their family physician.[14] Even where HMO members are offered a choice of physician, it is difficult for patients to establish a one-on-one relationship because physicians leave HMOs, companies change health care providers, and patients change jobs (often meaning they now have a different health care provider, if their new employer even offers health care benefits).

THE CUSTOMER ROLE IN SERVICE TRANSACTIONS

Let me now turn to the customer role under both relationships and encounters with an eye to understanding how it impinges on balancing work and family obligations.

The Customer Role in Service Relationships

Middle- and upper-class families often have many different service relationships. In fact, many of the kinds of service typically available in relationships are used almost exclusively by the more affluent members of society. For example, few of the poor have a personal lawyer, stockbroker, tax analyst, architect, gardener, nanny, housekeeper, or manicurist. To cite a personal example of a relationship, I have had the same dentist for about over a decade. Although he is in Los Angeles (L.A.) and I work in Tucson, he is reasonably flexible in fitting me into his schedule on the days I will be in L.A. (typically, Monday mornings). I have chosen to keep the same dentist even though it would definitely be more convenient to have a dentist in Tucson because, like other customers who have a good relationship with a service provider, I believe he is highly competent, takes pride in doing good work, knows me and my idiosyncrasies, and, I believe, genuinely cares about my "dental well-being."

Customers often believe that the expertise of their chosen provider is somewhat unique—that the provider brings to the relationship special talents, experience, and the like. In their mind, not all providers are created equal, nor are they functionally equivalent. Thus, in return for past service and anticipated future good service, customers may be willing to expend "extra" time and money on the relationship: they may be willing to wait longer for a relationship provider than they would for an encounter, for example, or spend more money for the transaction. They are typically willing to accommodate the provider's needs in exchange for knowing that the provider will, in return, accommodate theirs. For example, a family who expects a housekeeper to do extra work for a party might be just as willing to give the housekeeper time off to accommodate her or his family obligations.

Relationships have costs for customers as well as benefits. One disadvantage of relationships is the transaction costs of maintaining them, one of which is financial. I argue that relationships often come at a financial premium that not everyone can afford. But there are other costs, too, including finding a provider, having limited access to the provider, fitting one's needs to the provider's schedule, sometimes waiting for the provider, finding a "new" provider if the "old" provider is not satisfactory, and finding a substitute provider when one's usual provider is sick or away on vacation. While a customer-provider relationship is not the same as a friendship or kinship relationship, it does carry some of the same baggage, due in part to the common characteristic of repeated interactions with the same person in a particular role. Of the various costs, probably the greatest involves finding a satisfactory provider and, by extension, finding a new provider if the old one is not satisfactory. For example, finding a new baby-sitter or live-in nanny is a major ordeal for two-career families. The difficulty in establishing a good service relationship is one reason why, when I moved to the University of Arizona, I maintained a variety of service relationships in Los Angeles (where my family lives). Not only my dentist, but also my tax analyst, hairdresser, and manicurist are in Los Angeles. Although I have lived in Tucson for seven years now, I have not found the time to establish these service rela-tionships here, and I am quite satisfied with the relationships I have in L.A.

Good service relationships can do a lot to assist families. Indeed, upper-middle-class professional families with small children are increasingly relying on a bevy of service relationships (with, e.g., nannies, housekeepers, gardeners, accountants, stockbrokers) to allow both mother and father to concentrate on demanding careers while maintaining a comfortable home life for themselves and their children. While this dependence on service providers to create the ''free'' time to devote to their careers has received some public attention (e.g., concerns about the lack of Social Security contributions to the live-in house-keepers of two of President Clinton's nominees to his cabinet, dubbed ''Nan-nygate''), researchers have generally not studied this. In contrast to the scant attention paid by researchers, a number of businesses have opted for service relationships in order to attract busy customers. For example, some retail stores provide personal shoppers for professionals who do not want to take the time away from work or family to be well dressed.[15] And while most banks that promise a ''personal banker'' provide no such thing, some small banks are seeking to reestablish service relationships with customers as a way of compet-ing with banking giants such as Bank of America and Citicorp.[16]

The Customer Role in Service Encounters

Not only middle- and upper-class families, but also their poorer counterparts, engage in service encounters. Families in all income ranges have come to depend on getting money from ATMs or a meal from a fast-food restaurant at any time and at just about any location. (Over 50% of Americans live within 5 minutes of a McDonald's restaurant, for example.)[17] Families who belong to HMOs are often pleased to be able to go to the medical facility and see a physician or a nurse when they need one. They need not depend on any particular physician's availability. Encounters are designed to be quick and efficient, and indeed, many of them are. To the extent that they are quick and efficient, they can help families balance work and family obligations because they allow for the purchase of goods and services without using a lot of that increasingly valuable resource, time.

In encounters, customers are an integral part of an encounter system (i.e., a system designed to rationally and efficiently deliver goods and service to cus-tomers). Thus, the customer role, like the provider role, has been examined, analyzed, and structured by encounter systems designers so that customers' behavior contributes to the overall efficiency of the system. Indeed, customers are often considered "co-producers" of service because their efforts contribute to the service they receive. In return, their efforts reduce the costs of the transaction and raise the potential for profits if the organization is a profit-making endeavor.

If encounters are designed to be efficient, then more efficient encounters are likely to win out over less-efficient encounters. One example of this, I believe, is the growth in mail-order products, which give added flexibility to busy families. Family members can order goods or services, sometimes 24 hours a day, without leaving home. This is much more efficient than going to a mall where one also has encounters, not relationships with service providers.

While there are many characteristics of encounter systems, let me focus on four of them: customers as co-producers, customers as interchangeable parts, customers as stereotypes, and the efficiency of encounters.[18] In doing so, I want to question the extent to which encounters really make it easier for families to manage work and family responsibilities.

Customers as Co-producers. Co-production refers to the fact that the customer typically engages in some activities that facilitate or contribute to the completion of the transaction (i.e., helps to produce a transaction). Thus, customers can be viewed as an "efficiency-maximizing opportunity."[19] Customers who are willing to do some of the work of producing or delivering a service are relatively low in cost and thus desirable for organizations. Heskitt wrote: "Supermarket shoppers spend time and money to drive beyond the corner grocery store, inform themselves about various products, and transport their purchases home. The success of more recently developed warehouse stores requiring even more customer effort attests to the importance of such customers."[20] Examples of co-production are filling out forms in a bank, pumping gas, punching keys and filling out a deposit slip at an ATM, picking out and bagging groceries or other goods in a discount store, dialing and redialing the telephone, listening to digitized voice instructions, and punching buttons to get information. The important point for this chapter is that although services can be viewed as saving the valuable time of family members, for a variety of good reasons, managers of many service organizations are actively looking for ways in which customers can do more of the work of the service encounter. Thus, families who engage in encounters are not being "served" in the old-fashioned sense of being waited on; instead, they "work" in order to obtain the services or goods they are purchasing.

Interchangeability of Customers. Another important characteristic of encounters is the interchangeability of customers. Where providers are functionally equivalent, in essence, so are customers. That is not because organizations or encounter providers are uncaring or cold; it is an inherent structural property of encounter systems. Because there is no asset specificity attached to any customer and the product or service is uniform, one customer is pretty much like any other. What is important for the organization is that there are plenty of customers in encounters, but typically no one customer is all that important. It really does not make any difference who buys McDonald's hamburgers as long as plenty of people do. Similarly, although tax preparation will vary from one customer to another, the important point for H&R Block is that enough people want tax preparation help to keep the firm in business.

Although customers in encounters are more or less interchangeable, organizations and their providers often go to great lengths to make each person feel like an individual, and not an interchangeable cog, because they often assume that people *expect* to be treated like individuals. Robin Leidner used an oxymoron, "routine individuality," to refer to the fact that organizations try to personalize service in encounters—often in five minutes or less.[21] Machines, too, now personalize service, as when an ATM machine addresses the customer by name. Nonetheless, any one person who shows up at an ATM machine is, like any one person who shows up at the Department of Motor Vehicles window, pretty much like any other.

Stereotyping of Customers. Despite the fact that encounter providers often attempt to personalize an encounter, customers can easily be, and often are, stereotyped on the basis of their dress, race, sex, and similar traits because the only real basis for making inferences about customers is the broad visible social categories to which they belong. In general, this hurts women more than men and minorities more than majorities (i.e., any lower-status person will be hurt more by stereotyping than a higher-status person because more positive stereotypes are associated with high-status than low-status people). For example, although women have no more leisure time than men on average,[22] men are sometimes given more prompt service and/or served first when a woman and man arrive for service at the same time.[23] In a relationship, the provider knows who is busy and who does not mind waiting, or knows times when a customer is especially busy (i.e., is on the way to pick up child from child care service or needs to get back to work). But the provider in an encounter does not know these things and can therefore seem insensitive to the customer, although in reality, he or she simply lacks sufficient information to respond more appropriately to a customer's preferences or needs. The lack of information is inherent in the encounter structure, not the personality of the provider, but that may be of small consolation to a busy parent concerned about getting to the day care center before it closes.

The Efficiency of Encounters. Perhaps the main selling point of encounters is that they are efficient; that is, they take little of the customer's time relative to what they do for the customer. Encounters are designed to be *operationally efficient,* defined as the amount of materials or the number of products, parts, or people processed per labor or machine input time. This is a standard of efficiency used in many organizations, but from the customer's point of view, this is not a very good definition. For customers, two other efficiency measures, *completion time* and *process efficiency,* are much better. Completion time is simply the total amount of time it takes to complete a transaction (not an encounter). Process efficiency is the ratio of the time in which a product or person is being processed to the time the product or person is in the production system.[24] For the customer, the total time it takes to complete a transaction is what matters, including standing in line, waiting on the phone, or carrying out multiple encounters to complete the transaction. If one has to wait 20 minutes listening to a message saying that all operators are busy helping other customers, the fact that the actual transaction takes, say, 2 minutes is unimportant. In fact, it is likely to be especially aggravating because process efficiency is extremely poor; the customer was in the system for 22 minutes to complete a 2-minute transaction. Only 9% of the total time in the system was spent engaged in the transaction. One might contrast the process efficiency of an inefficient encounter with someone who waits 45 minutes to see a family physician but then spends 45 minutes with the physician. In that case, 50% of the time in the system was spent engaged in the transaction, which is hardly a model of efficiency, but still substantially better than some encounter transactions.

CONCLUSIONS

It is time to return to the original question: how does the customer role and the emergence of encounter systems for delivering services and goods fit into an overall understanding of work-and-family issues? The notion that American society is, first and foremost, a consumerist society is hardly a new idea, but the customer or consumer role and the time it takes have generally not been integrated into the study of major adult roles. As customers we are now awash in choices, many of which are of a trivial nature. For example, the number of different telephone systems do provide a choice of options, but that requires learning all the available options and then learning one's particular system, which is likely to be different from the other phones one has at home and different still from the phone system at work. And what other activities could a parent be doing while he or she is checking telephone options and learning the different features on each of the phone systems the family uses?

I should start by noting that many people seem to be perfectly happy with the customer role; many people apparently enjoy shopping, and it is a true leisure activity for some. But what about the people who feel truly pressed for time and don't particularly relish standing in lines, waiting in phone queues, and pushing shopping carts through miles of aisles, and/or those who do not consider shopping together their idea of a family activity?

Utilizing service relationships is one way for families to cope, but in general, service relationships are expensive and thus not available to many two-earner or single-parent families. While some families of moderate means may be willing to do without in certain areas in order to pay for service relationships, this option is not a possibility for many families whose incomes provide only the basic necessities—or less.

Utilizing service encounters is another way for families to cope, but encounters often represent a totally different way for families to manage work and family. In particular, they allow families to purchase services at all hours of the day or night, an option that is desirable on occasion, but if employed regularly, could result in ''stressed-out'' families with little true leisure.

A new movement toward simplifying one's life reflects another reaction to the increasing time and expense of being a customer. If it is too time-consuming to purchase goods and services and then maintain them, perhaps it is easier to forgo them and allocate the extra time to being with one's family or to productive work. This path may be more attractive to adults than to their children, and it may also be more attractive to adults who can afford whatever services and goods they want to purchase than those who feel deprived in a consumerist society.

Perhaps a more practical and broad-ranging solution is for organizations to recognize the time-consuming role of being a customer and help their employees balance work and family by making services easily available to them. Among the examples I have encountered are the following: (1) providing car-washing services: employees turn over their car in the morning and it is returned, cleaned, before they leave work; (2) providing dry-cleaning services: a dry-cleaning establishment is available in a designated place (e.g., a side lobby) either early in the morning, in late afternoon, or both; (3) exercise and stress reduction courses: after-work or lunchtime classes are offered on-site; (4) banking services: an ATM is available on-site; (5) catering services: one Los Angeles company, Rhino Records, contracts with a gourmet catering service and provides subsidized lunches several days a week. (Since many employees take their gourmet lunch back to their desk where they work through the ''lunch hour,'' this service does not actually cost the company.)

These examples represent the tip of the iceberg in what could be available. While not usually considered a work-and-family initiative, such services are easy and usually inexpensive to implement and would, like more traditional family-oriented services such as child care facilities or referral services, help families. Rather than providing direct family-support services, these services help to create more off-work time that mothers and fathers can spend with their families— doing something other than shopping.

NOTES

1. Described in detail in B.A. Gutek, *The Dynamics of Service: Reflections on the Changing Nature of Customer/Provider Interactions* (San Francisco: Jossey-Bass, 1995), where I describe both the customer and provider role. In this chapter, I focus on selected aspects of the customer role; see also B.A. Gutek, ''Service Workers: Human Resources or Labor Costs?'' *Annals of the American Academy of Politics and Social Science* 554 (March 1995): 68–82.

2. See, for example, Suzan N.C. Lewis & Cary L. Cooper, ''Stress in Dual-Earner Families,'' in B.A. Gutek, A.H. Stromberg, & L. Larwood (eds.), *Women and Work: An Annual Review*, vol. 3 (Newbury Park, CA: Sage, 1988), pp. 139–168.

3. J. Schor, *The Overworked American* (New York: Basic Books, 1991).

4. Gutek, *The Dynamics of Service*, ch. 9.

5. E. Appelbaum & R. Batt, *The American Workplace: Transforming the Work Systems in the United States* (Ithaca, NY: ILR Press, 1994); "Productivity: The U.S. Remains the Leader of the Pack," *Business Week*, December 21, 1992, p. 18.

6. C.H. Lovelock, *Services Marketing* (Englewood Cliffs, NJ: Prentice-Hall, 1984), p. 29.

7. "Consumers in the Information Age," *Futurist*, January-February 1993, pp. 15–19.

8. Figures cited in this paragraph are taken from Gutek, *The Dynamics of Service*.

9. Schor, *The Overworked American*, p. 107.

10. Ibid.

11. Gutek, *The Dynamics of Service*.

12. Ibid., chs. 2, 3.

13. "They Rub Customers Just the Right Way," *Tucson Citizen*, November 18, 1993, p. 3B; M.J. McCarthy, "Stranded at O'Hare? Well, You Can Drink or Leave the Airport," *Wall Street Journal*, June 1, 1995, pp. A1, A6.

14. J. Erikson, "Newborn Care: Dangers Seen in HMO Pressure for Short Hospital Stays," *Arizona Daily Star*, September 19, 1995, pp. 1A–2A.

15. A.M. Jaffe, "Retailing's New Strategy: I Can Get It For You Personal," *New York Times*, August 13, 1995, p. F8.

16. G.B. Knecht, "Norwest Corp. Relies on Branches, Pushes Service—And Prospers," *Wall Street Journal*, August 17, 1995, pp. A1, A9.

17. J.F. Love, *McDonalds: Behind the Arches* (Toronto, Canada: Bantom Books, 1987); George Ritzer, *The McDonaldization of Society: An Investigation into the Changing Character of Contemporary Social Life* (Thousand Oaks, CA: Pine Forge Press, 1991).

18. The other characteristics are detailed in Gutek, *The Dynamics of Service*.

19. D.E. Bowen & G.R. Jones, "Transaction Cost Analysis of Service Organization–Customer Exchange," *Academy of Management Review* 11(4) (1986): 428–441.

20. J. Heskitt, *Managing in the Service Economy* (Cambridge: Harvard Business School Press, 1986), p. 48.

21. R. Leidner, *Fast Food, Fast Talk: Service Work and the Routinization of Everyday Life* (Berkeley: University of California Press, 1993).

22. United Nations, *The World's Women: 1970–1990*, Social Statistics and Indicators, Series K., No. 8 (New York: United Nations, 1991).

23. See, for example, G.M. Zinkhan & L.F. Stoiadin, "Impact of Sex Role Stereotypes on Service Priority in Department Stores," *Journal of Applied Psychology* 69(4) (1984): 691–693.

24. B.J. Pine, *Mass Customization* (Cambridge: Harvard Business School Press), pp. 110–111.

PART III

Legal and Cultural Perspectives on Work-Family Relationships

CHAPTER 9

An International Perspective on Work-Family Issues

Suzan Lewis

The acknowledgment that work and family are interdependent underpins research and practice in relation to the work-family interface. However, it is also important to recognize that work and family systems operate within, influence, and are influenced by wider social systems, which incorporate cultural norms, state institutions and public policies. This chapter explores work-family issues and some social and organizational responses across a number of different national contexts. A truly international perspective would be an enormous undertaking, well beyond the scope of this chapter. No claims are made, therefore, to be exhaustive, either in terms of the countries represented or the issues covered. Inevitably, what follows is selective, focusing on industrial societies and with a particular emphasis on Europe. The chapter begins with a discussion of some of the ideological/cultural dimensions on which countries vary in relation to work and family and their impact on social policy. The relevance of sociopolitical context is then discussed with particular reference to the situation in Europe. Organizational responses to work-family issues are discussed in relation to different policy contexts. Barriers to effective organizational responses, some of which transcend national context, and related research and practical issues are considered.

CULTURAL AND IDEOLOGICAL CONTEXTS AND SOCIAL POLICY

The expanding role of women in the labor market throughout the industrialized world, together with changing family and gender roles, create issues relating to the balancing of employment and family roles for individuals, families, corporations, and society. Social and organizational responses to these issues are rooted in, and informed by, cultural values and norms, as well as economic imperatives to change. Economic factors, especially the need for women's labor, have been a major impetus for social change and, in some cases, for social policies, such as child care provisions, parental leaves, and rights and opportunities for part-time workers, to address work-family issues. However, the ease with which governments and/or employers can address these economic needs is also influenced by cultural attitudes, and these shape the nature of, and perspectives on, work-family issues in different contexts. The exact definition of culture has been the subject of much debate, but it is defined in this chapter as consisting of historically rooted shared values, norms, and dominant ideologies.[1] A number of these ideological dimensions, which are of relevance to work and family issues and to social and corporate policy, are discussed in this chapter.

Ideology of the Role of the State: Family as Individual or Collective Responsibility?

Countries differ in their beliefs about the role of the state in relation to work and family. In the United Kingdom, like the United States, successive governments have emphasized individual responsibility for the family and minimal intervention or support from the state. The state does intervene in the family, for example, to ensure paternal financial support for children from a previous marriage, but not in the provision of child care, which is viewed as the responsibility of individual families. Government policy is also made to impose minimal regulations on employers. Hence, there is no statutory right for family leave if a family member is ill, or to paternity leave, and there has been little employment protection for part-time workers. In other European states, social policy is underpinned by a greater sense of communal responsibility for family welfare, including child care, and hence a more proactive role for the state in helping people to manage work and family.

Ideologies of the Family and Childhood

Cross-national variations in the dominant ideology of the family also impact social policy. In the United Kingdom, for example, the lack of paid leave for sick child care, minimal provision of publicly funded child care and the prevailing philosophy of care in the community, which relies heavily on informal care of the elderly and vulnerable, all derive from the assumptions that there is someone (i.e., a woman) at home to provide this sort of care or that a woman's income is not essential for the family. Elsewhere in Europe, social policy is based on the assumption of a modified single-breadwinner family, with women as secondary earners (e.g., Germany and the Netherlands) or on the dual-earner family as the norm (e.g., France, the Scandinavian countries, and Eastern and Central Europe in the former communist countries). Similarly, countries differ in their dominant beliefs about the needs of children and the role of parents.

The social construction of the ideal mother in the United Kingdom and Ireland, for example, as one who provides full-time mothering for young children creates guilt, which exacerbates work-family conflict and is particularly pernicious in the context of the growing need for two incomes.[2] This guilt is alien to women in other contexts, where maternal employment is regarded as the norm and considered to be in the children's interest. European countries that recognize and encourage men's family roles and women's income-generating roles place less emphasis on the need for full-time parenting and regard the provision of adequate care for children as an essential support.

The exclusive role of the mother in the care of children also receives less emphasis in many Far Eastern countries, where family support systems are deeply embedded in extended family structures.[3] While child care is less problematic in the context of extended families in many Eastern contexts, elder care presents a more pressing issue.[4] Often there is a strong tradition of the care of elderly relatives by daughters or daughters-in-law, and strong cultural constraints against nonfamilial care. Indeed, cultural norms may militate against the social construction of care of the elderly as a "problem" in traditional societies. It is easier, culturally, to address the elder care and work issue in the West, particularly in countries that construct female employment as the norm and family as a collective responsibility. However, in countries such as the United Kingdom, which emphasize the male-breadwinner family pattern and individual responsibility for family, cuts in public spending and policies of informal care in the community exacerbate conflicts between work and family in respect to care of the elderly and other vulnerable family members.[5]

Ideologies of Equality

Countries differ, crucially, in the extent to which they are ideologically committed to a notion of equal opportunity that incorporates the ideal of modifying the role of men and women within the family as well as the workplace. This has important implications for the ways in which work-family dilemmas are conceptualized. The Scandinavian countries are the most developed in terms of endorsing the ideal of equal roles in all spheres.[6] At the other extreme, in more traditional societies such as India, Israel, Spain, and many others, the role of the woman in the family remains paramount.[7] Some assistance from men may be envisaged, but the notion of equal role sharing is inherently in conflict with cultural beliefs. Thus, debates on work and family issues in the former contexts will include a consideration about how to encourage greater participation of men in family life, and this is translated into social policies, such as statutory parental and family leave, that encourage equal responsibility for parenting and other family roles, as well as in the public sphere.[8] In cultures nearer the traditional end of the continuum, the issue is more often articulated as determining how to help women to balance work and gendered family responsibilities, and public policies are directed at helping women to accommodate employment with their primary family roles.[9] Many societies, of course, fall somewhere between the two extremes and exhibit considerable ambivalence about gender and family roles.

The Process of Ideological and Social Development

Although ideology and policy are clearly related, there is little systematic comparative research to explain the processes of ideological and policy development in different contexts, and the direction of causality between cultural ideology and public policy for work and family remains unclear. Giele argues that the actual experience of women in bridging the work family divide, rather than attitudes and ideology, has been important in shaping social policy over the past century.[10] In the United Kingdom and United States, the labor force participation of women in the late 19th and earlier parts of the 20th century were relatively low compared with other parts of the world. Hence, British and American social policies have developed around the male-breadwinner model. Giele points to other countries, such as France and Finland, that lack a strong bourgeois-housewife tradition; France, because women made up 30 to 40% of the labor market in all sectors during this period, and Finland, because it remained predominantly agricultural until the 1960s, and home and work life were not strongly differentiated. Consequently, in both these societies, social policy has developed on the assumption that mothers are also workers, rather than a view of women as dependent on men.[11]

INTERNATIONAL INFLUENCES ON PUBLIC POLICY AND PRACTICE

More recently, national policies on work and family have also been influenced by international institutions such as the International Labor Organization (ILO). The ILO is a body of the United Nations, which, as part of its charter, develops international standards to improve working life. Australian work-family policy, for example, is based upon ILO convention 156, on workers with family commitments. This convention was adopted by the ILO in 1981 and recognizes that helping employees balance work and family issues is important for both male and female employees as well as for employers, unions, governments, and the economy. It was ratified by Australia in 1990. This requires the Australian government to develop and extend existing initiatives towards these ends, and to report regularly on its progress to the ILO. Thus, ratification of the ILO convention demonstrates a commitment to work and family balance and a means of encouraging development.

The European Union (EU) provides another example of an international organization with the potential to influence national governments on work and family issues. This is an interesting case because some tensions exist between national cultures and policies, on the one hand, and a drive for harmonization of social policy, on the other. While the ratification of ILO convention 156 is a deliberate strategy for addressing these issues, membership of the EU is sought for political and economic, as well as social, reasons. European social policy, particularly in relation to work and family issues, is largely embraced by some states and resisted by others, notably the United Kingdom.

Social policy in European Union member states is influenced by both European and national governments. Work-family issues are very much on the agenda of the European Commission, although the responses of individual member states vary. The terminology used in European debates involves the "reconciliation" of employment and family life. Moss notes that the term *reconciliation* has been subject to some criticism on the grounds that it implies restoration of some former harmonious relationship, which, by implication may be lost due to women entering the labor force.[12] The European Commission, he argues, is quite clear that this is not intended, but rather that the term *reconciliation* implies an attempt to harmonize different activities so that they can be conducted with minimal friction and stress. The term does, however, recognize that there are potential or actual conflicts of interests between the worlds of work and family.

The political commitment at the EU level to the reconciliation of work and family responsibilities is driven by an objective of gender equality in the labor market as well as social and economic goals.[13] European Commission (EC) publications have emphasized the role of public policy, but more recently, they have also addressed the need for workplace change and for more egalitarian family relationships to support reconciliation.[14] Thus, a partnership approach to reconciliation is being adopted. Governments, employers, trade unions, and families are all considered to have a role to play.

EU activities relate primarily to public policy, although this in turn has the potential to influence both workplaces and the family. An agreement on social policy annexed to the Treaty of European Union (1992) formalized "social dialogue" between the European trade unions and employer associations and enables any agreements reached to be implemented in legislation. An agreement on parental leave has been reached by this process and will result in all member states (except the United Kingdom, which opted out of this aspect of the treaty) being required to implement an entitlement of at least three months' parental leave. European management and labor are now attempting a similar process on the protection of atypical workers. Certain aspects of European employment law and health and safety law have considerable potential to influence work and family reconciliation.[15] Reconciliation has been interpreted in different ways across Europe, depending on the various national starting points. The different responses of member states to the issue of reconciliation and to EU initiatives can be illustrated in relation to the provision of leaves for family purposes and of atypical work arrangements (i.e., non–full-time work).

Family and Parental Leaves

All European countries have statutory paid maternity leave, although the length of the leave and the pay attached to it varies. In the United Kingdom, the provisions have recently been improved to remove conditions of entitlement, bring the law further into line with that of other European states, and meet the requirements of European health and safety law (the "Pregnant Workers" directive). This illustrates the impact of European initiatives. The majority of (but not all) member states have already developed some form of parental leave. The use of parental leave benefits by men is much lower than by women, and this is of particular concern in the Scandinavian countries. Approximately one-third of Swedish fathers take parental leave, a figure that is high by international standards but regarded as too low by Swedish policy makers. In an effort to increase fathers' participation the Swedish government has recently modified the long-standing parental leave provision to include 30 days specifically for fathers (at 90% pay), which cannot, under usual circumstances, be transferred to mothers.

Atypical Working Hours

Long, rigid hours of work pose a barrier to the reconciliation of work and family. However, options of part-time or reduced hours of work have traditionally been associated with reduced benefits and opportunities. A number of factors are combining to challenge this model in Europe. It has not been possible to reach a consensus on a European Commission draft directive that would have given all part-time workers employment rights equal to those of full-time workers, but again, many European states have such legislation.

In the United Kingdom, part-time and flexible working schemes are increasingly being used by employers as a way of cutting costs, with an increasing use of temporary contracts, which is developing forms of work that are anything but family friendly as they do not fulfill families' basic needs for economic security. Although the government is reluctant to improve conditions attached to part-time work, case law and the influence of European antidiscrimination law are challenging this position. A recent case taken to the British House of Lords by the Equal Opportunities Commission found that current legislation was in breach of European sex discrimination law by not giving part-time workers (who are mainly women) equal employment protection with full-time workers.[16]

The decision that denying part-time workers equal employment protection is unlawful has the potential to enhance the quality of part-time work in Britain, and may serve to discourage employers from regarding those who work less than full-time to reconcile work and family, or for other purposes, as expendable workers who are marginal to the organization.[17] Other recent cases suggest that European-based discrimination law may have the potential to encourage employers to adopt more flexible ways of working. Although one recent case found that it was not discriminatory to refuse to allow a woman returning from maternity leave to job share, two other cases have ruled that the refusal of requests to return to part-time work were in breach of discrimination law. Thus, while there is still the possibility that some employers may be able to justify decisions not to allow more flexible forms of work, discrimination law, based on European provisions, does, nevertheless, have the potential to challenge assumptions about the norm of full-time work.

European law may help to bring about changes in practice, but it is not clear whether it will bring about changes in values. There is evidence of some shifts in attitudes to the ideal of continuous full-time work in some contexts, but European pressures could, at most, be one of a whole range of factors contributing to these shifts. The trade unions' traditional opposition to atypical work patterns as a potential threat to conditions of work is changing to a certain extent in parts of Europe. For example, the trade unions in the Netherlands are making a concerted effort to encourage "fully valued part time work, that is, atypical work with equal pay and benefits, rights and responsibilities." Based on the view that it is no longer meaningful to talk of the standard employee with standard hours of work, evidence of aspirations of a growing number of men as well as women to vary their working hours over their life cycle, and the argument that part-time work can play an important role in achieving a fairer distribution of work across society, the Dutch unions recommend that fully valued part-time work should be available in all sectors and occupations.[18] The German trade unions have also supported a departure from standard hours, in terms of a reduction in the number of full-time hours, as a form of work sharing in the context of threats of unemployment.[19] A number of collective agreements have been concluded in the private and public sectors in which employees and works councils agreed to reduce full-time standard hours in order to avoid redundancies. In some cases, reductions have taken place on the basis of full income compensation, but with future increases being smaller than they would have been without this reduction, and a saving to employers in terms of redundancy payments. Similar agreements have been negotiated in France. These initiatives have not come about in response to work and family issues, but have the potential to challenge traditional models of working time and to support employees with family commitments.

National culture and ideology, national public policy, and in some cases, international policy and pressure, therefore, all have a potential impact on the scope of organizational initiatives and employee experiences of work and family.

ORGANIZATIONAL RESPONSES IN DIFFERENT SOCIAL CONTEXTS

Social values and policies in turn influence the demand for organizational work-family policies and the ways in which employers can respond, although again, the nature of the relationship is not always clear. Do family-friendly social policies, such as publicly provided child care or mandated leaves, absolve employers from responsibility for considering work-family issues, or do they provide a floor of rights on which employers can build? It can be argued that in the absence of public supports for work and family, the reliance on employers will be greater, and that this both creates a tradition of corporate welfare and also sensitizes employees to feel entitled to support for work-family demands from employers.[20] Although the public provision of child care is minimal, some employers in the United Kingdom, as in the United States, are developing innovative ways of assisting with child care demands, which are rarely considered by employers elsewhere in Europe, where there exists an infrastructure of public child care provisions. For example, child care vouchers, which are provided by some British firms have not been adopted in other European countries. The problem of a corporate approach, however, is that access to child care is limited and uneven, being provided mainly by large firms or public sector organizations, and not available to the majority of employees.

An alternative argument is that the public provision of family-friendly policies demonstrates the importance attached to family well-being by government, and/or reflects a culture of valuing parenting and family care, which encourages employers to build upon this effort. Where statutory leaves exist in Europe, employers are often willing to enhance statutory provisions through collective agreements. The availability of statutory benefits can free employers to take on other roles. For example, in Denmark, where child care is provided by local authorities for the majority of children, employers often provide alternative support such as flexible hours. Some employers play an advocacy role, as illustrated by the Danish State Railways, which obtained government funding in 1989 to campaign for longer opening hours of local child care facilities to meet the needs of working parents.[21] In France, where there is an excellent infrastructure of quality child care, some companies extend the parents' choice and offer alternatives that are competitively priced or supplement existing provisions. Public provisions and entitlements thus ensure a basic level of rights, but enable progressive employers to build on these to retain a competitive edge in recruitment and become an employer of choice.

The development of family-friendly employer policies in the United Kingdom and Denmark illustrates the two approaches within Europe and makes an interesting contrast. Organizations in the United Kingdom operate in a context where, despite broader European support for the reconciliation of work and family there is little national social-policy support. To some extent, the government is prepared to act as a role model, and the civil service is one of the employers that voluntarily implements family-friendly policies, but there is no legal requirement for companies to do so. Nevertheless, some employers have started to address work and family issues in response to a business orientation argument. Predictions of demographic changes and skills shortages made at the end of the 1980's warned of the costs to businesses, in terms of recruitment and retention, of not taking steps to enable parents to remain in the workforce.[22] The argument was expressed in terms of retaining and recruiting women, and the subsequent policies were also aimed primarily at women. The recession largely obscured the issues of skills shortfalls, but the importance of retaining valued skills remains the major argument for organizational change toward more family-friendly policies and practices. Where policies to support work and family are implemented, therefore, this is primarily for business reasons and targeted at women. In the context of ideological ambivalence about family roles, and of the social construction of families as a private concern, work-family discourses in the United Kingdom remain dominated by business imperatives.

Danish companies have not traditionally been expected to take any direct responsibility for family welfare. Family is assumed to be a public responsibility, and hence, the reconciliation of work and family is the topic of considerable political interest. The main focus of these discussions, and the coherent family policy that results, are on the child, and support of the family to ensure children's well-being.[23] To this end, day care is publicly provided, and there are statutory rights to parental leave and leave to take care of a sick child. Parental leave here, as elsewhere, is taken more often by women than men, but there is much discussion about how to encourage men to be more involved in fathering. More recently, however, there has been a growing political interest in finding ways in which private companies can participate more actively, thus taking on some social responsibility. The government has, for example, funded research to explore how companies could become more family friendly. Work-family discourses in Denmark, therefore, are dominated by concern for family, and especially the children's well-being, and while the business advantages of supporting the reconciliation of work and family remain important motivators for organizational change, a sense of corporate social responsibility is also emphasized.

WORKPLACE CULTURES

The relationship between ideology and behavior is rarely straightforward, and multiple cultures and ideologies can coexist within national and workplace contexts. While supportive social policies may provide a floor of rights for families and some organizations may build upon these rights to assist in the reconciliation of work and family, a gendered workplace culture often remains a crucial factor in limiting the potential impact of family-friendly social and corporate policies. Workplace culture and employee responses to organizational initiatives are often influenced by a traditional gender ideology, even when this is at odds with prevailing social ideals. The traditional male model of work, which defines the ideal worker as one who works full time and continuously and does not allow family to interfere, remains widespread in Europe despite pockets of change, and can undermine policy intentions. This limits the use of family leaves and flexible working hours, especially by men, whether these are organizational policies or statutory rights.[24] A survey of organizational "father friendliness" in

Sweden did find some organizations that took a positive attitude toward men's involvement in family life, either for ideological or economic reasons. However, many companies retained a traditional orientation to fatherhood and work.[25] In the traditional firms, although men were legally entitled to take time to participate in family life, this participation was expected to be limited, and men were expected to put work before family.[26]

The impact of gendered workplace culture is also illustrated by Danish research, which demonstrates that while employees in female-dominated workplaces develop informal, flexible practices to help each other to manage work and family, in male-dominated workplaces, informal flexibility can be used for other purposes, such as the demands of a second job, but not for family reasons.[27] Workplace culture thus interacts with both public and company policies and can be a barrier to the reconciliation of work and family, regardless of other factors.

Another aspect of workplace culture that can constitute a strong barrier to the effectiveness of work-family policies is the way in which time is defined in the workplace. Research in the United Kingdom and United States of America reveals that time spent visibly in the workplace tends to be regarded as indicative of productivity, commitment, and value.[28] This serves to marginalize employees who reduce their time input for family reasons. These attitudes to time in the workplace do not appear to be universal, however. For example, Raabe quotes interviews with German managers who recognize the value of shorter working hours and the fact that long hours in the workplace can be indicative of inefficiency rather than productivity.[29]

SENSE OF ENTITLEMENT TO ASSERT WORK AND FAMILY NEEDS

The impact of aspects of workplace culture on the demand for, and use of, work-family policies suggests that even in countries with a strong ideological commitment to gender equality and the valuing of family roles, many people do not have a strong sense of entitlement to challenge traditional patterns of work for family reasons. Women currently feel more entitled than men to use these benefits, but many do not have a sense of entitlement to be able to both modify work for family reasons and to achieve occupational advancement. Men often feel more entitled to withdraw from family demands than to modify working patterns. An important question for further research is how to empower men and women to feel a greater sense of entitlement to demand the conditions that will enable them to make optimum contributions in both the private and public domains. It will be important to consider the relative contributions of cultural ideologies, public policy, and workplace policy to this sense of entitlement and to identify the conditions under which the sense of entitlement, and autonomy, to be able to combine work and family, can flourish.[30]

CONCLUSIONS

Social policy support for the accommodation of work and family has emerged earlier in countries with ideologies supporting equal roles in the family as well as the workplace. Supportive social policies may enable corporations to build on these provisions, moving on to flexible work and other provisions with the potential for modifying the traditional work structures associated with the male model of work. However, it is apparent that these modifications will not be successful in achieving radical change without concomitant changes in workplace cultures. This does not follow automatically from supportive ideologies and social provision, nor from changes in formal workplace policy.

Clearly, ideological, social, and organizational contexts interact. Future progress is thus likely to rely on a partnership approach that encompasses the employee, family, organizational, and social policy levels. This will require a shared vision of the sort of organizations and communities that are desired in the future. One such vision, suggested by a British report on ways of achieving sustainable business growth in the face of global competition, is that tomorrow's company will adopt a more inclusive approach to the definition of success, taking account of the needs of all stakeholders: employers and employees, families and shareholders, customers, clients and others.[31] It is unlikely that the shared vision of desired outcomes would be identical across national contexts. Nevertheless, attention to lessons learned in other contexts helps to highlight alternative strategies and possibilities, and to identify current ideological, social policy, and organizational barriers to the reconciliation of work and family systems. Currently, our understanding of causal relationships between ideologies, policies, and outcomes remains limited. Further research comparing work and family issues and organizational responses cross-nationally will be useful to further our understanding of the processes and consequences of organizational and social change in a range of contexts.

NOTES

1. Concerning the debate, see H. De Cieri & P. Dowling, "Cross Cultural Issues in Organizational Behaviour," in C. Cooper & D. Rousseau (eds.), *Trends in Organizational Behaviour* (Chichester, UK: Wiley, 1995). On the definition used here, see M. Tayeb, *Organizations and National Culture* (London: Sage, 1988).

2. Concerning work-family conflict, see S. Lewis & C.L. Cooper, "Stress in Two-Earner Couples and Stage in the Life Cycle," *Journal of Occupational Psychology* 60 (1987): 289–303.

3. U. Sekaran, "Middle-Class Dual Earner Families and Their Support Systems in India," in S. Lewis, D.N. Izraeli, & H. Hootsmans (eds.), *Dual Earner Families: International Perspectives* (London: Sage, 1992), pp. 46–61.

4. Ibid.

5. F. Laczsco & S. Noden, "Eldercare and the Labour Market: Combining Care and

Work," in F. Laczsco & C. Victor (eds.), *Social Policy and Elderly People* (Aldershot, UK: Avebury, 1992), pp. 39–60.

6. K. Sandqvist, "Sweden's Sex Role Scheme and Commitment to Equality," in S. Lewis, D. Izraeli, & H. Hootsmans (eds.), *Dual Earner Families: International Perspectives* (London: Sage, 1992), pp. 80–98; L. Haas, & P. Hwang, "Company Culture and Men's Usage of Family Leave Benefits in Sweden," *Family Relations* 44, (1995): 28–36.

7. Sekaran, "Middle Class Dual Earner Families and Their Support Systems"; D. Izraeli, "Culture, Policy and Women in Dual Earner Families in Israel," in S. Lewis, D. Izraeli, & H. Hootsmans (eds.), *Dual Earner Families: International Perspectives* (London: Sage, 1992), pp. 19–45.

8. Sandqvist, "Sweden's Sex Role Scheme"; Haas & Hwang, "Company Culture and Men's Usage of Family Leave."

9. Izraeli, "Culture, Policy and Women."

10. J. Giele, "Women's Changing Lives and the Emergence of Family Policy," in T. Gordon & K. Kauppinen-Toropainen (eds.), *Unresolved Dilemmas: Women, Work and the Family in the United States, Europe and the Former Soviet Union* (Aldershot, UK: Avebury, 1994).

11. Ibid.

12. P. Moss, "Reconciling Employment and Family Responsibilities: A European Perspective," in S. Lewis & J. Lewis (eds.), *The Work-Family Challenge: Rethinking Employment* (London: Sage, 1996), pp. 36–59.

13. Ibid.

14. European Commission, *European Social Policy: A White Paper* (Luxembourg: Office for Official Publications of the European Community, 1994).

15. J. Lewis, "Work-Family Reconciliation and the Law: Intrusion or Empowerment?" in S. Lewis & J. Lewis (eds.), *The Work-Family Challenge: Rethinking Employment* (London: Sage, 1996), pp. 60–81.

16. Ibid.

17. Ibid.

18. FNV, *Part-time Work. The Dutch Perspective: Policy and Perceptions of the Netherlands Trade Union Confederation* (Amsterdam: Netherlands Trade Union Confederation [FNV], 1994).

19. A. Hoff, "Work Sharing in Germany: Provisional Solution or Part of a Long-term Strategy to Combat Unemployment?" (paper presented at the International Society for Work options conference, Amersfoort, the Netherlands).

20. Concerning the tradition of corporate welfare, see J. Gonyea & B. Googins, "The Restructuring of Work and Family in the United States: A New Challenge for American Corporations," in S. Lewis & J. Lewis (eds.), *The Work-Family Challenge: Rethinking Employment* (London: Sage, 1996), pp. 109–137.

21. L. Hogg & C. Harker, *The Family Friendly Employer: Examples from Europe* (London: Daycare Trust, 1992).

22. B. Berry Lound, *Work and the Family: Career Friendly Employment Practices* (London: IPM, 1990).

23. V. Pruzan, "Denmark: Focus on Child Policy," in European Commission (ed.), *Social Europe: The European Union and the Family* (Brussels: Directorate General Five [DGV], 1994), pp. 51–53.

24. Concerning organizational policies, see S. Lewis, " 'Family Friendly' Employ-

ment Policies: Organizational Culture Change, or Playing Around at the Margins?'' in *Gender, Work and Organizations* (London: Sage, 1997).

25. Haas & Hwang, ''Company Culture and Men's Usage of Family Leave Benefits.''

26. Ibid.

27. H. Holt, ''The Influence of Workplace Culture on Family Life,'' in S. Carlsen & T.E. Larson (eds.), *The Equality Dilemma: Reconciling Working Life and Family Life, Viewed in an Equality Perspective* (Copenhagen: Danish Equal Status Council, 1992), pp. 53–66.

28. Lewis & Taylor, ''Evaluating the Impact of Family Friendly Policies''; L. Bailyn, *Breaking the Mold: Women, Men and Time in the New Corporate World* (New York: Free Press, 1993).

29. P. Raabe, ''Constructing Pluralistic Work and Career Arrangements That Are Family and Career Friendly,'' in S. Lewis & J. Lewis (eds.), *The Work-Family Challenge: Rethinking Employment* (London: Sage, 1996), pp. 247–270.

30. Concerning the relative contributions, see S. Lewis, ''Sense of Entitlement,'' in H. Holt & I. Thaulow (eds.), *The Role of Companies in Reconciling Working Life and Family Life* (Copenhagen: Danish National Institute of Social Research, 1996), pp. 17–42.

31. Royal Society of Arts (RSA), *Tomorrow's Company: The Case for an Inclusive Approach*, RSA report (London: RSA, 1994).

CHAPTER 10

The Work-Family Interface in India

Meera Komarraju

In India, as in many other countries, traditional assumptions regarding the work-family interface are currently being challenged as an increasing number of women seek educational and employment opportunities. This is particularly true of the urban, organized, industrialized sector, which employs a growing proportion of educated middle- and upper-middle-class women in the technical, professional, and managerial ranks as bankers, administrators, nurses, teachers, professors, lawyers, and engineers. About one-third of these women are married and are members of a two-earner couple. This growth of the dual-earner family is a response to the joint forces of advancing urbanization and industrialization, rising inflation and cost of living, and a desire for a higher standard of living, as well as professional development.

CONTEXTUAL FACTORS INFLUENCING THE WORK-FAMILY NEXUS

The lives of dual-earner families are influenced by various contextual factors. These have been organized into three categories to provide a framework that captures the complex interplay of work-family issues. These three categories are as follows:

- the legal changes that have created a more supportive environment for working women by defining and addressing their concerns;
- the human resource policies in various organizations that determine on-the-job flexibility, which is crucial to the daily functioning of dual-earner families;
- the social and cultural institutions that outline the traditional norms regarding marriage, family, and sex-role expectations.

The Legal Environment

On the legal front, in addition to the Indian constitution, which guarantees equal rights for males and females, specific industrial laws have been passed that offer support to working women in dual-earner families. The Equal Remuneration Act (1976) requires equal pay for male and female workers doing the same work, and prohibits any other discrimination against women on the grounds of gender. The Factories Act (1948) requires an employing organization to have a creche or on-site child care center for infants and children under the age of 6 at sites where there are 30 or more female employees. It also tries to ensure the safety of women by prohibiting the carrying of more than prescribed weights, and prevents women from cleaning or adjusting heavy machinery while it is in motion. The Contract Labor Act (1970) requires any labor site with more than 20 female laborers to provide a creche or day care facility. The Mines Act (1952) prohibits the employment of women in underground mines.[1]

The Maternity Benefits Act (1929, 1961) allows women to take leave with full pay for 6 weeks before and 6 weeks after childbirth, as well as two nursing breaks before the child is 15 months old. These benefits apply for up to three births in a woman's career. A pregnant woman is also exempt (at no loss of remuneration) from arduous work and standing for long hours (which may interfere with the pregnancy) for a period of 72 days prior to her delivery date. Further, 6 weeks of paid leave are also given to a woman who has a miscarriage. These leave benefits apply to women who have worked for at least 160 days during the preceding 12 months.

All of these laws attempt to address the major concerns of families in which both spouses work by providing legislative support to employed women. They recognize the constraints under which women work and attempt to ameliorate them. Some researchers argue that even though the government has implemented numerous legal changes, the social system continues to perpetuate a patriarchal ambience, which does not give priority to women's problems.[2] However, it has to be acknowledged that, as in the West, social change takes time. A few generations will have to go by before all legal changes have been internalized and enacted in women's daily lives. This is particularly so in the Indian context, which has an ancient culture with a past going back thousands of years. It is noteworthy that changes are already very visible within the urban society and are trickling into rural lives, too. As women become more aware of their rights and assertively demand them, legal changes are likely to become more of a reality.

Human Resource Policies

At the workplace, particularly in state and federal public sector organizations, as well as in the large unionized business and financial organizations, certain human resource policies offer a great deal of support to dual-earner families.

For example, the policy of granting job "confirmation" after undergoing an initial "probationary" period of employment, provides workers with a certain level of job security. Also, as Sekaran points out, the practice of valuing "seniority" when making promotion decisions reduces the amount of stress and anxiety associated with career advancement.[3] Other benefits that ease some of the complications of a dual-earner family and add to flexibility in planning family events include one month's paid vacation yearly for all permanent employees, as well as travel support for vacations every two years. In addition, there are a relatively large number of days for "casual leave," elected holidays, and the availability of unpaid leaves of absence for advanced study or other approved purposes. In general, employers are quite accommodating of employees who occasionally seek time off for taking care of family needs such as sick children or elderly relatives and visiting family. Taking such leaves of absence is not held against the employee when the time for promotion comes. In fact, an employee who gives priority to family duties is given respect.

Social and Cultural Environment

The social and cultural factors that are unique to Indian society have the greatest degree of influence on the work-family issues faced by individuals in a dual-earner lifestyle. At this point it is helpful to identify the traditional norms and values that determine the basic assumptions regarding appropriate behavior for those trying to balance home and work responsibilities.

Collectivism. Indian culture, which could be identified as collectivistic on an individualism-collectivism continuum, places great emphasis on maintaining social relationships.[4] Retaining membership in a network of family and friends is the guiding theme underlying most human transactions. Throughout an individual's life, obedience, duty, sacrifice for the in-group (here, *in-group* refers to the particular family, caste, language, and religious group into which the individual is born), cooperation with the in-group, favoritism toward in-group members, and acceptance by the in-group are important considerations. Separation from the in-group or going against the wishes of its members is avoided for fear of social ostracism. Family integrity is crucial and mutual interdependence among members is maintained, as it helps to nurture relationships. Most Indians are family oriented and willing to live through problematic situations in order to preserve the integrity and cohesiveness of the family.

Concept of Marriage and the Family. To assess work-family linkages in India, it is crucial to understand the role of marriage and family in an individual's life. An early study of working women by Kapur concludes that the prevalence of the authoritarian joint family and caste system does not provide much scope for the recognition of personal factors.[5] Marriage is not undertaken for individual gratification. Instead, after they marry, the husband and wife attempt to carry out their duty to society. Wagner, Clack, Tekarslan, and Verma explain that arranged marriages are acceptable.[6] Spouses occupy complementary roles with separate identities and a clear division of labor. Typically, a husband and wife do not compete to establish superiority over the other, as there is a mutual acknowledgment of the different, yet important, contributions each makes to the family unit. While there are some current changes as the extended family gives way to the nuclear family, certain basic assumptions persist.

Role of Women. As regards the role of women, Dhruvarajan offers a description of the idealized view of womanhood offered in traditional Indian society.[7] In a family system that is patriarchal and patrilineal, marriage is a must for women, and motherhood provides a legitimate role that reinforces their identity and place in society. While this is the traditional role expectation, contemporary society is beginning to expect women to obtain an education as well as employment so as to contribute substantially towards the well-being of the family.

Based on a comparative study of Indian and American families, Luthar and Quinlan found that, relative to American families, in Indian families, deference, loyalty, and conformity are expected of women.[8] Indian cultural views place greater emphasis on a woman's social duties than on her individual rights. In particular, the Indian woman experiences herself in contextual and relational terms rather than in a separate and individual way.

Current Challenges to Traditional Expectations. It appears that while traditional norms have a strong influence on how men and women live life, there is increasing evidence that the dual-earner lifestyle is creating different expectations. Due to increased urbanization and a rising cost of living, males are seeking and preferring matrimony with employed women. They are beginning to make adjustments to new role demands. Further, Kapur notes that women are demanding self-respect, attempting to develop their personality, and even seeking to marry by choice.[9] They are working hard to fulfill their twin responsibilities at home and at work. With working wives, men are experiencing problems in adjusting to the increased demands on their time, particularly as they have few role models to guide them.

Sunder Rajan addresses this issue of changing roles when she points to the emergence of the new Indian woman in the media as one who is primarily an urban, educated, middle-class, career woman.[10] Advertisements for consumer goods depict her as an attractive, educated, hardworking, and socially aware individual who can successfully balance modernity with traditional roles as wife, mother, and homemaker.

THE DUAL-EARNER LIFESTYLE

Over the past 15 years, a growing body of literature has documented the dynamics emerging out of the dual-earner lifestyle. These research findings have been organized into various themes and described in the sections that follow.

The Benefits for Working Women

Why do women work, and how do they manage to integrate their identities as employees and homemakers, particularly as qualities needed for occupational success seem to be at variance with the qualities needed for social success? Kumar proposed a theoretical analysis to respond to these questions.[11] She categorized working women into four groups:

- *Existential women*: These women have to work for survival; they work before and also after marriage.
- *Professional women*: They are better educated and use work as an expression of self. They find that marriage prevents career progress. They are willing to accommodate their career to marriage realities, yet they generally want to marry as it gives them some advantages in the workplace. They tend to have a better economic status, so they can get domestic help.
- *Transitional women*: They are typically in occupations such as telephone operators, typists, tellers, receptionists, and so forth. They are urban, middle class, and are not looking for promotions. They handle both home and work responsibilities. Before marriage they work to collect dowry money, and after marriage they work to supplement the family income.
- *Reluctant women*: These women grow up traditionally. At some point in their lives, circumstances force them to work. They usually work from home: they may sew clothes or quilts or make book covers or bangles. Their work is not recognized or respected. They tend to be poor and uneducated.

The next question addressed in the same study was whether the working world discriminates against women and whether women discriminate against themselves in the workplace. The answer to this question seemed to be tied into the issue of how a woman's work role fit in with her gender identity. Existential women had no conflict between their work role and gender identity as they kept these two identities separate and perceived work as an external demand. Professional women also had no conflict. In fact, their work role was integral to their self-image. The professional woman prepared herself for her work role and maintained it as continuous with her self. The transitional woman had some conflict due to role overload, as she tended to accommodate to rather than change the circumstances regarding marriage and work. For the transitional woman, there were no attempts toward career building or development of skills. Her work was based on permission given by male authority to make money. The reluctant woman had no work identity and found her work life to be painful.

This theoretical analysis was applied to an empirical study of 62 women (existential, professional, and transitional). It was found that those who considered work as an integral part of their self (such as the professional women) and who were active in making networks (changing circumstances) assimilated success at work into their personal identity. The most problems seemed to be experienced by transitional women, who kept the two worlds of work and family separate.

There are some studies that attest to the benefits experienced by employed women. For example, Sekaran studied 100 career women and found that their work provided them higher status among relatives, allowed them to bargain for a reduced load of housework, gave them professional satisfaction, and helped obtain respect from other men and women.[12] She describes the Indian family structure as being based on a strong sense of "duty" or "dharma," wherein the emphasis is not on "I" or "my," but on "our" needs. Relationships are close, and women get a lot of help from friends, neighbors, and relatives in handling child care, in addition to hiring domestic help when economically possible.

Nathawat and Mathur studied the marital adjustment of 200 educated housewives as compared to 200 working women from Rajasthan in western India.[13] They found that working women had significantly better marital adjustment and subjective well-being relative to educated housewives. They had better general health, life satisfaction, and higher self-esteem. This was accompanied by less hopelessness, anxiety, and insecurity. Employment appeared to serve as a buffer from the less-desirable housework. While these are the privileges of working, the authors state that working women are faced with the complex issue of balancing home and work. In particular, the Indian woman's guilt and conflict deepen in response to religious traditions, customs, and folklore that stress the virtues of the domestic role.

There is further evidence of the positive impact of employment on women. Bala and Lakshmi, who studied 150 employed and 150 educated, nonemployed women from Bihar in eastern India, found that employed women had a more positive self-concept compared to the nonemployed women, particularly those in occupations having higher status (doctors) and requiring more education (college teachers).[14] Employment made these women more self-confident in their abilities, made them feel economically secure and independent, increased professional individuality, and provided the opportunity for greater social interaction.

Employment also serves to increase the power of women in dual-earner families. Shukla and Kapoor studied a sample of 130 upper-middle-class women in dual-earner families (approximately half were employed).[15] Employed women with higher education and more resources (education, income, and occupational prestige) had more power compared to nonemployed women. Husbands of employed wives had relatively less power in the family compared to husbands of nonemployed women. However, across families, the power between husbands and wives did not differ significantly. Egalitarian relationships seemed to be present in affluent families, perhaps because husbands who were more educated were exposed to the egalitarian husband-wife relationships in the West. What was of interest was the finding that having more power was not correlated with greater satisfaction in the marriage. In fact, in marriages where husbands dominated or shared decision making, there was greater marital satisfaction. In marriages where the spheres of decision making were separate/autonomous, there was medium marital satisfaction. In families where decision making was wife dominated, there was low marital satisfaction.

Handling Work and Family Effectively

Results regarding the positive effects of employment for working women are not consistently supported. Some researchers have found that on certain dimensions, there are very few differences between working and nonworking wives. This is particularly the case because working wives seem very keen on fulfilling their homemaker role, too.

An early in-depth case analysis of 300 working women in northern India (doctors, teachers, and office workers) led to the conclusion that being employed did not affect marital adjustment as long as the women and men were satisfied that the wife was performing both her roles satisfactorily.[16] Even though 86% of the husbands were supportive of their wives' employment, the major complaint of employed wives was that they could not cater adequately to their husbands' and children's needs. Happily adjusted wives were those who could combine both roles well and did so happily. There was disharmony in the family if the wife gave too much importance to her work role, especially if the husband wanted her to concentrate on the home. The wife generally expressed satisfaction in doing things for others.

Similar results were obtained in a much later study by Shukla, who studied women in 130 single-earner families and 125 dual-earner families from northern India who worked in professional careers (professors, doctors, lawyers, engineers, scientists, and administrators) regarding their satisfaction with various marital role behaviors: provider, housekeeper, kinship, therapeutic, child care, and child discipline.[17] Results showed that due to normative role expectations, women had greater marital satisfaction when they were satisfied with their performance as housekeepers and with their husbands as providers. Women obtained much satisfaction from housekeeping and from caring for and disciplining children, and not as much from the provider role. Men evaluated themselves more positively in the provider role. For both spouses, marital satisfaction was dependent on agreement with each other's spousal role.

The importance of balancing family and work responsibilities is communicated through the findings of Shukla and Verma, who studied 100 middle-class employed wives and 100 nonemployed middle-class wives from a variety of occupations, including doctors, professors, clerks, bank employees, telephone operators, and radio and television workers.[18] They found that employed wives and housewives did not differ in terms of mental health. In India, housewives are not looked down upon, as they are perceived to be devoted and dutiful women. In regard to the impact of age of children on working women, those with preschool children managed quite well, as they had a lot of help from kith and kin or hired help. Those with "empty nests" had the fewest constraints; they were happy at work and also had time to maintain good relations with relatives, which was very important to them. Those with adolescent children had, relatively, the most problems in dealing with their responsibilities as a parent and as an employee. These research findings offer support for the notion that Indian working women feel satisfied and successful when they are able to fulfill their family and work responsibilities effectively. Though there is not yet much empirical evidence, the issue that needs to be addressed is the cost that is incurred in maintaining such efforts. Employed women experience some degree of stress, fatigue, and exhaustion as they tackle all the demands on their time, at work and at home. Given the relative lack of an infrastructure providing a reliable supply of electricity, water, and time-saving, modern-day kitchen and other household appliances, the dual-career life does take its toll on its family members. Though there are relatives to share the problems, the costs are still quite high. Further, employed women also tend to sacrifice their opportunities for professional development and subdue their career aspirations in order to maintain an atmosphere of harmony at home.

The Role of Husbands in Dual-Earner Families

There is a growing body of research addressing the role of husbands in dual-earner families. This literature suggests that while males are supportive of their wives' employment, they still have difficulty taking on typically "feminine" household chores. Further, both males and females seem to prefer to have males retain the dominant position in the household. In a comparative study of Indian husbands from 245 dual-earner and 245 single-earner families from southern India working in three large public sector enterprises, Ramu found that husbands of employed wives were more egalitarian than husbands of nonemployed wives and contributed 30% more of their time to housework.[19] However, they avoided traditional "women's" work such as cooking, cleaning, and laundry. Further, employed wives did not encourage their husbands to do any housework, as this might reflect on their incompetence at household tasks. They strongly desired to be good wives and mothers. In supporting their husbands' avoidance of domestic work, wives encouraged their husbands to develop a "cultivated incompetence" regarding domestic work. Employed wives rated the provider role as the most important role for an ideal husband. It appeared that women wanted to serve men and sought employment mainly for economic reasons. They resisted change because of persistent traditional gender-role orientations. It is anticipated that with increased education, fertility rates will drop, and more women will opt for work. As a consequence, men are likely to experience pressures to change their expectations and behavior.

Some supporting results are also evident from a study conducted by Roopnarine, Talukder, Jain, Joshi, and Srivastav, who observed 34 single- and 54 dual-earner families in their interactions with children at home.[20] They found no differences between fathers in these two types of families. Mothers were still primary caregivers, and female relatives were greatly involved in the care of infants. Fathers tended to remain distant from care giving and engaged in little domestic work. The traditions and customs of such a patriarchal society seem slow to change. Traditional cultural definitions of male and female roles place constraints on who will do what. Women avoid too strong a career orientation because of disapproval from their husband and relatives about the neglect of children.

Are the husband and wife willing to be copartners? Indiradevi, who addressed the issue in a study of 80 employed and 80 nonemployed wives in southern India, found that husbands seemed reluctant to accept equality in decision making.[21] But for women, education tended to lead to more egalitarian conjugal role performance and decision making. Still, when it came to financial decision making, men dominated. With regard to carrying out feminine tasks, men stayed away. Further, while males preferred joint families, females tended to prefer nuclear families, as this seemed to be more compatible with an increasing demand for an individualistic way of life and lesser conformity to authority by employed women.

CONCLUSIONS

This analysis of the legislative, human resource, and sociocultural factors that impact the behavior of dual-earner families suggests that traditional assumptions regarding work and family life are being challenged and are undergoing rapid change. Employed women are enjoying the privileges that accompany employment and experience relatively less time pressures as compared to their Western counterparts because they can still call upon kith and kin and hired domestic help in juggling their dual responsibilities at work and at home. However, they are not entirely free from the work-family conflicts typical of the dual-earner lifestyle. In particular, the major source of conflict for employed Indian women seems to be their difficulty in integrating their work role into their identity as a "good" and dutiful wife and mother. Their desire to try and fulfill traditional role expectations while being employed full time seems to be taking its toll. They overwork and feel stress in trying to do everything for everybody: spouses, growing children, and aging relatives. With the passage of time they need to identify their priorities and decide on what they can and cannot do—and what other members in the family need to do. This will not be easy, as being assertive is not necessarily viewed positively in the Indian cultural context. Finally, though males in dual-earner families are supportive of their working wives, they have not adjusted completely to their new role demands and need to contribute more substantially toward improving the quality of the dual-career lifestyle as well as toward providing role models for future generations.

NOTES

1. M. Shastri, *Status of Hindu Women: A Study of Legislative Trends and Judicial Behavior* (Jaipur, India: RBSA Publishers, 1990).

2. See, for example, I.P. Singh, *Women, Law and Social Change in India* (New Delhi, India: Radian Publishers, 1989).

3. U. Sekaran, "Middle-class Dual Earner Families and Their Support Systems in Urban India," in S. Lewis, D.N. Izraeli, & H. Hootsmans (eds.), *Dual-earner Families: International Perspectives* (London: Sage Publications), pp. 46–61.

4. Concerning this continuum, see H.C. Triandis, H. Betancourt, S. Iwao, K. Leung, J.M. Salazar, B. Setiadi, J.B.P. Sinha, H. Touzard, & A. Zaleski, "An Etic-Emic Analysis of Individualism and Collectivism." *International Journal of Applied Cross-Cultural Research* 18(3) (1993): 13–17.

5. P. Kapur, *Marriage and the Working Woman in India* (Delhi, India: Vikas Publications, 1970).

6. W. Wagner, F. Clack, E. Tekarslan, & J. Verma, "Male Dominance, Role Segregation, and Spouses' Interdependence: A Cross-Cultural Study," *Journal of Cross-Cultural Psychology* 21(1), 48–70.

7. V. Dhruvarajan, "Religious Ideology, Hindu Women, and Development in India," *Journal of Social Issues* 46(3) (1990): 57–69.

8. S.S. Luthar & D.M. Quinlan, "Parental Images in Two Cultures: A Study of Women in India and America," *Journal of Cross-Cultural Psychology* 24(2) (1993): 186–202.

9. Kapur, *Marriage and the Working Woman in India*.

10. R. Sunder Rajan, *Real and Imagined Women: Gender, Culture and Postcolonialism* (London: Routledge, 1993).

11. U. Kumar, "Indian Women and Work: A Paradigm for Research," *Psychological Studies* 31(2) (1986): 147–160.

12. Sekaran, "Middle-class Dual Earner Families and Their Support Systems in Urban India."

13. S.S. Nathawat & A. Mathur, "Marital Adjustment and Subjective Well-being in Indian-Educated Housewives and Working Women," *Journal of Psychology* 127(3) (1992): 353–358.

14. M. Bala & S. Lakshmi, "Perceived Self in Educated Employed and Educated Unemployed Women," *International Journal of Social Psychiatry* 38(4) (1992): 257–261.

15. A. Shukla & M. Kapoor, "Sex Role Identity, Marital Power, and Marital Satisfaction among Middle-class Couples in India," *Sex Roles* 22 (11/12) (1990): 693–706.

16. Kapur, *Marriage and the Working Woman in India*.

17. A. Shukla, "Marital Role Behaviors and Marital Relationships among Single- and Dual-career Families," *Indian Journal of Clinical Psychology* 15(1) (1988): 84–88.

18. A. Shukla & V. Verma, "Influence of Employment on Mothers' Work and Home Attitudes and Mental Health," *Psychological Studies* 31(2) (1986): 142–146.

19. G.N. Ramu, "Indian Husbands: Their Role Perceptions and Performance in Single- and Dual-earner Families," *Journal of Marriage and the Family* 49 (1987): 903–915.

20. J.L. Roopnarine, E. Talukder, D. Jain, P. Joshi, & P. Srivastav, "Personal Well-

being, Kinship Tie, Mother-Infant and Father-Infant, Interactions in Single-wage and Dual-wage Families in New Delhi, India,'' *Journal of Marriage and the Family* 54 (1992): 293–301.

21. M. Indiradevi, *Women-Education-Employment: Family Living* (Delhi, India: Gian Publishing House, 1987).

CHAPTER 11

Cultural Diversity in Organizations: Implications for Work-Family Initiatives

Donna Klein

If we believe that families are the seedbed of society, some would argue that our future looks a little grim. While "Corporate America" has done a commendable job over the last decade to integrate family-friendly policies and programs, in actuality, the population that has been served is the population that is usually served most often and best, the middle- to upper-middle-class professional workers, who benefit from company contributions, pension plans, medical coverage, and a plethora of family-friendly programs, which creatively and flexibly help them to balance the demands of their work and family lives.

Left behind and eternally struggling, however, are those diverse groups of families who are represented by shift workers, housekeepers, hotel workers, chefs, guards, waiters and waitresses, nurse's aids, and so forth. While the parallel emergence of the diversity and work-family agenda in the United States has assisted some of the diverse members of the middle and upper class in achieving their goals, the parallel rise of both issues has done next to nothing to enhance the ability to achieve for the working-class population, which has a far greater degree of diversity and a corresponding lower level of education. However, if we recognize that the professional working families in the United States are stressed in creating some balance in their lives, the complexity of life for these diverse working-class families is correspondingly almost incomprehensible.

This chapter will attempt to address the overlap between diversity and work-life issues where they complement each other, but will also attempt to create a sense of just how much we have left unattended as we proclaimed ourselves family friendly. What has gone unaddressed is not only the uniqueness of ethnic groups, but also economic groups and groups defined by education level and work shifts.

EARLY STAGES OF DIVERSITY

Early stages of the promotion of diversity first became part of the management parlance because diversity was visible. It was easy to look around the executive committee conference table and note the striking differences in mannerisms and behavior when a woman or minority was present. To look at any corporate head-quarters building in America from the 1970's to the present, it was possible to note by sight the presence of females, African Americans, Asians, and Hispanics. Second, of course, these visible differences and the widely documented ramifications of differences in terms of opportunity and advancement resulted from much needed legislation (i.e., the Civil Rights Act of 1964 and Executive Order 11246 in 1965). These directly supported the ''advancement for minorities'' spirit and intent of the U.S. Constitution and Bill of Rights. While this legislative support re-sulted in some impact in terms of numbers of females and minorities in manage-ment positions, the successes have, in real numbers, been minimal. The work environment that was needed to succeed was pretty much ignored during those early years, and the latitude to account for cultural and personal life differences was not taken into account. It was still the case of a square peg forced into a round hole—the corners had been rounded a little, however.

EMERGENCE OF WORK AND FAMILY

And the mismatch continues to a great extent. In most organizations, diversity and work-family issues are separate agendas, vying for a small percentage of finite attention that senior executives expend on what are still determined to be ''soft'' issues with soft, and many times, immeasurable benefits. The issue of diversity in most companies can be looked at as a ''traditional'' one. It reflects the integration of women and minorities of color into the executive ranks. It manages the physical (i.e., visible) differences in workers, and counts its vic-tories based on that uniqueness. What has been ignored is the unseen, invisible private person which is, in all likelihood, more strongly correlated to success than skin color or gender. To fragment the issues of diversity and work-family into discrete management agendas dilutes the impact that could be made by managing them synergistically.

To truly address the issue of diversity and create an environment within which each worker has an opportunity to achieve, one must recognize and take into account the work–personal life differences that impact success. The definition of diversity must be expanded to include not only gender and race differences. Of equal importance are differences in marital and parental status, socioeco-nomic background, religious persuasion, and sexual orientation. When the def-inition of diversity is expanded to be more inclusive, then we can complete the cultural transition to support our demographic mix.

At the current point in time, the field of work-life/work-family in Corporate America is doing a commendable job in support of the professional worker who has become assimilated into the white, upper-middle, and upper-class lifestyle. The knowledge worker is being supported with services as wide-ranging as child and elder care resource and referral to on-site child care, corporate schools, and concierge service to assist in the delivery of the all-important ''career maker or breaker''—the department dinner party. We in the field of work-family have made progress in serving those who have ''made it,'' but we are underserving the traditionally underserved. Particular among the underserved in the population are those who are economically disadvantaged, which correlates indirectly with the degree of ethnic diversity. As we go down the economic scale, we find proportionally increasing ethnic differences.

Lower socioeconomic status in the United States results from:

- lower levels of education
- single parenting
- nutrition deficiencies
- youth parenthood[1]

These factors, in turn, result in:

- single parenthood
- poverty
- nutrition deficiencies
- low levels of education
- low attainment
- poorer health
- higher incidence of Alzheimer's disease

Thus, there is a cyclical, downward-sloping trend. The more we continue to underserve, the greater grows the number of underserved.[2] Moreover, research has indicated that employees with low incomes and low levels of education are less likely to participate in dependent care programs than their more highly paid and highly educated coworkers.[3]

While support of a broad definition of diversity and its corresponding work-life/work-family issues is not addressable in one volume, let alone one chapter, this section will hopefully demonstrate the need for such breadth of definition if the evolution of work-life programs is indeed going to be successful in creating equitable opportunities.

A BUSINESS CASE

One Fortune 100 Service Company, which is very active in the work-life arena and a leader in the attempt to define work-life solutions for its ethnically

Table 11.1
Ethnic Breakdown of the Workforce

	Hourly Employees	Management
White	50.0%	85.0%
Hispanic	19.0%	4.0%
African American	24.5%	8.0%
Asian	6.0%	2.8%
American Indian	.5%	.2%

diverse and lower-income hourly population, serves as a good model of the direction in which work-life solutions for a truly diverse workforce (typified by 150,000 hourly employees) need to expand. This corporation's experience is used as an example of the breadth of considerations programs need to evaluate in the design stage, if they are to be truly equitable to all groups. The example is not meant to be representative of corporations in general. (See Table 11.1 for an ethnic breakdown of the workforce.) In fact, the profile shown below is a representation of the extreme in diversity. Some key top-line statistics include:

• the corporation employs approximately 180,000 employees; 53% are female
• 80% of the 180,000, or 144,000, are hourly workers
• the mean age is 33
• the median hourly wage is approximately $7.40
• 26 primary languages are spoken
• 40% of the population have children under 12 years of age
• 15% have children under 5 years of age

The traditional work-family/work-life solutions offered by most American corporations are addressing the needs, therefore, of perhaps 20% of the American workforce (100% of the management staff and the high end of the hourly staff), because the baseline assumptions behind the design of these traditional work-family programs are:

1. employees are able to understand and accept assistance from the corporation, and
2. they can afford to pay for the services (child care, elder care, concierge, etc.).

Both of these assumptions are invalid with the largely diverse hourly population defined above.

The first year of implementation of the business plan for work-family benefits at the corporation cited represents painful and profound learnings. A partial list and the history of the initial program rollout at this corporation is highlighted below:

- Nationwide Childcare Resource and Referral was rolled out and heavily monitored for two years, with a fraction of percent of usage.

- A center-based child care discount program was developed, giving the employee who used center-based care a 10% discount on fees, it reached approximately 800 employees per year.

- A quarterly newsletter was developed, distributed nationwide and published in two languages, English and Spanish. However, 30% of the hourly population and over 10% of the management population were unable to read it since they were not literate in English or Spanish.

- Product discounts were negotiated with a leading manufacturer, which enabled another 600 families to afford to purchase high chairs, car seats, strollers, and other children's products.

- Management training was developed to encourage workplace flexibility (hours of work), and alternative work arrangements were developed corporatewide, resulting in increased opportunities for flexibility for 20% of the employee base in management positions. It wasn't recognized that little flexibility other than part-time work could be utilized by the hourly population. They could not, for example, use telecommuting because their work location was prescribed. They could not work a compressed work-week because of the limitations in hours established by the Fair Labor Standards Act. They could use a reduced workweek (i.e., part-time hours), and in some cases, flextime. If statistics were available, they would have shown that:
  - hourly workers worked more days, anyway;
  - the tasks they perform are directly related to customer needs; therefore,
  - they have less control over hours;
  - many already hold multiple jobs.[4]

An additional complexity making communication of any new policies on scheduling a major challenge is that the industry estimates a 48% illiteracy rate.[5] One must remember that service industry hours are driven by the needs of the customers, which change on a weekly basis. If a property is fully booked with morning wedding receptions one week and evening bar mitzvahs in the next, the staff schedules for these weeks will be entirely different. The incidents do not drive the schedule; the customer needs do. Multiple jobs, also a characteristic of the population, impact an employee's availability. If one job is inflexible (or totally flexible), the impact on the second job becomes negative.

  In summary, the "traditional" work-family solutions were minimally effective in meeting a population as diverse and economically challenged as the one this corporation employed. It was relatively easy for the firm to conclude that a paradigm shift in the work-family field, which would take into account the economic, cultural, and literacy challenges as factors in program design, was required if the work-family initiative was to include its hourly workers.

CURRENT FOCUS AND EXPERIMENT

Considering profit margins of 2.5 cents on each dollar of sales, it became clear that regardless of the money available for program implementation, the impact would be minimal at best. The profit margins were clearly too small to offer direct child care subsidies. But it was also clear that the services that were available in the community were not being utilized by the people for whom they were targeted.

For example, one focus group identified 35 hourly employees who were eligible for child care subsidy through state block grants. Only 1 employee was receiving a subsidy, although an excess in funding was available. The eligible employees were unaware of how to apply, and also unaware of their eligibility. They did not understand the program, and many were even suspicious of it.

This scenario was repeated many times over when an investigation of other community-based services throughout the country was made. It was determined that the new paradigm must create a bridge to correct the existing disconnects and ensure that existing services, both company-based and community-based, were made available.

As a result of this lack of continuity between needs and access to services already available, a nationwide program was designed, which functions as a holistic approach to family support. Called the Associate Resource Line, this new development in the work-family arena merged the traditional Employee Assistance Program (EAP) response employed by many corporations nationally with a full continuum of work-family programs. The need for the merger resulted from a conclusion reached through the analysis of the failed child care resource and referral implemented in the first year of work-family services in the business case described here. The anecdotal data from the unsuccessful program attempt indicate that the lower-income families that the corporation employed had many acute issues that complicated their daily existence. It became unrealistic to attempt to focus these families on requested licensed child care when acute issues such as eviction, Immigration and Naturalization Service (INS) issues, and transportation challenges were a part and parcel of everyday problem solving.

The Associate Resource Line was designed to be a holistic approach to full family support. The concept of family included any and all aspects of an employee's personal life, and was not limited to the traditional family configuration.

The availability of the service was communicated in four languages during the first six-month pilot project launched in Florida (English, Spanish, French, and Haitian Creole), and telephone counseling was available in these languages as well. The second pilot expanded to Chicago, Atlanta, and the state of Texas. After 18 months, usage was nearly 9% (benchmarked against traditional EAP usage numbers generated from a professional population), and calculations on business impacted indicated a nearly five-to-one payback on the investment. The program was subsequently approved and is in operation in all 50 states. In addition to being an ongoing family intervention, this program serves as a daily data collection tool and provides ongoing information about the family issues and trends.

A second experiment in collaboration with competitors was also initiated in a major southern market. Three competing companies formed an umbrella non-profit corporation to create full family support services, to be delivered through a venue that additionally provides childcare for 250 children, the majority of whom need subsidizing. In addition to care, the center will provide immunization, parent education, nutrition counseling, resource and referral, and other services bridged directly from the community.

These experiments in collaboration, partnership, and leveraging continue. The issues of a diverse population, many times of lower socioeconomic status, present barriers that are not only financial, but cultural and communications-oriented as well. The challenge has only begun to be investigated. The solution will take cooperation and collaboration from all sectors of the economy—public, nonprofit, and private. The corporation cited here feels confident that the answers lie within the framework of corporate and community partnerships. After all, the economics of the issue preclude either a corporate-only or community-only model. However, the communities must be redeveloped, and the corporate community must assist in the redevelopment so that bridges can be created between employers and the community. Only collaboration will be able to provide the greatest support for the employees, who are also citizens of the community. It will take effort, understanding, and new behavior.

NOTES

1. A. Bridgman & D.A. Phillips, *Child Care for Low-income Families* (Washington, DC: National Academy Press, 1996).

2. E. Galinsky, J.T. Bond, & D.E. Friedman, *The Changing Workforce: Highlights of the National Study* (New York: Families and Work Institute, 1993).

3. Ibid.

4. J. Swanberg, "Walking a Fine Line: A Preliminary Description of How Low-wage workers Balance Work and Family Life" (unpublished ms., Boston University Center on Work and Family, 1995).

5. R. Foley, remarks made at meeting of the Educational Institute, American Hotel and Motel Association, East Lansing, MI, 1996.

CHAPTER 12

A Legal Perspective on Work-Family Issues

Eileen Drake

This chapter looks at the interplay of three areas of employment law with work-family issues: (1) the federal Family and Medical Leave Act (FMLA) and similar state leave laws, (2) federal and state wage and hour laws, and (3) legal issues associated with the increasing use of temporary or leased workers ("contingent workers"). The first two areas, the family leave and wage and hour laws, were intended to be employee protective. In theory, these laws were intended to limit perceived "abuse" of employees by either requiring or encouraging employers to recognize the needs of employees to take time for nonwork demands and interests. In practice, the statutes only partially achieve their goals and in some respects actually are counterproductive. The third area, the expanding use of contingent workers, reflects a shift in the basic employment relationship with as-yet unknown significance for the positive integration of work and family life.

INTRODUCTION

The federal Family and Medical Leave Act and similar state leave statutes are said to reflect an increasing societal concern that the demands of work balance with family needs. Workers, it is argued, should not be forced to choose between keeping their jobs and meeting their own or their family's health care needs. Employers, it is claimed, are more concerned with the "bottom line" than with the well-being of their employees.

In reality, we are a society with changing demographics and values. One recent study indicates that less than 10% of American families conform to the "traditional" pattern of one male wage earner in the paid workforce married to a female spouse who stays home to provide unpaid home and child care. The most common family types now in the workplace are dual-wage earners and single-parent families. Parents with children under the age of 18 make up roughly half the total workforce in the United States. Of these families, approximately one-quarter are single-parent households.[1] These types of households often have conflicting work and family demands.

Employees also face "family-life" needs beyond those involving children at home. As the "baby-boomers" age, so do their parents. The caregiver role often reverses, with children required to spend more time helping parents and in-laws through illness or major life changes. Adult children may return home because of financial or employment problems, frequently bringing their own children with them. Even in households without children or aging parents, employed individuals may want more free time, greater schedule flexibility, or both. Added to these demographic changes are technological developments that make it possible to "bring work home" (or elsewhere) in a new sense—via computers, modems, cellular phones, and facsimile machines.

If we agree that one important goal of our society is to improve the balance of work life and family life and that this goal should be approached from all possible perspectives, it also is important to recognize that "the law" does not—and probably will not ever—get us there.

Our laws, whether statutes passed by Congress and state legislatures or common law theories developed by the courts, do reflect societal values. For the most part, though, these legal directives are adopted as after-the-fact attempts to solve broad problems with generalized solutions. As such, they neither fix the problem nor advance the societal goal. The civil rights laws from the 1960's and 1970's are prime examples: 20 to 30 years later, our civil rights agencies and courts still are flooded with discrimination claims and, more importantly, we remain a society focused more on our differences than our commonalities.

The federal Family and Medical Leave Act, enacted by Congress in 1993, is no different. Although "birthed" with bipartisan support, it is only a partial solution to the challenge of blending family and work that, two years later, has benefited only a small percentage of U.S. workers. Furthermore, other employment laws, particularly the wage and hour laws, actually hinder employer attempts to offer more flexible work arrangements to employees or encourage employers to shift to using more temporary, part-time, or leased employees.

FAMILY LEAVE LAWS

FMLA Eligibility and Leave Rights

The federal Family and Medical Leave Act of 1993 (FMLA) covers private sector employers with 50 or more employees and public employers with 2 or more employees. However, an employee of a covered employer will be eligible for leave only if the employer has 50 or more employees within a 75-mile radius of the facility where the employee who needs leave works and the employee requesting leave has worked for the employer for at least 12 months and at least 1,250 hours in the 12 months preceding the start of the leave.

An eligible employee may take up to 12 weeks of leave in a 12-month period (a calendar year or a "rolling" year either running forward from the time the leave starts or looking backward from the prospective leave date, as set by the employer's policy) for any of the following reasons:

- birth of a child or adoption or foster placement of a child under the age of 18;
- the employee's own serious health condition; or
- the serious health condition of certain immediate family members.

This leave is unpaid, except to the extent that the employee chooses (or the employer requires him or her) to use accrued vacation or personal time off or the employee qualifies for use of sick leave or disability benefits under the employer's policy or a collective-bargaining agreement. The employer must continue group health benefits for an employee on FMLA leave on the same basis as if the employee were still at work.

At the end of the leave period, the employee must be reinstated to his or her former position or an equivalent position, with pay and benefits generally resumed as if there had been no leave. If the former position has been eliminated for legitimate business reasons, the employee may be laid off only if the employee would have been laid off had he or she been at work instead of on leave.

Leave may be taken in whatever increments an employee needs—hourly, daily, or weekly; in consecutive blocks of time or intermittently; or by working a reduced schedule (e.g., shifting from full time to part time). An employee taking an intermittent or reduced work schedule leave may be transferred by the employer to another position where the latter can better accommodate the leave needs, provided the employer maintains the same level of pay and benefits for the employee (subject to normal reductions if the employee has shifted from full time to part time).

The employee must give advance notice if the need for leave is anticipated (normally, 30 days). In cases of emergency, the employee's notice may be given after the fact. An employer can require medical verification for any leave needed for an employee's own serious health condition or that of a family member and may require other appropriate verification for leave for birth, adoption, or foster placement.

An employer may not count family leave absences against an employee for attendance policy purposes. In essence, FMLA leave is a federally mandated "excused" absence.

Practical Implications and Limitations

Despite its socially progressive tone, the FMLA is a flawed law. It is at once too broad and too narrow. It is too broad in its definition of "serious health condition.'' Under the FMLA, and the final rules adopted by the Department of Labor (DOL) in January 1995, a serious health condition is a medical condition requiring inpatient hospital care of any duration (even an overnight stay for observation) or continuing treatment by a health care provider for more than three days or which, if left untreated, would result in more than a three-day absence from work or a long-term chronic condition requiring any length of absence. The term includes routine prenatal care, as well as pregnancy-related disabilities; absences for substance abuse treatment (but not absences caused by the substance abuse itself); and absences for mental conditions exacerbated by work-related stress (but not absences due solely to ''stress''). It excludes voluntary or cosmetic treatments, routine physical exams, and routine illnesses or injuries treatable with nonprescription medications or bedrest.

Although the final DOL rules tightened up the definition significantly to correct an earlier definition that would have allowed the use of leave for ''stress'' and for such routine illness as colds and flu that resulted in absences of more than three days, the final definition still is broad enough to cover medical conditions that in the past would not have fit the common understanding of what is a serious health condition. For example, strep throat may last no longer than a bad bout of the flu, but the former could be considered a serious health condition because the employee requires antibiotics, while the latter would not be because the only cure is bedrest. Similarly, if an employee is hospitalized overnight for observation of a head injury for a possible concussion, this technically is a ''serious health condition.'' If, however, the same employee were to be sent home for bedrest and observation by a family member, it would not be a ''serious health condition.'' Such distinctions not only make no sense, but also make it difficult for employers to manage attendance in cases of employees looking for an excuse to stay away from work.

On the other hand, the FMLA is too narrow in several respects. The definition of ''family member'' includes common-law spouses, children, parents, and persons who act ''in loco parentis'' (who provide, or have provided, care to a child not their own). There are two significant gaps in this coverage. First, not all states recognize common-law marriages, thus conditioning coverage on the vagaries of somewhat arcane state laws. In other states (and even where common-law marriage is recognized), individuals in other forms of domestic partnerships not ''sanctified'' by a marriage license do not qualify for FMLA leave. Unless an employer voluntarily extends leave benefits to individuals whom it determines to be in a relationship equivalent to that of a spouse, the narrow definition of spouse excludes many relationships in which the burden of providing care for a serious health condition is just as real as in a marriage setting.

Second, the FMLA also is unnecessarily narrow in limiting coverage to ''parents'' and excluding parents-in-law. A son-in-law, for example, could not use FMLA leave to provide care for his spouse's mother—even if his spouse were deceased and the mother-in-law had no remaining direct family members. Since the impact of care needs on employees can be just as difficult with in-laws as with parents, this omission is puzzling at best. (Compare, for example, the Oregon Family Leave Act, which includes parents-in-law in the definition of family members covered by that state's law.)

Another significant omission from the FMLA lies in the purposes for which the leave may be used. While recognizing the burden associated with adding a new family member in its parental leave provisions, the law fails to cover some of the more significant needs associated with an employee's elderly parents. For example, there is no provision for leave to allow an employee to provide assistance to a surviving parent in moving or managing financial affairs after the death of the spouse. Similarly, an employee whose child may never have a serious health condition but who has a continuing pattern of routine health problems, resulting in the parent having to take time off from work, has no protection under the federal law.

Finally, initial studies by the Bureau of Labor Statistics (BLS) indicate that few U.S. workers actually took advantage of the FMLA in its first year in effect. One survey commissioned by BLS reports that only about 11 percent of U.S. employers (employing approximately 59% of U.S. workers) are actually subject to the FMLA. A second BLS survey of U.S. employees indicates that only 17% took leave for a reason that would be covered by the FMLA.[2]

WAGE AND HOUR LAWS

Despite the flaws in the FMLA—and leaving aside any discussion of major problems in coordinating the FMLA with state leave laws—the FMLA is significant as a statement of societal and governmental recognition of the changing workforce demographics and as an attempt to balance work and family-related needs. The same cannot be said for this country's outmoded wage and hour laws. The federal Fair Labor Standards Act (FLSA) and similar state laws, which set minimum wage and overtime pay requirements, were passed after the Depression and last updated in the 1970's. One of the original purposes of the wage and hour laws was to discourage employers from requiring employees to work extraordinarily long hours, to the detriment of the latter's personal and family lives. The laws do this, not by imposing direct limits on the number of hours employees may be required to work, but through a financial penalty in the form of legally mandated "extra" compensation for overtime work by employees in certain classifications.[3]

Under these laws, all jobs in the workplace are classified either as "nonexempt" (i.e., subject to the overtime rules) or "exempt" (i.e., not subject to the overtime rules). The wage and hour laws pose no significant compensation problems for employers who wish to offer flexible work schedules to hourly, "nonexempt" employees. By definition, these employees may be compensated for hours actually worked, with deductions taken from base pay for hours not worked in excess of any paid vacation or sick leave benefits. Nonexempt employees, therefore, may easily work flexible schedules with direct pay adjustments based on hours worked.

However, "exempt" employees (generally, salaried employees in executive, professional, or administrative positions whose work involves the exercise of independent judgment and discretion) face extra hurdles in arranging flexible work schedules. Courts recently have found even high-level professional employees to be "nonexempt" (and therefore, eligible for overtime pay) if an employer makes any deductions from pay for an absence of less than one full day. (The underlying legal theory is that if an employee is "salaried," then he or she should be paid the same amount regardless of how many hours are worked in a given workday.) This forces too many employers to think in terms of controls on flextime work schedules intended to get them their "money's worth," rather than making it possible to be more flexible in arranging schedules.

This "salary" factor also poses a problem for an exempt employee needing less than a full day's leave for FMLA purposes. The FMLA itself provides that an employer may allow an exempt employee to use FMLA leave in hourly increments without negating the individual's exempt status. However, the FMLA provides this as an exception only to the FLSA and does not override state laws. Many states have wage and hour laws with exemption tests that mirror the FLSA classifications. Since the FMLA does not preempt state laws, an employer still will have a problem under state law if the exempt employee is allowed to use leave in hourly increments. This leaves employers with the unsatisfactory alternatives of requiring the employee to take a full day off when only a few hours are needed or not counting the time off against the employee's FMLA allotment.

State laws may place further barriers on flexible work schedules. For example, California wage and hour laws require employers to give overtime pay to nonexempt employees who work more than eight hours in a workday. (The FLSA requirement is only to pay overtime for hours in excess of 40 in one workweek.) State regulations provide that, if one employee wants to work a flextime schedule (e.g., four ten-hour days), the employer will have to pay overtime for the ninth and tenth hours worked each day, unless: (1) all employees in the affected job classification are asked to vote on the flextime schedule by secret ballot; (2) a majority of the employees vote in favor of the schedule change; and (3) the schedules of all of the affected employees are changed to the flextime schedule.

Such nonsensical rules, while originally adopted to protect employees against employer abuse, actually work against both employers and employees. We need to rethink our wage and hour laws in light of today's needs and goals and make sure they facilitate, rather than hinder, flexible work arrangements.

CONTINGENT WORKERS

One of the more significant employment trends of the 1990's is the increasing use of workers other than a company's own regular or temporary employees (either through temporary agencies or longer-term employee-leasing services). These arrangements may offer advantages for both employers and the so-called "contingent workers." This represents a fundamental change in the employment relationship: the employer of record may have no direct involvement in the actual work done by its employees, while the business for whom the work is provided may disavow any direct responsibility for the workers.

It is too soon to project the impact of the use of contingent workers on work and family issues. For some, these arrangements raise the specter of the "disposable" employee with, not only limited job security, but also a loss of benefits and flexibility—a new class of "itinerant" workers subject to the individual whims and largesse of the business contracting for their services. On the other hand, these arrangements can meet legitimate employment objectives for both employees and employers. For employers, advantages include greater flexibility in meeting cyclical increases in production demands, easier fill-in for absent employees, and cost reductions associated with shifting responsibility for some benefits and liabilities. For the workers, advantages can include greater flexibility in scheduling workdays or moving in and out of the workforce as family needs permit.

Employers who look at such arrangements, however, also should be aware that they are not risk free and should not be entered into as a means to avoid the responsibilities and liabilities commonly associated with the direct employment of workers. Many employment laws, particularly those adopted in recent years, recognize the concept of "joint employer" and extend coverage to both the "primary employer" (the temporary or leasing agency) and the "secondary employer" for whom the contingent workers provide services. The FMLA, for example, expressly imposes responsibility on both the primary and secondary employer for making leave benefits available to eligible contingent workers. Furthermore, as employers expand the use of contingent workers, they should expect a similar expansion of other labor and employment laws to cover their relationships with these workers as well as their regular employees.

CONCLUSION

While it may be interesting—and even intellectually stimulating—to debate the adequacies and inadequacies of labor and employment laws, employers and employees alike should not make the mistake of thinking that laws and regulations are the path to reach our societal goals. Even the best of employment laws set only the minimum standard for work relationships. The law, in general, is merely a set of "thou shalt nots"—setting the minimal level of acceptable behavior and the penalties for going below that level. The law neither answers questions nor solves societal problems in and of itself. Even Title VII of the Civil Rights Act of 1964, the most sweeping piece of civil rights legislation of this century, is merely a list of prohibitions rather than guidelines for capitalizing on diversity in the workplace.

It is up to our business and community organizations, more than our governments, to set the standards and define the values for how people should work and live together in our society. The challenges and the goals, and the means to reach both, lie, not in our employment laws or in this chapter, but in the ideas, efforts, and experiments detailed throughout the rest of this book.

NOTES

1. N.E. Dowd, "Work and Family: Restructuring the Workplace," *Arizona Law Review* 431 (1990): 439–445.

2. " 'FMLA' Results in Employer Policy Changes," *Oregon Labor Letter*, December 1995, p. 8.

3. Overtime pay at time and one-half the employee's regular rate for hours worked in excess of 40 in one work week under federal and state laws and, under some state laws, for hours worked in excess of a set maximum in one workday.

PART IV

Work-Family Initiatives and Career Development: Problems and Promise

CHAPTER 13

Telecommuting as a Response to Helping People Balance Work and Family

Francine Riley and
Donna Weaver McCloskey

Changes in family structures and work environments have contributed to the need for more flexibility in balancing the conflicting roles of work and family. Traditional families with a working husband, a stay-at-home wife, 2.2 children, and a pie in the oven are now down to 10% of American families.[1] The growth of both dual-career parents and single-parent families has made it even more difficult to meet both work and family demands. In addition to working, child care needs, and family responsibilities, many employees must now care for elderly friends and relatives.[2] Along with the changing family structures, our work lives have become more demanding. Both men and women are working longer hours, resulting in more conflict between work and family obligations.[3] The strain created from trying to balance seemingly incompatible roles contributes to negative work outcomes, including higher absenteeism, job dissatisfaction, and turnover. This leads us to wonder whether organizations can develop and keep better employees by providing them with the flexibility to balance their work and family commitments.

Along with other family-responsive programs such as dependent care, compressed workweeks, and job sharing, telecommuting is an organizational response to helping employees balance work and family commitments. There is not a universally accepted definition of this term, as it is constantly evolving and may vary across departments, companies, industries, and researchers. In the most general sense, telecommuting is a means of using technology so that work can be completed without regard to physical location. It is a work arrangement that allows an employee to work at a distant location, frequently from home, under specified conditions, for a designated number of days during normal business hours.

The interest and growth in telecommuting has been further spurred by advances in technology and recent legislative mandates. Technological advances and the reduction in hardware and software costs have made this work option a feasible reality. Telecommunication and network technology enable many employees to work at home seamlessly.[4] Data, graphics, and video can easily be sent from one location to another, making knowledge and information jobs less location dependent. In addition to providing other benefits, telecommuting also allows organizations to comply with recent legislation, including the Clean Air Act[5] and Americans with Disabilities Act.[6] It is therefore not surprising that there has been tremendous growth in telecommuting. Although the statistics in this area are a bit muddled due to differences in definitions, it is clear that remote-work options, including telecommuting, have been growing. LINK Resources Corp., a New York–based market research firm which has been following the work-at-home trend since 1986, estimates that in 1989, 26.6 million Americans (23% of the total work force) were doing job-related work at home at least part of the time.[7] By the year 2000 it is estimated that at least 25 million employees will be participating in the telecommuting trend, and by 2030, it is estimated that there will be over 90 million telecommuters in the United States alone.[8]

As telecommuting becomes a more needed and accepted form of flexible work, it is necessary to understand the factors that contribute to positive outcomes. This chapter addresses the potential advantages and disadvantages of telecommuting and suggests factors to consider in designing a successful telecommuting work arrangement. The results from a pilot telecommuting program conducted by GTE, a Fortune 500 company, will be used to illustrate the benefits of this work option as a response to balancing work and family demands. Individual case histories are offered as additional evidence of the potential positive results of this work arrangement.

GTE is a large, highly competitive telecommunications firm with over 100,000 employees and operations in 48 states and many countries worldwide. The corporation conducted a six-month telecommuting pilot study from January through June 1993 at the telephone headquarters in Dallas, Texas. The pilot study was announced via E-mail to all of the employees at GTE's telephone headquarters, along with a call for volunteers. Union employees were not permitted to participate, resulting in most participants coming from managerial areas. Volunteers were required to have the permission of their supervisor to participate. Ultimately, the pilot study consisted of 120 employees from diverse job responsibilities. Participants were allowed to work at home one day per week for a six-month time period. Telecommuting was not permitted on Mondays or Fridays in an attempt to limit the impression that this work arrangement was a way of taking a long weekend. The organization provided the equipment and other support services. The participants, their supervisors, and their customers provided feedback on various aspects of the work arrangement through a comprehensive survey administered at the midpoint and at the conclusion of the pilot study. In addition to presenting the related literature in the area, the following sections trace the results and outcomes of this pilot telecommuting program.

BENEFITS OF TELECOMMUTING

Work and Family Balance

Work-family conflict has been associated with job dissatisfaction, job stress, increased turnover, and decreased productivity, all of which are factors that have a negative impact on the organization.[9] Organizations have recognized the need to assist employees in balancing work and family commitments. Providing more work-schedule flexibility is one way organizations may help alleviate work-family conflict, as it allows individuals to balance demands from both areas of their lives. In addition to direct organizational benefits, 75% of the 120 participants in the telecommuting pilot study conducted by GTE reported increased feelings of satisfaction with their home life, 44% reported having more quality time with their family, and 33% reported less work-related stress after they began telecommuting. The following case further demonstrates how telecommuting allows individuals to successfully meet both work and family demands.

Phil White, manager of the Associate Development Program, is responsible for recruiting and developing over 100 college hires every year. It is an incredibly busy job. Phil's wife had ailing, elderly parents who lived out of the state. Her frequent visits to stay with them left Phil responsible for caring for their five sons, ranging from age 3 to 14. Phil is able to work from home on the days that his wife visits her parents and stays in touch with the office through the telephone and, using a modem, through a computer connection. This work arrangement benefits both Phil and the organization. He is able to complete more work because there are no planned interruptions. Yet his schedule is flexible enough to accommodate milk and cookies and homework reviews in the late afternoons with his sons.

Productivity Gains

Increases in productivity have been reported from 10% to an astounding 150–200% as a result of telecommuting.[10] There are a variety of reasons why telecommuting contributes to increased employee productivity. Workers are more productive when they are not distracted and constantly interrupted. Additionally, employees who are able to work at home are more likely to work longer hours, because they are appreciative of the flexible work schedule and because it is more convenient. During the telecommuting pilot study, GTE found that the telecommuters were making productivity gains. Of the 120 participants in the study, 97% of the participants and their supervisors reported higher productivity while telecommuting. The work arrangement was also found to decrease customer response time, with 99% of the telecommuters' clients reporting improved service levels. In addition to their doing more work, there is evidence that the work completed was of higher quality. Both employees and their supervisors reported higher quantity and quality of work on their telecommuting days.

Employee Morale

In addition to quantifiable benefits, such as productivity gains, family-supportive work arrangements may also benefit the organization in terms of improved employee morale, job satisfaction, and organizational commitment. Employees feel grateful for the opportunity to telecommute and are therefore more committed to the organization, less likely to leave, and more likely to work harder and longer.[11] When the GTE pilot program participants were asked whether they feel better about GTE because they were allowed to telecommute, 96% agreed and 77% reported increased job satisfaction.

The morale of the employees who do not telecommute must also be considered. There would be a potential detriment to employee morale if these workers felt they were "picking up the slack" for telecommuters. GTE tracked this very carefully and found that the telecommuters were very conscientious about making sure this did not happen. Morale was low, however, among those employees whose managers would not permit participation in this work arrangement.

Absenteeism and Retention

Finding qualified employees is becoming more difficult, as the pool of younger workers is shrinking, while older workers who are trained and experienced are continuing to retire.[12] In this competitive work environment, providing flexible work options may be a necessary means of attracting and retaining valued employees.[13] In addition to attracting and retaining employees, telecommuting has also been found to contribute to reduced absenteeism.[14] The work arrangement allows employees who are ill, disabled, or have family commitments to continue to work at times when conventional office work would not have been feasible. GTE found that telecommuters were grateful for the opportunity to have flexible hours, which helped to relieve stress in their lives. The employees were more likely to work extra hours without pay, work on days when they weren't feeling very well, and remain committed to the organization. Gigi's case, which follows, illustrates how retention can be a direct result of telecommuting.

Gigi was a valued support staff member. After the birth of her third child, she was continually under stress from trying to meet the commitments of both her job and her family. Recognizing the importance of alleviating some of this stress, the organization sought ways of allowing her more flexibility to meet all of her commitments. Leaving work early a few days a week and completing work at home in the evening hours has allowed her to meet her baby-sitting arrangements. Gigi readily admits that had she continued in her old schedule the stresses in her life probably would have continued to grow, eventually resulting in her leaving the organization and seeking a more flexible job. The flexible work arrangement has been very positive for everyone involved: Gigi, her children and family life, her supervisor, and the organization. Gigi was able to keep a job she enjoyed, meet the demands of her family life, and spend more time with her children. Her supervisor is satisfied with the work arrangement because Gigi is very conscientious and completes her work. The organization has benefited because the flexible work arrangement has enabled the retention of a skilled and valued employee. Originally, Gigi had been a secretary, but she has since been promoted twice and is now part of the managerial staff.

Cost Savings

In cases where employees work at home permanently, significant financial savings are possible for the employer due to the need to maintain less office space. Gus Bender, second vice president of data processing for the Travelers Co., estimates that with cost savings, related expenditures, and productivity gains, the company saves as much as $11,600 per telecommuter per year.[15] Part-time telecommuting programs may also result in cost benefits from the ability to retain highly skilled workers who, due to such factors as family demands, health problems, or distance, can no longer work in an office environment. Allowing these people to work from an alternate location allows the company to increase retention and minimize the costs associated with hiring and training.

Environmental Concerns

When the concept of telecommuting was first introduced, it was estimated that for every 1% of the workforce who gave up urban commuting by car, the United States would save 5.4 million barrels of oil per year. If one in seven commuters opted to work full time from home, the United States would have had no need to import oil.[16] Recent environmental legislation has again sparked an interest in telecommuting. The Clean Air Act requires companies with 100 or more employees to reduce the number of single-occupancy vehicles arriving at the work site.[17] Compliance can be met with a variety of programs, such as encouraging the use of mass transit or compressed work weeks. Telecommuting is also a very viable option for many organizations. At GTE, senior management support was solidified when the local department of transportation began seeking corporate partners for a telecommuting pilot project to see if traffic and air pollution could be reduced by having employees work from home one day a week. This work option was seen as providing advantages to the employees and the organization, as well as environmental benefits.

LIMITATIONS AND CONCERNS ABOUT
TELECOMMUTING

Successful Employee Characteristics

Telecommuting is not a work arrangement that will be positive for everyone. The employee must be self-disciplined, a good time manager, organized, and able to work without structure. The potential advantages of telecommuting will never be realized if the wrong employees are allowed to participate, or if the right employees are allowed to participate but for the wrong reasons. The employees who are permitted to telecommute, particularly for a pilot study, must possess the qualities to be successful in a flexible work environment and have a clear understanding of the expectations concerning the work arrangement. Experts have recommended allowing only employees who are comfortable and capable in their positions to telecommute.[18] A written policy concerning the guidelines and expectations for the telecommuting arrangement may also contribute to success.[19] To some extent, GTE identifies telecommuting as a "reward." It is a work option that is available to employees who have their supervisor's approval. Additionally, the company provides each telecommuter with a written policy concerning expectations and guidelines.

Management by Objectives

Just as certain employee characteristics can contribute to a more successful telecommuting arrangement, there are also management styles that can contribute to success. The management of telecommuters requires the ability to manage by outcomes, as opposed to "line of sight." Managerial focus needs to be placed on the quantity and quality of the work completed, as opposed to the number of hours worked and when and where the work is done. To manage telecommuters successfully, managers must be able to break jobs down into tasks, set timetables, monitor output, and provide effective feedback.[20] To participate in the GTE pilot study, employees were required to get the approval of their immediate supervisor. Some work groups were categorically denied participation by their managers, suggesting that not all managers are ready to manage in a flexible work environment.

Child Care Issues

Telecommuting allows employees to balance their work and family commitments, not to meet demands from both areas concurrently. Simultaneously trying to work and perform child care responsibilities results in increased stress for the employee.[21] This is exactly what we were trying to eliminate! GTE's policy states that telecommuters are not to be responsible for child care during work hours. Including this restriction in a telecommuting policy has been recommended by other experts.[22]

Career Advancement Prospects

Many employees feel that telecommuting will reduce their career advancement prospects due to their not being "visible" at the workplace.[23] This fear was identified among the GTE pilot study participants, with 89% being neutral or negative when asked whether telecommuting would help their advancement within their work groups. Researchers have suggested that having telecommuters work in the office several times per week will prevent telecommuters from being passed over for promotions and will contribute to their continued identification with the corporate culture and objectives.[24]

GTE found that if the telecommuting program is designed correctly and has support from management, it will not have a negative impact on an employee's career advancement prospects. The strong career potential of employees taking advantage of flexible schedules is evidenced in the cases provided in this chapter. Both Faye and Gigi have been promoted since they began telecommuting.

Faye was faced with a dilemma. She was marrying a farmer who lived over 120 miles from her place of employment. She loved her job and was a valued employee, yet it was important for her to live with her husband. The organization was facing a dilemma as well. If Faye left the organization, a job freeze meant that it could not replace her. In an attempt to retain her, GTE's first flexible work option plan was developed. In conjunction with her supervisors, Faye developed a plan for telecommuting. The experience has been very positive. Faye's supervisor estimates that her productivity has increased 10 to 15% since beginning this work arrangement. Shortly after she began telecommuting Faye was promoted from administrative manager to manager of the Finance Associate Development Program. Faye is very pleased with this work arrangement and her career advancement. When she had her first child, a few modifications to her schedule allowed her to live on the farm with her husband, care for their child, and continue her promising career with the organization.

Overwork and Burnout

Another potential disadvantage of telecommuting is that if the work site is very convenient, particularly within the home, employees may tend to overwork.[25] Studies have found that with compulsive overwork, health care costs rise, productivity plummets, family satisfaction decreases, and job dissatisfaction grows.[26] It seems we are back to where we started: stressed-out employees who have low productivity and job satisfaction. This is not necessarily the case, however. These potential problems can be minimized with an effective telecommuting plan and employee training. For example, maintaining a separate area in the home that is used solely for work has been suggested as a way of providing both physical and mental boundaries.[27] Additionally, setting regular work hours may limit the tendency to overwork and help to meet family expectations.[28]

TELECOMMUTING PROGRAM GUIDELINES

Telecommuting can potentially offer a number of benefits. Businesses view telecommuting as a means of reducing costs and increasing productivity, whereas employees view it as a way of decreasing stressful commutes and maintaining flexibility to meet both work and family demands. The following guidelines concerning the design and implementation of a telecommuting program may increase the likelihood of success.

Support from Management

Lack of support for telecommuting from management will most likely result in isolation, dissatisfaction, and limited career advancement for the telecommuters. A telecommuting program can only be successful if management is supportive of the work option.

Comprehensive, Written Telecommuting Policy

Telecommuting provides employees with flexibility and autonomy within company-defined boundaries. In addition to covering legal issues and human resource policies, a telecommuting policy should address expectations and guidelines, including whether it is acceptable to have simultaneous child care responsibilities and whether a private work area must be maintained.

Selection of Participants and Supervisors

As futurists have pointed out, not everyone will enjoy, or benefit from, telecommuting.[29] Participants should be selected based on both their interest in participating in telecommuting and their ability to be successful in a flexible work environment. Likewise, managers should be trained in how to effectively manage, motivate, and monitor employees who spend some or all of their time working at physically distant locations.

CONCLUSIONS

The results of the telecommuting pilot study conducted by GTE were very positive. Because of the success of the pilot program, GTE has developed a formal policy that enables workers to telecommute with the permission of their supervisor. It is estimated that the corporation now has over 1,000 employees who are either formally or informally telecommuting. The success of this experiment led to other pilot programs for flexible work arrangements, which have also been well received.

Employees are finding it increasingly difficult to balance both work and family demands. This results in negative consequences for both the individual and the organization. Organizations are attempting to offer more flexibility to minimize these consequences. Telecommuting is one very viable option among the available flexible alternative structures that are evolving in the workplace. Technology allows work to be completed without regard to location, allowing the employee more flexibility in meeting multiple demands from work and family. When designed and implemented correctly, telecommuting may also offer a number of additional benefits to the organization and the telecommuters.

NOTES

1. B. Schepp, *The Telecommuter's Handbook: How to Work for a Salary without Ever Leaving the House* (New York: Pharos Books, 1990).

2. B. Vanderkolk & A. Young, *The Work and Family Revolution: How Companies Can Keep Employees Happy and Businesses Profitable* (New York: Facts on File, 1991).

3. A.R. Hochschild, *The Second Shift* (New York: Avon Books, 1990).

4. J. Martin, "ISDN in the Home Will Revolutionize Telecommuting," *PC Week*, April 17, 1989, p. 68.

5. K.L. Rose & S. Parker, "Surviving the Clean Air Act: Creative Uses of Work/Life Initiatives," *Compensation and Benefits Management*, Autumn 1994, pp. 35–41.

6. J.H. Foegen, "Telexploitation," *Labor Law Journal* 44(5) (1993): 318–320.

7. D.C. Bacon, "Look Who's Working at Home," *Nation's Business* 77(10) (1989): 20–31.

8. K. Barnes, "Tips for Telecommuting," *HRFocus*, November 1994, pp. 9–10; R.B. Wilkes, M.N. Frolick, & R. Urwiler, "Critical Issues in Developing Successful Telework Programs," *Journal of Systems Management* 45(7) (1994): 30–34.

9. On the association of worker-family conflict with these negative factors, see S. Parasuraman, J. Greenhaus, & C. Granrose, "Role Stressors, Social Support and Well-being in Two-Career Couples," *Journal of Organizational Behavior* 13 (1992): 339–356; L.T. Thomas & D.C. Ganster, "Impact of Family-Supportive Work Variables on Work-Family Conflict and Strain: A Control Perspective," *Journal of Applied Psychology* 80(1) (1995): 6–15.

10. J.M. Weiss, "Telecommuting Boosts Employee Output," *HRMagazine*, February 1994, pp. 51–53.

11. G. DeSanctis, "Attitudes toward Telecommuting: Implications for Work-at-Home Programs," *Information and Management* 7(3) (1984): 133–139; J. Goodrich, "Telecommuting in America," *Business Horizons* 33(4) (1990): 31–37.

12. B. Olmsted & S. Smith, *Creating a Flexible Workplace: How to Select and Manage Alternative Work Options* (New York: American Management Association, 1992).

13. Goodrich, "Telecommuting in America"; N. Solomon & A. Templer, "Development of Non-Traditional Work Sites: The Challenge of Telecommuting," *Journal of Management Development* 12(5) (1993): 21–32.

14. D.R. Dalton & D.J. Mesch, "The Impact of Flexible Scheduling on Employee Attendance," *Administrative Science Quarterly* 35 (1990): 370–387.

15. M.J. Dziak, "Telecommuters Do Their Best Work at Home," *Telephone Engineer and Management* 97(12) (1993): 48–50.

16. J.M. Nilles, *The Telecommunication Transportation Tradeoff* (New York: John Wiley and Sons, 1977).

17. Rose & Parker, "Surviving the Clean Air Act."

18. L.F. McGee, "Setting Up Work at Home," *Personnel Administrator*, December 1988, pp. 58–62.

19. B.J. Farrah & C.D. Dagen, "Telecommuting Policies That Work," *HRMagazine* 39(7) (1993): 64–71.

20. Goodrich, "Telecommuting in America"; G. Gordon & M.M. Kelly, *Telecommuting: How to Make It Work for You and Your Company* (Prentice-Hall, 1986).

21. Schepp, *The Telecommuter's Handbook.*

22. A.J. DuBrin & J.C. Barnard, "What Telecommuters Like and Dislike about Their Jobs," *Business Forum* 18(3) (1993): 13–17.

23. Ibid.

24. G. Dutton, "Can California Change Its Corporate Culture?" *Management Review* 83(6) (1994): 49–54.

25. W. Atkinson, *Working at Home—Is It for You?* (Chicago: Dow Jones–Irwin, 1985); Foegen, "Telexploitation."

26. E. Danzinger & L. Reinhart, "Overcoming Overdoing," *Training and Development* 48(4) (1994): 38–42; R.I. Hartman, C.R., Stoner, & R. Arora, "Developing Successful Organizational Telecommuting Arrangements: Worker Perceptions and Managerial Prescriptions," *SAM Advanced Management Journal* 57(3) (1992): 35–42.

27. Atkinson, *Working at Home.*

28. D. Brown, "Working at Home: Too Much of a Good Thing?" *Executive Female* 17(1) (1994): 76.

29. J. Connelly, "Let's Hear It for the Office," *Fortune* 131(4) (March 6, 1995): 22–23.

CHAPTER 14

Family, Sex, and Career Advancement

Jeanne M. Brett

The family structure that appears to provide the best support for advancement in a managerial career is one with a male head of household and either no children or children plus a wife who is at home caring for the children. This conclusion, based on empirical data, suggests that despite the attention paid to issues of work and family in recent years, including the passage of the U.S. Family and Medical Leave Act, family remains a drag on career advancement. In this chapter, I review three important findings from a long-term research program inquiring into the relationships between work and family. After describing the studies, I begin to trace the micro-mediating relationships between having children, reluctance to relocate, and career advancement. I then review the research on males' family structure and career advancement and summarize findings relating to females, both with and without children. The conclusion discusses what workforce factors are holding the preference for traditional male managers in place and what it will take to change these preferences and open traditional career patterns to women and dual-earner men with children.

RESEARCH PROGRAM

My research on work and family has focused on the experiences of relocated employees. The careers of relocated employees provide an excellent window into corporate human resource strategy and individual career advancement. Relocation is an opportunity provided by the company to the employee. The costs are substantial. (The Employee Relocation Council estimates that it costs a company on average $45,373 to relocate a home-owning current employee.[1]) Thus, corporations are making significant investments in employees' careers when they relocate them. Likewise, employees are making investments in a company when they accept relocation. In the career patterns of relocated employees, we can see the strategies that companies use to advance their most valued employees.

The research program, which was sponsored by the Employee Relocation Council, began in 1978, when Jim Werbel and I studied the effect of relocation on employees and their families.[2] In 1988, Linda Stroh, Anne Reilly, and I convinced the Employee Relocation Council to support a follow-up study.[3] We reasoned that a great deal had changed or was changing in the demographic composition of the workforce involved in relocations, in the nature of jobs (because of organizational restructuring and communications technology), and in the structure of organizations and human resources strategy (because of global competition). My conclusion, that the family structure that provides the best support for advancement in a managerial career is one with a male head of household and either no children or children plus a wife who is at home caring for the children, was drawn from these studies of relocated employees and their families.

Both studies used similar methods for sample selection. The 1978 study involved 350 employees from 10 of the Fortune 500 companies. Each company participating in the study provided a list of all employees relocated domestically in the prior two years. Fifty employees were selected at random from each list. The response rate was 71%. The 1989 study used the same methods to select 1,000 employees from 20 of the Fortune 500 companies. The response rate was 67%.

In 1989 we made two changes in the sampling. We were concerned that limiting the study to 10 companies would not reflect the diversity of the membership of the Employee Relocation Council in 1988, so we doubled the number of participating companies from 10 to 20. We were also concerned that employees with special demographic characteristics, for example dual-earner employees or female employees, might be underrepresented in our random sample if they were less likely either to be offered a relocation or to accept one if offered. To avoid this potential bias, we oversampled as many as 150 other randomly selected employees from each company, asking them to participate in the study if they were dual-earner or single, and especially if they had children. We added 359 employees to the study in this way.

The two-study design is a cohort design, not a longitudinal design. We made no effort to study the same companies or employees in 1978 and 1989. There were three reasons for this, the foremost being that a longitudinal study did not suit our research questions. Of course, had we wished to follow up on the 1978 companies in 1989, we would have had extreme difficulty doing so, due to the rash of mergers, acquisitions, and restructurings that occurred in the 1980's. Finally, the employees we had studied in 1978 were unlikely to all be working for their 1978 employer 11 years later, given retirements, restructuring, and reemployment.

DEFINING CAREER ADVANCEMENT

In order to deconstruct my thesis that the family structure that best supports career advancement is one with a male head of household and either no children or children plus a wife who is at home caring for the children, we must first define the terms, and then look at the data. The place to begin is with a definition of a career. A career is a series a work experiences not limited to a single organization or even a single occupation.[4] Career advancement implies a series of work experiences in which responsibilities, skills, authority, commitment, and changes in level of reward increase in a relatively linear fashion over time.[5] I visualize a traditional career as an upward, inward spiral of work experiences, which increase in responsibility and in organizational centrality, though they need not be within the same organization. A nontraditional pattern of career development implies a protean career.[6] I visualize a protean career pattern as a series of lateral loops, either connected or disconnected. Level of responsibility and centrality may change from one experience to another, but there is no consistent upward and inward pattern to the experiences as in a traditional career pattern.

The prototypical indicator of career advancement is increases in salary, or more recently, with the movement to variable pay, increases in salary plus bonus, over time, controlled for years in the workforce and industry. This is typically termed *salary progression.*

The traditional family, with the husband as the economic provider and the wife as the homemaker, is rapidly becoming obsolete in the United States. The demographic profile of the randomly selected managers in these studies was quite different in 1989 than in 1978. In 1978, 96% of the managers were male, 93% were married, and 31% were in dual-income relationships. In 1989, 82% of the managers were male, 79% were married, and 47% were in dual-income relationships. Although there was no significant difference in the average age of married employees in our sample (average of 37 years old), the married employees in the 1989 study were less likely to have children than those in the 1978 study (64% of married managers in 1978 had children living at home, compared to 54% of married managers in 1989). The decade brought into the workforce more female managers, more dual-earner managers, and more managers without children.

CHILDREN, RELOCATION, AND CAREER ADVANCEMENT

Relocation plays a major role in career advancement. The presence of children in the family has a significant impact on whether a manager is available for relocation. Relocation impacts career progression because managers who are willing to relocate can compete for more job opportunities than those who are not willing to relocate. Furthermore, employees who are willing to relocate signal commitment to their careers and to their organizations. Our data show that employees who relocate more frequently reach higher levels in their organizations than those who relocate less frequently, and that employees who relocate more frequently also earn higher salaries than those who relocate less frequently.[7] These results remain when the data are controlled for human capital and industry differences.

The single most important factor in an employee's willingness to relocate domestically or internationally is the spouse's willingness to relocate.[8] We have always sent a separate questionnaire to spouses and not relied on managers' reports of their spouses' attitudes about a potential relocation. The feelings of each spouse are therefore measured independently. The correspondence between husband's and wives' willingness to relocate decreased from the 1978 to the 1989 study. Spouses' attitudes toward moving were less tightly linked, or correlated, in 1989 than in 1978. This greater independence in spouses' attitudes toward moving in the 1989 sample allowed us to test the direction of the causal influence between employee and spouse willingness to relocate.[9] Testing causal direction in survey research is one of the most difficult tasks, both methodologically and statistically, but it can be done with a two-stage least-squares statistical technique. With this statistical technique, we asked whether the data best fit (1) the model of spouses' attitudes responding to those of managers, indicating a spillover of a manager's career pressures to family; (2) the model of managers' attitudes responding to those of their spouses, indicating a spillover of family values to career; or (3) an equilibrium model of joint influence, in which each spouse's attitudes reciprocally affect those of the other spouse. We found that spouses had an influence on managers' willingness to relocate, but managers had little influence on their spouse's willingness to relocate.[10] These results support the model of spillover of family values to career.

We then tried to trace the sources of spouses' feelings about relocation. Eight percent of the trailing spouses in the study were males, yet sex did not distinguish between spouses who were, and those who were not, willing to relocate.[11] Forty-seven percent of spouses were employed, but employment status did not explain spouses' willingness to relocate. Neither employment per se, part- versus full-time employment, nor career versus job orientation accounted for spouses' willingness to relocate either domestically or intentionally.[12]

Spouses' willingness to relocate was closely tied to the presence of children in the home. When there were children at home, spouses were less willing to relocate domestically or internationally, regardless of their own employment status.[13] Children were also a primary reason given by employees for withdrawing from a relocation opportunity or turning down a transfer.[14]

Thus, through a chain of connections beginning with children in the home and extending to the spouse's willingness to relocate, managers' family status is linked to career advancement. Managers who were earning higher salaries and being promoted more frequently were those who had moved geographically more frequently than others, and those who moved were those who were less likely to have children.

Dual- and Single-Earner Males, Children, and Career Advancement

Family has another significant effect on career advancement, but one that is not mediated by relocation. Dual-income males with children at home earn less than single-income males with children at home. Traditional family status benefits career advancement for male managers.

This is a well-documented finding. Pfeffer and Ross observed that being married had a positive effect on men's wage attainment, but that having an employed wife had negative effects on both wage attainment and occupational status.[15] Their findings were based on a 1966 data set and did not control for the presence of children. Of course, in 1966, dual-income status was rare among managers. It seemed unlikely that this negative effect of family structure would prevail in our 1989 data set. We were wrong; it did.[16] Schneer and Reitman have also independently identified this effect with contemporary data.[17]

We analyzed married male managers' salary progression over five years, controlling for the presence of children by only including in the study "dads" with kids at home.[18] We also controlled for workforce experience and industry differences. The average increase in dual-income males' total compensation (salary plus bonus) was 59%. Single-income males' compensation increased 70% over the same period. The difference was statistically significant.

We ruled out several possible explanations for the results statistically. We considered the possibility that dual-income males' compensation lagged because they had less human capital in terms of educational credentials and firm-specific work experience. We reasoned that greater responsibility for child care and housework, as is characteristic of dual-income males, might give them less time to acquire higher education than single-income males, who do less child care and housework.[19] We also thought that the dual-income males might have less firm-specific human capital as a result of possibly changing organizations to accommodate a spouse's career. Education and company tenure (our indicators of firm-specific human capital) did account for salary progression, but did not account for the discrepancy in salary progression between dual- and single-income dads.

We recognized the possibility that the dual-income males in our study might be working fewer hours than traditional males, due to their family responsibilities, and thereby be signaling less effort and less organizational commitment than traditional males. Here, we found a partial, but not complete, explanation for the differences in salary progression. Dual-income males were working slightly fewer hours per week on average than traditional males (51 hours versus

53 hours). This difference correspond with, and accounted for, some of the difference in salary.

We were frankly astounded that so small a difference in hours would translate into so large a difference in salary progression. After all, the employees in our study were managers, not hourly workers. However, in managerial work, which is difficult to evaluate, evidence of effort is often used as a surrogate for success. And hours worked is used as a signal of effort.

Hours worked, however, did not account for all of the discrepancy in salary progression between dual-income and traditional males. We could not rule out that having a wife at home serves as a resource for the traditional manager. Kanter outlines the ways in which a wife can serve as a resource to her husband's career: (1) as a direct substitute—she does work he is expected to do; (2) as an indirect support—by entertaining and building social networks; (3) as a consultant—discussing and advising on job-related matters; and (4) as an emotional support—keeping the husband motivated for work.[20]

Although nonemployed wives undoubtedly contribute to their husband's careers in all of these ways, we find it difficult to believe that many wives are actually doing part of their husbands' work. Likewise, we find it difficult to believe that employment makes a woman unfit to be a consultant or to provide emotional aid. This leaves Kanter's category of indirect aid as the most likely resource that nonemployed wives provide their husbands and that employed wives do not.

If the nonemployed (though certainly working) wife is truly managing the family, she is providing her husband with time to spend working, or in personal or social activities, and with psychological freedom from concern about family matters.[21] Time overload is a major stressor for dual-income men and women.[22] Thus, a major indirect support that a wife can supply her husband is time.

Given the wide-scale publicity this study has received, it has done a great deal to establish the link in people's minds between family structure and career advancement. As a result of the publicity, the study has also attracted some criticism. There is little question that the gap exists; however, the cause of the gap remains open. Clearly, time management is one factor, as it was shown statistically to reduce, but not wipe out, the difference in salary progression of dual- and single-earner males. The alternative causal explanation is that the wives of the dual-earner males are in the workforce because their husbands are earning less, and those of the single-earner males are not in the workforce because their husbands are earning more. This is a possible explanation; however, both dual- and single-earner males were earning substantial incomes—more than $60,000 annually in 1989 when the data were collected. It seems unlikely that any of the dual-earner wives "had to work." In addition, settling in after a move, which all of the families in the study had experienced in the two years prior to data collection, is an excellent reason to stay out of the workforce. The dual-earner wives appear to be in the workforce because they want to be there.

FEMALES, WITH AND WITHOUT HUSBANDS AND CHILDREN, AND CAREER ADVANCEMENT

Schwartz describes the "career and family woman" as willing to trade some career growth and compensation for freedom from the constant pressure to work long hours and weekends.[23] In our study, companies did not seem to distinguish between women who had children and those who did not. We compared the career experiences of dual-earner female managers with children with the career experiences of dual-earner female managers without children.[24] We also compared their career experiences with those of male managers.[25] The two groups of women were similar in all respects: education, company tenure, family power (proportion of family income: 74% were income leaders in their families), years of workforce experience, number of jobs, and number of companies worked at. Not surprisingly, there were no significant differences in the rate of career advancement for these two groups of women. On the other hand, female managers' wages (salary plus bonus) lagged behind those of male managers by 11% over the five-year period studied.[26] Female managers' salaries over five years increased by 54% compared to male managers' salaries, which increased by 65%. These results show that male and female managers' wages are on different trajectories. To the extent that raises are based on percentage increases, any early differences get compounded over time, and early differences that may be insignificant increase over time.

Part of the explanation for this salary lag was that female managers were relocating less frequently than male managers.[27] Female employees were not significantly more likely than the males to either withdraw from transfer opportunities or turn down transfers. Female managers with children were actually somewhat better off than female managers without children in terms of receiving opportunities to relocate, but neither group received the opportunities extended to the males in the sample. There was no evidence that companies were discriminating against dual-income females with children any more heavily than dual-income females without children. However, compared to male managers, female managers' careers were advancing more slowly.

More recent evidence based on a 1991 follow-up study shows female managers leaving their organizations proportionately more frequently than male managers (26% as compared to 14% of male managers).[28] However, even though female managers who leave their organizations improve their wages compared to those who stay, the same effect holds for male managers.[29] Thus, the differences in trajectory between male and female managers' salary progression remains, despite the females' seemingly greater willingness to change companies.

CONCLUSION

Taken together, our studies of career advancement indicate that males are benefited over females, and married males with children are benefited over other males when their wives are not employed outside of the home. Although children do not appear to exert the same drag on the careers of women in our studies as they do on those of men whose wives are employed, females' careers lag behind those of all males, regardless of whether they have children.

Workforce demographics changed rather dramatically during the 1970's. Career dynamics, however, continue to benefit employees who fit the old profile of the "organization man." How long will this continue? It probably depends upon the economy. One scenario is that career patterns will bifurcate, like so many other aspects of our society. One pattern—the traditional upward, inward spiral—will continue to be followed by a small group of powerful men and a few women who are devoted to their careers, and whose families, if they have families, serve as career resources, not career anchors. If women are going to participate equally in this scenario, there will have to be changes in their opportunity structure as well. The other pattern—the protean series of connected or disconnected career loops—will be followed by the majority of managers and professionals, males and females alike, who have family structures that conflict with, or are believed to conflict with, the traditional image of the committed employee. These men and women will suffer from the stress of managing work and family, of making compromises in their careers to cater to the needs of their families, and of making compromises in their families for the sake of their careers. Women will be hardest hit for the following reasons: they experience greater work-family stress than men;[30] they see their careers as of equal priority to those of their husbands, while their husbands see their own careers as higher priority;[31] and they remain the primary caregivers of children and protectors of family values.[32]

This two-pattern career system describes where we are today. If this scenario is to change, there will have to be both a major expansion of the economy that cannot be managed without utilizing larger numbers of people in protean career tracks and a restructuring of managerial work to accommodate those who wish to balance work and family. I am not optimistic about the likely occurrence of either change.

As long as there are adequate numbers of managers and professionals who are willing to emphasize work over family, organizations will take maximum advantage of their work involvement and reward them with career opportunities. Business schools throughout the world are turning out large numbers of such managers. There are young Americans, even in business schools, who espouse the desire for a more balanced and less stressful life than their parents, who tried to have it all. These are not necessarily the values ascribed to by nationals of other countries, who are making a significant human capital investment in an American business school education. Moreover, with their international perspective, their American educations, and their traditional work and family values, foreign nationals are competitive for upward-spiral careers. It seems reasonable that organizations will fill their fast-track jobs with foreign nationals before making the effort to restructure jobs to accommodate the needs of Americans pursuing a work-family balance.

Restructuring jobs to accommodate family almost always means spending less time in the office. Yet somehow, time in the office has come to represent effort, and longer effort has come to mean higher quality, whether the inference is correct or not. Time in the office also brings opportunities to those who are present when the opportunity arises. If jobs are to be restructured to accommodate the family, evaluations of effort and performance and consideration for opportunities like relocations must be decoupled from the employee being physically in the office, and from the assumption that to do the job requires spending 12-hour days and six-day weeks in the office. The competitive pressures that have caused the downsizing of corporate staff and have left more work for fewer managers, of course, lead in the opposite direction.

There is one environmental development that may bring about this decoupling of "face time" and career advancement. We are seeing a vast internal restructuring of organizations and, in some cases, a significant change in human resources policies. The financial pressures of the 1980's and the global economic pressures that have followed have led some organizations to reduce their reliance on relational employment strategies, where tasks and performance criteria are left unspecified and employees exchange loyalty (and the willingness to do what it takes to get the job done) for secure employment and career development opportunities. Organizations are subcontracting more and more of their work. Contract work, by its very nature, is transactional. Concrete tasks are specified in advance, and performance standards are precise. Assuming that their skills are in demand, contract workers can negotiate their jobs to accommodate their family. If contract workers are working side-by-side with regular employees, differential treatment may cause conflict. It is within the realm of possibility that the organization will allow employees with families greater latitude in restructuring work in order to equalize employment between transactional and relational employees.

Some commentators (e.g., Handy) foresee future organizations being staffed by a few permanent employees (presumably those following inward, upward career trajectories) and large numbers of contract workers (presumably those following protean careers).[33] Frankly, I think this vision of the future rather unlikely, because of another concurrent aspect of organizational restructuring. Organizations are flattening their hierarchies, pushing decision making down to lower levels in the organization and to task forces and teams. Less hierarchy means less time to monitor, and so, organizations must rely on socialization and informal control mechanisms for coordination and control. Contract workers, who have not been socialized by the company and have no related long-term future career aspirations, are not subject to these informal control mechanisms. Thus, staffing a company with large numbers of contract workers is inconsistent with flattening hierarchies and decentralizing decision making.

I wish I had greater optimism that changes in organizational structures are going to make the relationship between work and family easier to manage by making accommodations both automatic and without prejudice. Organizations do seem to be negotiating individual accommodations more readily than in the past. However, these accommodations are not without prejudice. They move the employee off the upward, inward career trajectory and onto a protean career track. Whether one can, once on a protean career track, negotiate back onto the upward-inward track without changing companies is a question for future research.

These accommodations are also not without costs to the company. Negotiation increases human resources transaction costs, it presumes that employees know their priorities and are willing to concede lower-priority issues for higher-priority issues. It presumes that organizations can be flexible. Most critically, and least likely, it presumes that both individuals and organizations can predict and control the future.

NOTES

1. *Transfer Volume and Cost Survey of 191 Organizations* (Washington, DC: Employee Relocation Council, 1996).

2. J.M. Brett & J.D. Werbel, *The Effect of Job Transfer on Employees and Their Families* (Washington, DC: Employee Relocation Council, 1980).

3. J.M. Brett, L.K. Stroh, & A.H. Reilly, *Impact of Societal Shifts and Corporate Change on Employee Relocation* (Washington, DC: Employee Relocation Council, 1990).

4. J.H. Greenhaus & G.A. Callanan, *Career Management*, 2nd ed. (Fort Worth, TX: Dryden Press, 1994); N. Nicholson & M. West, *Managerial Job Change: Men and Women in Transition* (Cambridge: Cambridge University Press, 1988).

5. J.E. Rosenbaum, *Career Mobility in a Corporate Hierarchy* (San Diego, CA: Academic Press, 1984).

6. L. Bailyn, "Accommodation of Work or Family," in R. Rapoport & R.N. Rapoport (eds.), *Working Couples* (London: Routledge & Kegan Paul, 1978), pp. 159–174.

7. L.K. Stroh, J.M. Brett, & A.H. Reilly, "All the Right Stuff: Career Progression of Female and Male Managers," *Journal of Applied Psychology*, 77 (1992): 251–260.

8. J.M. Brett & A.H. Reilly. "On the Road Again: Predicting the Job Transfer Decision," *Journal of Applied Psychology*, 73 (1988): 614–620; J.M. Brett, L.K. Stroh, & A.H. Reilly, "Job Transfer," in C.L. Cooper & I.T. Robertson (eds.), *International Review of Industrial and Organizational Psychology*, vol. 7 (London: John Wiley & Sons, 1992), pp. 323–352; J.M. Brett, L.K. Stroh, & A.H. Reilly, "Pulling Up Roots in the 1990s: Who's Willing to Relocate?" *Journal of Organizational Behavior* 14 (1993): 49–60; J.M. Brett & L.K. Stroh, "Willingness to Relocate Internationally," *Human Resources Management Journal* 34, (1995): 405–424.

9. Brett & Stroh, "Willingness to Relocate Internationally."

10. Ibid.

11. Brett et al., "Job Transfer."

12. Ibid.; Brett & Stroh, "Willingness to Relocate Internationally."

13. Brett et al., "Job Transfer"; Brett & Stroh, "Willingness to Relocate Internationally."

14. Brett et al., "Job Transfer."

15. J. Pfeffer & J. Ross, "The Effects of Marriage and a Working Wife on Occupational and Wage Attainment," *Administrative Science Quarterly* 27 (1982): 66–80.

16. L.K. Stroh & J.M. Brett, "The Dual-Earner Dad Penalty in Salary Progression," *Human Resource Management Journal* (in press).

17. J. Schneer & F. Reitman, "Effects of Alternative Family Structures on Managerial Career Paths," *Academy of Management Journal* 36 (1993): 830–843.

18. Stroh & Brett, "The Dual-Earner Dad Penalty."

19. S. Yogev & J.M. Brett, "Patterns of Work and Family Involvement among Single and Dual-Earner Couples," *Journal of Applied Psychology* 70 (1985): 754–768; Schneer & Reitman, "Effects of Alternative Family Structures."

20. R.M. Kanter, *Work and Family in the United States: A Critical Review and Agenda for Research Policy* (New York: Russell Sage Foundation, 1977), pp. 110–111.

21. Ibid.; Schneer & Reitman, "Effects of Alternative Family Structures."

22. J.H. Greenhaus & N.J. Beutell, "Sources of Conflict between Work and Family Roles," *Academy of Management Review* 10 (1985): 76–88; P. Voydanoff, "Work Role Characteristics, Family Structure Demands, and Work/Family Conflict," *Journal of Marriage and the Family* 50 (1988): 749–761.

23. F.N. Schwartz, "Management Women and the New Facts of Life," *Harvard Business Review* 72(1) (1989): 65–76.

24. Brett et al., "Job Transfer."

25. Stroh et al., "All the Right Stuff."

26. Ibid.

27. Ibid.

28. L.K. Stroh, J.M. Brett, & A.H. Reilly, "Family Structure, Glass Ceiling, and Traditional Explanations for the Differential Rate of Turnover of Female and Male Managers." *Journal of Vocational Behavior* 49 (1996): 99–118.

29. J.M. Brett & L.K. Stroh, "Jumping Ship: Who Benefits from an Extended Labor Market Career Strategy?" Working paper, Kellogg Graduate School of Management, Evanston, IL, 1996.

30. Greenhaus & Buetell, "Sources of Conflict between Work and Family Roles."

31. S. Friedman, "Wharton Life Interests Project," Report 1 (Philadelphia: Wharton Business School, 1993).

32. J. Brines, "Economic Dependency, Gender and the Division of Labor at Home," *American Journal of Sociology* 100 (1994): 652–688.

33. C. Handy, *The Age of Unreason* (Boston: Harvard Business School Press, 1990).

CHAPTER 15

Gaining Legitimacy for Flexible Work Arrangements and Career Paths: The Business Case for Public Accounting and Professional Services Firms

Monique Connor, Karen Hooks, and Terry McGuire

PUBLIC ACCOUNTING: THE TRADITIONAL WORK ENVIRONMENT

The work environment in the largest public accounting firms has been relatively stable for decades. The ability to "attest" to the fairness of a company's financial statements is restricted to individuals and firms of certified public accountants. This limited access to the profession, combined with steady growth in the formation of new companies and the resultant demand for audits created by equity and debt financing, combined to create an environment of limited competition and consistent revenue growth. Consequently, the profession prospered and employees of the largest firms (known today as the "Big Six") enjoyed unique career opportunities. Larger revenues and demand for services resulted in greater demand for new partners (laws generally require accounting firms to be organized as partnerships, and the partners own the firm). As with other business organizations, white males have traditionally dominated public accounting firms at all levels, but particularly at the partner and other senior levels.

THE TRADITIONAL CAREER PATH

The traditional Big Six career path required a full-time work schedule with significant overtime hours. Upward career movement was an inflexible condition, so much so that the career path has always been known as "up or out": either you are "promoted on schedule" to the next level, or you are asked to leave. For those who enjoyed the nature of the work, a Big Six career has traditionally been very rewarding, and becoming a partner in a Big Six firm is a widely recognized measure of success. But given the long hours, frequent travel and pressure to advance created by the up-or-out career model, a Big Six career was (and still is) very demanding.

MANAGING TURNOVER—A CRITICAL BUSINESS ISSUE

One of the more significant consequences of the demanding work environment is high staff turnover. As with all businesses, some turnover of *selected* employees is desired by management. Unlike other industries, however, public accounting has traditionally experienced a relatively high level of *undesired* turnover. All of the firms recognize that undesired turnover is costly due to the large training investment made in staff and the disruptions it causes in client service. Despite this knowledge, there has also been a certain degree of acceptance that fairly significant turnover (i.e., 20% or more annually) is inherent in the profession. As a result, accounting firms have managed to work around this talent loss and, until recently, clients did not protest very loudly, either.

Environmental Developments

The convergence of several external forces has encouraged the Big Six to become more proactive in identifying ways to reduce undesired staff turnover and thereby respond to today's client service demands. These developments include the growth in demand for specialized services, the emergence in the use of technology to deliver services, and changes in the demographic makeup of new entrants to the workforce.

Specialized Services

One of the effects of the growth in mergers, acquisitions, and privatizations during the 1980's was a reduction in the demand for traditional audit and tax services. Pressure to enhance profits, downsize, do more with less, work smarter, and so forth became common business themes.[1] This climate forced the Big Six firms to shift their practices into more specialized, and profitable, service areas.

The large accounting firms responded by offering an array of new services, thus transforming themselves into "professional services firms." The expansion in the nature and scope of services has had several impacts. First, Big Six firms are increasingly adding new services designed to add value to their clients' businesses. Although "traditional" information technology and management consulting comprise a major part of this expansion, many new consulting services have grown from traditional audit and tax relationships. As a result, the firms are now being challenged to "unbundle" or separate their fees for specialized services from, for example, a regular audit fee in order to demonstrate additional value. Second, in order to provide these new services, the firms have been forced to become more proactive in finding ways to recruit and retain professionals with the requisite skills.

Given these new business challenges, managing undesired turnover has now become a major business issue. It is not very easy to replace a bank specialist with a retail expert. When an industry expert decides to leave the firm, there is a smaller internal pool of potential replacements from which to choose. Further, finding a replacement with the same skill set in the external market is typically more difficult and expensive than when hiring a "generalist." In order to provide the best business advice, an auditor or tax professional must be able to do more than understand a body of knowledge and related rules. She or he must have a deep understanding of the client's industry and business. Consequently, to enhance their career prospects, many individuals now choose an industry specialization, and professional services firms are seeking to lower turnover in order to develop this expertise. Clients are also more inclined to employ the provider that is best equipped to meet their needs without regard to their auditor relationship.

Technology

Another major environmental change affecting the Big Six and their efforts to retain and develop staff is the increasing use of technology. Before the era of increased technology and industry specialization, the turnover of less experienced employees was not the significant business issue that it is today. At that time there were more tasks appropriate for entry-level workers, and the pyramid staffing structure, characterized by a smaller head count at each higher organizational level, made good business sense. Many employees entered the profession with the intent to stay for the short term, with the implicit understanding that they would have to make the personal sacrifices required by the job in return for the training and marketability associated with Big Six work experience. Others began public accounting careers to gain the experience necessary to earn a Certified Public Accountant's (CPA) license and later move into industry. Still others chose to remain for the long term in order to be considered for, and hopefully admitted to, the partnership (i.e., become an owner of the business). With partnership status comes significant financial rewards, career challenges and prestige—and increased control over one's own life.

In today's environment, many of the time-consuming tasks typically performed by entry-level professionals have been automated by computers, resulting in the need for fewer entry-level staff. As a result, a graphic depiction of

Figure 15.1
Traditional and New Accounting Firm Models

Traditional Accounting Firm Staffing Model

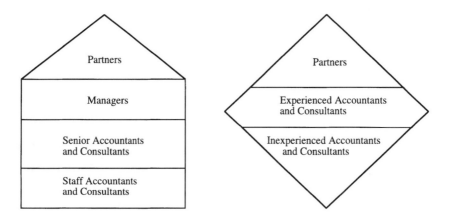

New Accounting Firm Models

the traditional Big Six staffing model, which traditionally resembled a pyramid, now more closely resembles a "house" or "diamond" (see Figure 15.1). Thus, in this environment, the development and retention of talent become even more critical. As a consequence of hiring fewer people at the entry level, and coexisting changes such as fewer students graduating with majors in accounting and changes in the composition of the workforce, the firms now have a strong business interest in retaining and motivating the staff they hire.

Workforce Changes

The third major change affecting the profession is the vastly different demographic makeup of new entrants to the workforce. In the mid- to late 1970's, women and people of color began to enter public accounting in larger numbers. Additionally, in response to the need for people with deep industry knowledge, more professionals with prior experience in industry began working for public accounting firms. These new entrants often had significantly different career expectations than the traditional workforce. All too often, these new employees did not ''fit'' into the existing culture and ultimately left the profession. Because many of these staff were hired to work in niche or strategic practice initiatives, this additional turnover was also very costly.

CURRENT WORK ENVIRONMENT

In today's more complex business climate, the Big Six now have more focused entry-level recruiting efforts and have also begun hiring a greater proportion of experienced professionals. The ''more with less'' phenomenon affects all levels within the firms, including partners, who are not immune to the increased pressure for greater productivity. Turnover at the partner level, once unheard of, is common today. Having observed the workload and ''lifestyle'' of today's partners, less experienced employees see a very different picture than their predecessors.[2]

The impact of all these influences and changes is readily apparent in today's Big Six workforce. When observing who works for the Big Six and the work schedules they generally maintain, the picture is very different from what existed in the past. As previously stated, the workforce is far more diverse. Women generally make up at least half of each group of new hires. Firms are also making significant efforts to hire members of minority groups, making competition for minority candidates particularly fierce. (Parenthetically, competition for top students and experienced professionals has become more intense in the current labor market, regardless of the candidates' race or gender. In addition to competing with each other, Big Six firms are also competing with other businesses equally committed to hiring the best employees.) Unfortunately, even when the firms are successful in their recruiting efforts, the high rate of turnover for women and people of color often takes its toll—causing firms to lose many of the ''best and brightest'' of these groups as well.

A number of factors beyond supply are also driving the Big Six's desire to add individuals with diverse backgrounds to their labor force. Although moral and cultural issues have an influence, the principal driver is profit. It is often said that Big Six firms sell the talents of their people and that as such, people represent intellectual capital. In order to best serve clients, it follows that the firms need to find and hire the most qualified candidates, regardless of majority or minority status, and retain them. Today, many of the most highly sought after candidates are women and/or people of color. Further, clients, government contract requirements, globalization, and overall social standards create pressure— in varying degrees of subtlety—for the Big Six to create a workforce that looks like that of the rest of the business world.

WHAT THE CURRENT ENVIRONMENT MEANS TO INDIVIDUALS

Although a Big Six career may be perceived by some as less desirable than in the past, many appealing characteristics have survived the environmental changes discussed here. Although revenues are not growing at historically high rates, they are still growing. Thus, the Big Six still provide superior opportunities for employees to advance when compared to many other industries. Although the rate of growth in partnership slots has slowed, new partners are admitted each year and the partner ranks are much more diverse than ever. Thus, the combination of continued revenue growth and partner turnover still makes for considerable "room at the top."

There are also more meaningful opportunities on the way to the top. The nature of the work in a Big Six environment is still appealing to many because of the challenges and excitement it offers. A Big Six career is a great opportunity for professionals who want a dynamic environment filled with complex client and business situations. This may be true even more now than in the past, due to the diverse types of services being provided by the firms and the higher-complexity work being assigned to employees earlier in their careers.

Many of the circumstances that affect individual workers today are fundamentally different from the past. The pervasive differences reflect changes that are not specific to the Big Six, or the accounting profession. These changes have occurred across the entire U.S. labor market. Changes in employment relationships have impacted employee expectations and attitudes in ways that affect turnover. For example, today few entry-level employees begin their careers expecting to stay with one employer. Becoming unemployed and changing jobs, whether initiated by the employer or employee, no longer has the stigma it once did. These new expectations and attitudes have changed the degree of loyalty employees feel toward their employers. As in other industries, Big Six employees, particularly many in the earlier years of their careers, expect accommodations from their firms. Many are part of dual-career marriages and expect to be able to meet both work and personal obligations. They want time for their families, and time for themselves.[3]

THE PROFESSION RESPONDS TO ITS NEW ENVIRONMENT

In order to meet the needs of clients *and* staff, the profession has embraced a number of initiatives designed to enhance retention and career satisfaction. Three of the more important initiatives utilized in our firm are:

- Flexible work arrangements
- Work/life balance programs
- Flexible career paths

Flexible Work Arrangements

Increasing numbers of Big Six staff are now taking advantage of an array of flexible work arrangements. The most prevalent of these arrangements are part-time schedules. Part-time schedules exist in many unique varieties. For example, a part-time arrangement might be a traditional "specified hours" schedule (with a target number of hours less than 40 per week); a phased-in return from a leave of absence, such as a maternity leave; a seasonally reduced schedule; or a reduced-hours schedule resulting from limiting the client or project load. While flexible work arrangements are widely available throughout the profession, the mechanisms for design and approval are more uniform and institutionalized in some firms than in others.[4] The success of these part-time arrangements is evidenced by the fact that some individuals—to date, all have been women—have been admitted to the partnership either after returning to full time from a part-time schedule or while still working part time. Several of the Big Six firms now have partners with flexible work schedules.

Flexible work times and locations are also fairly commonplace, although they tend to be informal arrangements and of limited duration. These arrangements are not radically new to the profession. The Big Six firms have traditionally afforded their employees some degree of flexibility by allowing them to work autonomously and altering their hours and/or work location as necessary. For example, employees frequently work overtime at night or on weekends and often have the option of taking work home rather than working in the office. A certain amount of workplace flexibility naturally exists since the majority of the work is performed at the client site, rather than in the office.

The flexibility inherent with the practice of public accounting has been augmented by technology.[5] The ability to pick up phone messages, send and receive faxes, and dial into a computer network from home and other locations has made the accountant's work far more portable. This in turn impacts the time and place in which work can be done. These developments have moved flextime and flex-place even more into the mainstream of Big Six work patterns. Most firms, including Price Waterhouse, are implementing various types of telecommuting arrangements. The practice of "hoteling," in which staff call a "concierge" to reserve office space, is now common among the Big Six. This practice tends to encourage more flexible work patterns and habits. Further, numerous maternity leaves have been "interrupted" (or enhanced, depending on one's perspective) by work done at home, with communications effected via phone, fax, and modem.

Work/Life Balance Programs

Work/life balance programs are another tool to provide greater staff support and reduced turnover. Often, these initiatives, which include 24-hour employee assistance programs, help employees deal with personal issues that impact workplace performance. Although these programs are not career path–specific, they may affect career path decisions. Current employee support programs typically provide information or services in areas such as child care, elder care, adoption assistance, school referrals, and so on. Obviously, the existence and effectiveness of these programs can affect the success of other programs such as flexible work schedules. Some of the firms also have employee-driven steering committees and local office groups to advise and direct various aspects of employee assistance programs and to sponsor seminars and other activities that address work/life balance issues.

Flexible Career Paths

Finally, public accounting and other professional services firms have recently begun to implement new career models to support the multiple career interests of their staff thus contributing to higher retention and development and client service.[6] This evolution in the employer-employee relationship is changing the face of the Big Six, with varying degrees of speed and in different ways. Despite the variety of approaches employed, the objectives for implementing new career models generally include:

- A desire to give employees the opportunity to advance through their careers at different paces while contributing to the success of the firm,
- A desire to give employees the opportunity to assume different workloads—either for a short- or long-term time horizon,
- A desire to give employees more flexibility to balance their career and personal life interests, and
- A desire to convey the message that the firm is willing to explore ways to meet individual needs *and* the needs of clients by embracing policies and practices that ultimately support higher retention.

At Price Waterhouse LLP, our Management Consulting Services (MCS) practice recently implemented a new career model. It emphasizes competencies and skills rather than tenure in evaluating employees.[7] Under the MCS model, a person is "promoted" when she or he demonstrates the predefined skills for movement to the next level. Staff who want to advance at a rate similar to the "lockstep" approach may do so, but this model also makes it acceptable to develop a broader set of skills or to pursue a more deep and narrow skill set. As a result, the flexible model is significantly different from the traditional public accounting career model, which requires that a person who's not ready to move up at the "appropriate" time leave the firm. In a mirror-image application, the competency-based model permits an individual who has acquired the requisite skills to move up more quickly than under the traditional career model. Our other service lines are now in various stages of implementing similar career models.

Legitimizing Flexible Career Paths and Other Arrangements

The recent changes in career paths provide expanded opportunities for staff members, professional services firms, and the clients they serve. We believe that flexible career paths contribute to cultures that are more supportive of employees who, for example, like their current roles but may not want to advance at the prescribed rates or become partners. Under these models, such employees are able to make valuable contributions to a firm while satisfying their career objectives. Flexible career paths can also provide greater job security without losing the benefits to the firm resulting from the motivational aspects of the up-or-out model. Also, employees are given more control over their own futures.[8] This is particularly the case when an employee selects a career path or schedule that results in slower skills development. For example, if an employee is working 80% of a full-time schedule, the reduced exposure and work experience might slow the rate at which his or her skills are attained. This is acceptable under a competency-based career path. In another scenario, an employee who works 80% of a full-time schedule and yet develops skills very quickly has the opportunity to be promoted more rapidly.

A major benefit to the firms from flexible career models is the ability to retain valued employees who might otherwise leave. This flexibility is also more consistent with the greater diversity that exists in the workforce. Examples of high-level employees make this benefit very clear. One example is the employee who would otherwise be "ready" to be admitted to the partnership, based on the traditional time-in-grade model. If, due to the business and economic environment, there are no partnership slots available for that individual at that time, or if, developmentally, he or she is not yet deemed to be ready, under the traditional model the individual would often leave the firm. A competency-based model allows for greater flexibility, permitting the firm to retain such a person until the situation for partnership admission improves. Another example is an employee with "deep" technical knowledge who may not possess the broader skill set needed for promotion (e.g., sales or interpersonal skills may be lacking). Competency-based models encourage such individuals to continue their careers with the firm by valuing their contributions. Such models also encourage firms to retain staff who have skills that are difficult and costly to replace. To the extent that these staff are happier and more productive, clients benefit as well.[9]

Other initiatives designed to support higher retention and career satisfaction in the fast-changing work environment include diversity and gender-awareness training. These programs help employees embrace the wide range of flexible options available.

In view of the heightened interest in retention and development, most firms are committed to these new initiatives. Despite this greater overall commitment to retaining and developing staff, there are challenges to face. For example, the nature of the environment and culture creates communication challenges when attempting to share the availability of flexible work arrangements. In spite of brochures, announcements, and similar tools, there remain many employees who still do not know that flexible work arrangements are truly available or how to propose and implement such an arrangement. Additionally, many staff remain concerned about how the corporate culture will view them (and their commitment to career) if they are successful in crafting an arrangement that provides more flexibility. There are still too few ''success'' stories to tell; thus, many are dissuaded from pursuing these arrangements. Further, many employees who would otherwise work flexibly (such as by carrying a partial client workload) are unable to meet their financial obligations with the income often associated with working less.

Unlike flexible work arrangements, we believe that there are fewer challenges facing the acceptance of flexible career paths. Given the rigidity of traditional career models, combined with the perceived benefits to the firm and clients associated with the new models, most partners and staff welcome these changes. One challenge comes from the partners and staff who prefer the more structured, linear approach embedded in the lockstep career model. Among the specific reasons offered for staying with the traditional career model are the charge that the new models lack some of the elements that traditionally motivated superior staff dedication and performance (such as the ''carrot'' of partnership admission). Others fear that benefits from increased client and staff satisfaction may be offset by the additional compensation cost associated with retention (i.e., less ability to control costs through hiring less experienced people). Because these models are so new, many of these concerns have not been tested.

Each of these challenges is being addressed through efforts to improve communications, educate everyone in the firms, and establish and/or clarify accountability for results. Communications efforts are often aimed at facilitating greater understanding of the linkage between the retention and development initiatives and the overall business strategy, which is critical.[10] Education, largely in the form of new training courses, is also being used to change attitudes toward asking for (and responsibilities for facilitating) greater workplace flexibility. As an example, the historical manager role reflected a desire to avoid discussing flexible work arrangements in order to avoid ''problems.'' Today, however, many firms are sending the message (often through education and training) that one cannot be an effective manager without facilitating flexible arrangements. This is also an area where accountability plays a vital role. For example, individuals utilizing flexible work arrangements must be held accountable for fulfilling their part of the arrangement, particularly as it relates to continued productivity. Also, those who supervise people involved in flexible arrangements must be measured by their success in facilitating these arrangements. Those in leadership roles must be held accountable as well. Today's leaders are increasingly being evaluated (and compensation is being influenced) by the prevalence of flexible arrangements in their units, how well these programs are managed, and the satisfaction of those participating in these programs. Finally, the importance of these initiatives is reinforced by the CEOs of the Big Six, who now characterize the success of these initiatives as critical to overcoming the human resources challenges they face.

SUMMARY OF THE BUSINESS CASE

What do these changes mean to the individual pursuing a Big Six career? Can a successful career be crafted from a part-time schedule? Can success be defined as remaining at one level indefinitely? Is there an appropriate goal other than an equity-ownership position? Can individuals truly define success through their own eyes, and not those of management? Clearly, the firms want the answers to these questions to be yes. A key business objective of the firms is to reduce turnover and better manage the turnover that occurs. The motivating factor is the business case; if these things *can* happen, it will be good business for the firms and ultimately will enhance their profitability.

As professional services firms, the main business goal is to render superior service to clients. In order to reach that goal, firms must successfully leverage their highly qualified and motivated professionals—their intellectual capital. It follows that in order to offer services in an efficient and profitable manner, firms must reduce or eliminate unwanted turnover, and that to the extent that flexible work arrangements and career paths increase retention, these programs make good business sense. In addition to supporting existing client service efforts, it is becoming increasingly clear that improved retention contributes to client retention.

While there is growing evidence to support the belief that flexible work arrangements contribute to greater retention, the fact that most career model initiatives are so new provides limited data to measure the success of these initiatives. Price Waterhouse's MCS practice enjoyed moderately improved retention rates after its first year with a new career model. Given the heavy information-technology orientation of our consulting practice, the extremely "hot" market for talent that currently exists, and other human resource strategy changes that accompanied the new model, it is difficult to associate the influence of the new career model with this progress. Anecdotally, the prevalent belief is that the career model initiative has contributed significantly to the success of our human resource initiatives (i.e., having a new career model helped our recruiting efforts, and turnover might have been much worse without the new model). Further, with its increased emphasis on rewarding demonstrated competencies and skills, the new career model has contributed significantly to staff development.

Another growing ideology in the business world is the notion that flexible work arrangements and career paths can contribute to the attraction of new clients by supporting diversity within the workforce. This notion suggests that there is a strong business case for work-family and other programs that support the retention of all members of the workforce. While many work/life and diversity initiatives target the entire workforce, most of the Big Six firms are placing particular emphasis on ways to reduce undesired turnover for members of minority groups and women, since turnover within these groups greatly dilutes their visible diversity. Anecdotal stories now abound of proposal teams who are quizzed regarding why women and minorities are not a part of the team. Additionally, prospective employees are increasingly asking about the extent to which the firm's culture supports workforce diversity. If a firm cannot include high-level women or people of color on the proposal and engagement teams, it may not win or retain the engagement. Thus there is growing interest in using programs such as flexible work arrangements and career paths to help firms retain and develop minority and women staff members in connection with efforts to achieve competitive advantage.

Other business reasons clearly exist for going the extra mile to reduce the turnover of underrepresented groups. For example, within professional services firms, the emphasis on working in teams is increasingly becoming more important. Although it is certainly a generalization, women may be more effective in teamwork because of their tendency toward more inclusive, rather than authoritarian, management styles. Also, as suggested by James J. Schiro, chairman and senior partner of Price Waterhouse LLP, diversity brings together people with different backgrounds, experiences and approaches to work on firm projects. "Six people with different perspectives have a better shot at solving a complex problem than 60 people who all think alike."[11]

The implementation of flexible career paths and other initiatives that support diversity and reduce turnover enable the firms to do a better job in a more profitable manner. In this case, both the firms and their employees benefit. The policies and programs in place are directed toward accomplishing that objective. It may be too soon to tell what will happen to the careers of all the individuals who avail themselves of the opportunities being presented, but it is clear that firms are using these and other programs to keep their valued professionals.

NOTES

1. Price Waterhouse Change Integration Team, *Better Change: Best Practices for Transforming Your Organization* (New York: Irwin, 1995).

2. P.M. Flynn, J.D. Leeth, & E.S. Levy, "Accounting Labor Markets in Transition: Implications for Education and Human Resources" (unpublished ms., January 1995).

3. J.H. Boyett & H.P. Conn, *Workplace 2000: The Revolution Reshaping American Business* (New York: Plume, 1991).

4. K. Hooks, "Diversity, Family Issues and the Big 6," *Journal of Accountancy*, 182(1) (July 1996): 51–56.

5. P. Pritchett, *New Work Habits for a Radically Changing World* (Dallas, TX: Pritchitt & Associates, 1994).

6. AICPA Women and Family Issues Executive Committee, "Experiences and Views of CPAs in Industry: Career and Life Balance Issues" (unpublished report, distributed by the American Institute of Certified Public Accountants, 1995); "CPA Firms Explore Alternate Career Paths," *CPA Personnel Report*, February 1995, pp. 1, 5.

7. "PW Scraps Up-or-Out Model," *CPA Personnel Report*, March 1996, pp. 1, 6.

8. Pritchett, *New Work Habits for a Radically Changing World*.

9. S. Shellenbarger, "Family-Friendly Jobs Are the First Step to Efficient Workplace," *Wall Street Journal*, May 15, 1996, p. B1.

10. Hooks, "Diversity, Family Issues and the Big 6."

11. Ibid., p. 51.

CHAPTER 16

The Sex Difference in Employee Inclinations Regarding Work-Family Programs: Why Does It Exist, Should We Care, and What Should Be Done about It (If Anything)?

Gary N. Powell

Male employees seem to be less inclined than female employees to be associated with formal work-family programs that their employers offer. For example, men take less advantage of formal paternity leaves than women take advantage of formal maternity leaves.[1] Also, women represent two-thirds of all part-time workers in the American workforce.[2] Even when men participate in what may be considered a work-family program, they are more inclined than women to try to disguise the reason for their participation. For example, although men and women appear to use flextime for family-related reasons to a similar extent, men are more likely to let their coworkers and supervisors think that something else has motivated their change in schedule.[3] Thus, there seems to be a sex difference in employee inclinations regarding work-family programs. However, there is considerable dispute over why this sex difference exists, whether it should be a matter of concern, and what should be done about it.

In this chapter, I present two alternative perspectives regarding the difference in men's and women's inclination to be associated with work-family programs. These two perspectives focus on different explanations for why this sex difference exists. The first perspective suggests that it is of no particular concern and that nothing needs to be done about it in the workplace. The second perspective suggests that it is of concern and that employees of both sexes would benefit if something were done about it. The two perspectives are presented in the ''point and counterpoint'' format that was popularized on the television newsmagazine *60 Minutes* (and satirized on *Saturday Night Live*) a few years ago. First, here is the point.

THE SEX DIFFERENCE IN EMPLOYEE INCLINATIONS REGARDING WORK-FAMILY PROGRAMS: SO WHAT? WHO CARES? WHAT'S THE BIG DEAL?

Male employees are less inclined than female employees to be associated with work-family programs. However, that is not a matter of concern, because male employees in the workplace *need* such programs to a lesser extent than female employees do. Consider the following statistics:

1. Eighteen percent of all employed adult women who maintain families, but only 5% of all employed adult men who maintain families, do not have a spouse present in the household.[4] Single parents are probably the employees who have the greatest need for work-family programs, and the vast majority of such parents are women.

2. Thirty percent of all employed adult men who maintain families, but only 6% of all employed adult women who maintain families, live with a spouse who is not in the labor force.[5] As a result, men are more likely than women to have a spouse at home who is available to bear the primary family responsibilities, rendering their need for work-family programs less than that of women.

3. Of all employed adult women 2.6%, compared to only 1.5% of all employed adult men, are actively involved in caring for an elderly parent by providing assistance with tasks such as transportation, shopping, meal preparation, and more personal forms of care for someone who is severely impaired.[6] Further, 3.5% of women and 2.0% of men have obligations for both an elderly parent *and* a child.[7] Thus, work-family programs that enable employees to fulfill their responsibilities for elder care are also more likely to be needed by female than male employees.

4. Overall, although husbands do more housework than before, wives still spend twice as many hours daily on housework than their husbands.[8] Wives also continue to bear the primary responsibility for arranging day care for preschool children and after-school care for older children, handling children's sicknesses, buying and cleaning the children's clothes, arranging for or doing house cleaning, and so on. Even in dual-career households, women are more likely to need assistance from work-family programs than men because they bear the greater share of family responsibilities.

These statistics suggest that women need the help that work-family programs provide more than men do. Thus, it is appropriate that women be the employees who embrace such programs the most. The proper reaction to the sex difference in inclinations regarding work-family programs should be: ''So what? Who cares? What's the big deal?'' The world is in order: The people who need work-family programs the most are the people who are ready to be associated with them the most.

Now, here is the counterpoint.

THE SEX DIFFERENCE IN EMPLOYEE INCLINATIONS REGARDING WORK-FAMILY PROGRAMS: WHY WE SHOULD CARE AND WHAT CAN BE DONE ABOUT IT

The point that male employees may be less inclined to be associated with work-family programs than female employees because they have less need for such programs is well taken. However, male employees also seem to have different inclinations regarding work-family programs than female employees *with similar needs*. For example, even when companies offer paid paternity and maternity leaves, new fathers are much less likely to take a paternity leave than new mothers are to take a maternity leave.[9] Although the needs of new fathers are less than those of new mothers because women, not men, physically deliver the child, fathers have an adjustment to make in incorporating the new child into the household, which seldom leads them to take a formal paternity leave. Therefore, we have reason to wonder what it would take to get men to catch up to women in the inclination to act on their own needs and take advantage of programs that are intended to help them. What sort of remedial assistance do we need to offer men to get them to learn what women seem to have already learned, that when you need help and someone offers you help, you take it?

We could conclude that what is operating for men is simply adherence to the traditional masculine role, which places a greater emphasis on independence and self-reliance than the traditional feminine role.[10] This is seen, for example, in statistics about sex differences in health and health-related actions.[11] Women are more likely than men to go to a doctor when they are not feeling well. They use more prescription medicines and over-the-counter drugs. They spend about 40% more days per year in bed. But they suffer less from major physical ailments. Men suffer more from life-threatening diseases and experience more overall long-term disability due to chronic health problems than women. And men live about seven years less than women. These health-related data suggest that men are less good at seeking help or helping themselves than women are, and that they pay the price. Perhaps a related symptom of men's adherence to the traditional masculine role is that they are less inclined to take advantage of work-family programs that are intended to help them, even when they could use the help.

However, to place complete responsibility on traditional sex roles for men's reluctance to be associated with work-family programs would be too simple a conclusion. Not all men seek to adopt the traditional masculine role. Kathleen Gerson, in a book entitled *No Man's Land: Men's Changing Commitments to Family and Work*, reported the results of interviews with men in both white-collar and blue-collar jobs.[12] She concluded that the men she interviewed fell about equally into three categories. One category she called "breadwinners"; these are men who seek to play traditional roles in their work and family lives by being the primary earner, whether or not their wives hold paid jobs, while resisting involvement in care taking and domestic work. A second category she called "autonomous men"; these are men who seek to avoid parental responsibilities in their lives by opting not to have children or by becoming estranged from their children in the wake of divorce. The third category she called "involved fathers"; these are men who seek to become significantly involved in the care-taking aspects of parenthood as well as to provide economic support and who renounce workplace success as the sole measure of their manhood. According to Gerson, about two-thirds of men are looking for something out of life other than what the traditional masculine role offers. Involved fathers, who are striving to achieve some sort of coherence and balance between their work and family lives, are more likely to be receptive to work-family programs that help them to achieve such a balance.

Gerson examined men's preferences for how they would like to live their lives. We also need to consider employers' preferences for how employees live their lives. More and more, organizations are expecting their key male and female employees to act like traditional males. In the current era of "downsizing" and "rightsizing," employees who are fewer in number are expected to do the same amount of work that a larger number of employees did before, and they are increasingly expected to work extra hours until this work is done.

A story that I heard in a recent discussion of work-family issues in a part-time MBA course that I teach at the University of Connecticut dramatizes this point. A student, whom I shall call Jennifer, told this story: A couple of months before, on a Saturday, Jennifer held a 50th birthday party for her mother. She worked for several months in arranging the party and in getting her family to agree to the arrangements. She lined up the restaurant at which the party would be held. She arranged the group gifts and prepared for the continuation of the party to be held at her house afterward—the whole scenario. It was going to be a special day for Jennifer, her mother, and everyone else involved. However, on that Saturday morning, Jennifer received a call from her boss and was told that she had to come to work that day. When she began to describe her plans for the day, she was cut off and told: "The Board doesn't want excuses. The Board wants work." The 50th birthday party was held, but without Jennifer present. She spent the whole Saturday at work. And, according to Jennifer, it wasn't even an emergency that led her to be called to work.

This is an appalling story. It made me mad when I heard it, and it makes me mad as I write these words to tell it. Despite the laudable work-family programs described elsewhere in this volume, Jennifer's story represents the work-family program for both male and female employees in many organizations today. Employees in such organizations are expected to put work first and have a family life only when granted permission to take time off from work. I regard such organizations as abusive.

How could Jennifer's employer get away with treating her like that? When Jennifer was presented with what she saw as an unreasonable demand, she asked herself, "How dependent am I on this job?" At the time, the economy was very slow in the state of Connecticut. Over the previous five years, the state had experienced what at best could be called negative job growth. As a result, Jennifer was very dependent on her job. If she had lost it, she most likely would have had to relocate to find a comparable job. In a soft or declining economy, companies are more able to get away with treating their employees in an abusive fashion. If the local economy had been adding rather than shedding jobs, Jennifer might have responded differently and attended her mother's birthday party, even if it meant losing her job, because she would have felt more confident that she could obtain at least a comparable job without relocating. She might have even been able to find employment with an organization that acknowledged that employees actually have important lives outside of work.

Other than the fact that they can get away with it when the economy is doing poorly, why else might companies act in the way that Jennifer's company acted? Joan Kofodimos, a management consultant, suggested another reason.[13] According to Kofodimos, corporations tend to be run by workaholic top executives who strive for mastery and control in their lives and find that they are better able to control what's going on at work than at home. They tend to avoid intimacy in their relationships with others and are more than willing to sacrifice family and outside interests whenever business needs call, however minor the business needs may be. These executives in turn set the standard by which managers who are earlier in their careers are judged. The demands and responsibilities of lower-level managers' jobs are typically less than those of top executives' jobs. Nonetheless, lower-level managers are expected to mimic top executives in their unwavering and absolute devotion to work, no matter how unnecessary it may be and no matter how great the cost to their family lives. A manager in such an environment who expresses an interest in a work-family program is doing the equivalent of committing career suicide.

In fact, companies have been encouraged by some writers to let employees take advantage of work-family programs *only if* they don't expect to get ahead. Felice Schwartz, in a controversial *Harvard Business Review* article that received considerable media attention, recommended that companies classify their female employees as either "career-primary" or "career-and-family."[14] According to Schwartz, companies should push their career-primary women hard, just as hard as they push men. In exchange for the opportunity to advance in the management ranks, such women should be expected to place work first and foremost in their lives and to sacrifice family interests when the business need arises. In contrast, career-and-family women should be offered extensive work-family programs in order to retain them and enhance their productivity, on the principle that these are valued employees whom employers need. However, in exchange for the opportunity to utilize such programs, such women should be told that they shouldn't expect to advance very far in the company. Schwartz's recommendations led many women with an interest in career advancement to shy away from work-family programs.

Although Schwartz did not focus on men in her article, men also had strong reactions to its message. First, she presented an essential trade-off between work and family or, more specifically, between seeking career advancement and using work-family programs to help to address family needs. Having work and family interests being presented as in such opposition to each other was not likely to make men feel comfortable about using work-family programs or even acknowledging their potential interest in such programs.[15] Second, the approach that Schwartz encouraged companies to adopt with career-and-family women came to be dubbed "the mommy track"[16] although she did not use this term herself. This is not exactly a male-friendly term. As a result, many men were scared away from work-family programs by the attention that Schwartz's article received. When work-family programs are labeled as a corporate response to "women's issues" rather than to "employees' issues," men who might consider using such programs are inclined to run for cover.

Therefore, to conclude that all men are adhering to the traditional male role in their reluctance to be associated with work-family programs would be to oversimplify men's reactions. Indeed, some men are reluctant to use work-family programs because such programs are inconsistent with the role they choose for themselves; these are the men that Kathleen Gerson called "breadwinners." However, other men are reluctant to use such programs because they are afraid of retribution from their employers if they deviate from the traditional male norm; these are Gerson's "involved fathers." Many women leave the corporate world and start their own businesses because they don't want to have to "act like men" to get ahead. In the same vein, many involved fathers are inclined to do the same because they don't want to have to "act like traditional males" to get ahead.

What can be done by corporations to get more men as well as more women to consider work-family programs that would help them with their specific needs? Here are some radical and not-so-radical suggestions:

1. *Select top executives who lead lives that demonstrate more of a balance between work and family concerns.* This is the most radical suggestion. It would call for a complete change in what boards of directors are looking for in top executives and in what top executives are looking for from their lives. Jeffrey E. Stiefler, the president of American Express, left his job in 1995 because of his unwillingness to subordinate his family and personal life to what he saw as an all-consuming job.[17] Stiefler realized that he was fitting the profile of a workaholic top executive and decided to walk away from the job to spend more time with his family. However, that sort of stance by a top executive is rare. According to Joan Kofodimos, boards of directors are happy to select workaholics for top executive positions, and most top executives are happy to be workaholics.[18] This is not likely to change unless a drastic restructuring of the demands of top management jobs takes place, which is not likely to happen soon.

Nonetheless, when the problem starts at the top, we need to consider the possibility of change at the top.

2. *End the linkage between an employee's participation in a work-family program and the assumption that he or she has a reduced career commitment.* This is a less radical suggestion. It does not call for change in board or top executive behavior, but instead in what is expected of lower-level employees. It should not be necessary for men or women to lead uninterrupted careers in full-time jobs with no prior involvement with work-family programs to demonstrate that they possess the career commitment needed to succeed at higher-level positions.

3. *Encourage critical, as well as noncritical, employees to take advantage of work-family programs that meet their particular needs.* This will send a message to both male and female employees that participation in such programs need not hold back their careers. Also, it may make the most valuable employees who utilize the programs more productive and loyal than ever before.

CONCLUSIONS

If companies make at least some of the changes described in the counterpoint section, we can expect more men *and* more women to be willing to be associated with work-family programs. There will still be a gap between the proportions of men and women who actually use the programs. As the original point makes clear, women will still need the programs more than men do unless major changes occur in our society. However, we will have less reason to be concerned, because all employees will be less reluctant to use or express interest in programs that benefit them. As a result, the difference in inclinations regarding work-family programs between women and men with similar needs will be reduced. Both the point and counterpoint sections suggest that this would be a positive development.

NOTES

1. M.A. Ferber & B. O'Farrell, *Work and Family: Policies for a Changing Work Force* (Washington, DC: National Academy Press, 1991), pp. 122–123; J.H. Pleck, "Are 'Family-Supportive' Employer Policies Relevant to Men?" in J.C. Hood (ed.), *Men, Work, and Family* (Newbury Park, CA: Sage, 1993), pp. 217–237.

2. D.C. Feldman, "Reconceptualizing the Nature and Consequences of Part-Time Work," *Academy of Management Review* 15(1) (1990): 103–112.

3. Ferber & O'Farrell, *Work and Family*, pp. 127–128; Pleck, "Are 'Family-Supportive' Employer Policies Relevant to Men?"

4. Ibid., p. 28, Table 2-3.

5. Ibid.

6. Ibid., p. 74, Table 4-3.

7. Ibid., p. 73.

8. Ibid., p. 31.

9. Pleck, "Are 'Family-Supportive' Employer Policies Relevant to Men?"

10. R.D. Ashmore, F.K. Del Boca, & A.J. Wohlers, "Gender Stereotypes," in R.D. Ashmore & F.K. Del Boca (eds.), *The Social Psychology of Female-Male Relations: A Critical Analysis of Central Concepts* (Orlando, FL: Academic Press, 1986), pp. 69–119.

11. G.N. Powell, *Women and Men in Management*, 2nd. ed (Newbury Park, CA: Sage, 1993), pp. 55–59.

12. K. Gerson, *No Man's Land: Men's Changing Commitments to Family and Work* (New York: Basic Books, 1993).

13. J.R. Kofodimos, "Why Executives Lose their Balance," *Organizational Dynamics* 19(1) (1990): 58–73.

14. F.N. Schwartz, "Management, Women and the New Facts of Life," *Harvard Business Review* 89(1) (1989): 65–76.

15. Pleck, "Are 'Family-Supportive' Employer Policies Relevant to Men?"

16. E. Ehrlich, "The Mommy Track." *Business Week*, March 20, 1989, pp. 126–134.

17. G.B. Knecht, "As American Express Loses Its President, His Kids Gain a Dad," *Wall Street Journal*, November 22, 1995, pp. A1, A12.

18. Kofodimos, "Why Executives Lose Their Balance."

PART V

Moving Ahead: New Directions for the Work-Family Agenda

CHAPTER 17

Visioning the Future

Ellen C. Bankert and Sharon A. Lobel

Over the past decade, significant progress has been made in addressing the work-family issues confronting individuals and their employers. We have moved well beyond a focus on child care or women, and now recognize the diversity of personal life situations that result in conflict with the demands of the workplace. Within organizations, attention is often focused on meeting the current, programmatic needs of employees. While the responses from employers have been significant, it is clear that more meaningful change in the way we work and address our family and community responsibilities could be realized.

The purpose of this chapter is to look to the future of work and the family, addressing the driving forces that will have significant implications for how we define the intersection of these two worlds in the coming years. To do this, we will draw on the learnings of two different visioning processes completed by work-family managers from leading companies. We will also explore a set of guiding principles to which companies might aspire in order to maximize individual, family, and organizational health.

VALUE OF EXPLORING DRIVING FORCES

Many work-family champions have been successful in implementing changes within their organizations, without the luxury of exploring larger trends that have significant implications for this issue now and in the future. For employers, the traditional process used to develop work-family initiatives has been some type of needs assessment. This process often involves the collection of data through employee surveys and/or focus groups and interviews. There is often a task force formed to cull through the data and present recommendations to senior management for program and policy changes. While this step of determining specific employee needs is critical, there is significant value in looking at the work-family issue through a broader lens. It's not surprising that this is often overlooked, given the organizational context for work and family. In many cases, early activity by a company to address work and family issues has been driven by one champion, who has not been given a strategic mandate; rather, the individual or task force has been charged with the goal of implementing some specific program and policy changes that are hoped to meet both employee and organizational needs.

An obvious benefit of considering driving forces in a broader context is to ensure that the responses developed by organizations will have long-term value for both the employee and the company. For example, if we addressed the issue of telecommuting only in today's environment, we would neglect important changes in technology and work restructuring that are likely to make working from home or another off-site location a much more common and effective way of getting work done in the future. Considering future trends should also help to foster greater collaboration between individuals responsible for work and family issues and other change agents, both internal and external to the company. Finally, a future-oriented approach to work and family will enable the individuals responsible for work-family initiatives to anticipate and react to resistance to change.

IDENTIFYING INTERNAL AND EXTERNAL TRENDS

In 1993, corporate members of the Work and Family Roundtable at Boston University initiated a visioning process to explore large-scale business and social trends and their implications for work and family.[1] The visioning project was initiated to support a systems perspective on work and family issues, using a process based on the "scenario-building" work of Peter Schwartz, which highlights changes in both internal business and the external environment.[2] The objective of this exercise was to provide a context for long-range planning for practitioners responsible for the development of work-family initiatives, who don't often have the opportunity to consider the relationship between future trends and the current needs of the organization and its employees. The process involved four steps:

1. Brainstorming of external trends,

2. Brainstorming of business trends,

3. Mapping each trend onto a grid with axes labeled "level of impact" and "probability of occurring" (see Figure 17.1),

4. Ranking and selection of top two business and external trends in the high impact/ high probability cell.

In reviewing the list of trends, several arguments were made as to their placement with respect to probability of occurring or level of impact. For example, participants were divided as to whether society is experiencing a rise or decline in a feeling of a sense of common good and also on whether the pace of our work lives was picking up or slowing down. Others debated the level of impact that would be experienced from a declining faith in government or a changing definition of community. What's more important than settling these debates, however, is appreciating the breadth and depth of challenges facing organizations in the future and attempting to single out some issues that can be addressed in a meaningful way.

After a multistep voting process, members identified two trends in the business and external environments that, *through a work-family lens*, they rated highest in terms of probability of occurring and level of impact.

LEADING BUSINESS AND EXTERNAL TRENDS

Business	External
Globalization	Technological change
Flexibility	Family complexity

After further reflection, we agreed that globalization, technological change, and family complexity were indeed driving forces, while flexibility on both the part of individuals and employers was a necessary response to address these and other driving forces. While the goal of this process was to arrive at leading trends, it would also be useful to consider the implications of each of these trends for companies in general, and for the future priority areas for work and family. For example, the trend toward increased globalization is likely to result in more frequent travel demands for employees; an expanded business calendar of 24 hours per day, 365 days a year; and increased relocation of families around the world. To respond, companies will need to do a more extensive assessment of their programs and policies on a global basis, and determine the availability of local resources in various countries to meet the work-family needs of their changing employee population.[3]

FIVE BROAD THEMES AND IMPLICATIONS FOR WORK AND FAMILY

In the fall of 1995, Roundtable members revisited the theme of visioning. The steering committee reviewed the entire list of trends and decided to broaden the focus beyond the four most important trends identified earlier. Five themes seemed to capture the full range of items that had been brainstormed: *work, family, schools, citizenship*, and *technology*. The primary objective of this exercise was to arrive at specific action recommendations, related to each theme

Figure 17.1
External and Business Trends: Implications for Work and Family

HIGH IMPACT / LOW PROBABILITY

External

⇩ Volunteerism
⇨ Valuing of Employees
⇩ Apprentice Programs
⇩ Outsourcing

Business

⇩ Influence of Boards
⇩ Employee Ownership

HIGH IMPACT / HIGH PROBABILITY

External

⇨ Sense of Personal Safety
⇩ Dysfunctional Families
⇩ Fiscal Pressure, Government Debt
⇩ Focus on Educational Reform
⇩ Integrated Technology
⇩ Leadership Vacuum
⇨ Single-Parent Households
⇩ Sense of Common Good
⇨ Age of Baby Boomers/ ⬅ Life Span
⇩ Continuous Learning Requirement
⇩ Redefinition of Work
⇩ Economic Shift to Pacific Rim
⇩ Pace/ ➡ Leisure Time
⇩ Organized Special Interest
⇩ Non-Traditional Families

Business

⇩ Global Competition
⇩ Corporate Restructuring
⇩ Search for Meaningful Work
⇩ Pressure on Profits / Short-Term Mentality
⇩ Senior-Level Women
⇩ Recognition of Differences
⇩ Emphasis on Cost Reduction / Avoidance
⇩ Experience of Productivity / Quality
⇩ Need for Flexibility
⇩ Needs for Skills / Competencies
⇩ Business Role in Govt. / Community
⇩ Company Involvement in Personal Life
⇩ Teamwork
⇩ Decentralization
⇩ Lack of Trust

LOW IMPACT / LOW PROBABILITY

External

- ⇧ Nationalism
- ⇦ Sense of Common Good
- ⇧ Blending of Cultures

Business

- ⇧ Cost of Duplicate Services
- ⇧ Emphasis on Safety

LOW IMPACT / HIGH PROBABILITY

External

- ⇧ Attention Span
- ⇧ Debate over Immigration Policy
- ⇧ Angry Young Generation
- ⇧ Environmental Action
- ⇧ Pressure to Produce
- ⇧ AIDS
- ⇧ Faith in God
- ⇧ Underclass
- ⇧ Interactive Media
- ⇧ Expectation of Govt. Supports
- ⇧ Redefinition of Community

Business

- ⇧ Emphasis on Ethics
- ⇧ Violence in Workplace

- ⇧ Educational Standards
- ⇧ Shared Domestic Responsibility
- ⇧ Changes in Mgt. / Personal Style
- ⇧ Shareholder / Investor Concern in Social Responsibility

Source: Boston University Center on Work and Family. Roundtable Publication, 1994.

area, for companies to consider. In order to pursue these themes, members spent
the first day of a three-day meeting completing the following four steps:

1. In-depth exploration of theme area in small groups
2. Mixed-group discussions (one member from each theme area) to add new ideas
3. Identification of company action ideas in each area
4. Member voting on priority action ideas

The following action ideas received the highest priority voting by members:

- Tie a proportion of a supervisor's compensation to successful utilization of a work-family program
- Develop the case for how the business impacts family life and how family life impacts the business
- Broaden the definition of corporate citizenship to include employees (i.e., corporate citizenship does not only mean serving the external community)
- Measure performance based on results and develop tools to quantify results
- Educate employees so they are better equipped to ''self-manage''
- Conduct research to determine correlation between excellence in management and support for work-family programs
- Encourage employee commitment and involvement in community

Figure 17.2 provides a summary of other action strategies developed by the group.

While many of the action strategies listed were ideas that few companies have tried, the group discussed whether or not these action strategies go far enough. For example, with regard to making the business case for work-family, Faith Wohl, director of workplace initiatives for the U.S. General Services Administration, raised the question of why it is that work and family responses are held to different standards than most other ''investments'' by an organization. She shared an example from her recent experience in which she was asked to document the impact on productivity that resulted from the creation of several telecommuting centers around the country. She countered by asking who had measured the productivity rates of workers in other federal buildings, thereby highlighting the inequity of the demands and stimulating a broader analysis of employee productivity.

APPLYING VISIONING TO INDIVIDUAL ORGANIZATIONS

While it is valuable to bring leaders in the work and family field together to work in the aggregate on creative visioning, it is just as critical for individual work/life managers to apply a similar process to visioning within their own

Figure 17.2
Potential Action Strategies in Five Theme Areas

FAMILY

- Make a proportion of employees' appraisal and compensation dependent on achievement of personal objectives.
- Increase strategies to increase availability of work/family programs at the nonprofessional level.
- Increase company involvement with the development of public policy.
- Family time-management training.

TECHNOLOGY

- Structure "interactions" to promote community within the company.
- Make employment contract explicit on technology – create "trust."
- Develop strategy in schools – when to introduce children to technology; what limits to set.
- Conduct a human impact audit on effects of technology on individual and family.

WORK

- Develop strategies to support skill-based employment.
- Get employee input into work redesign; allow more autonomy for how work gets done.
- Challenge the way things have always been done.
- Expand upward feedback/appraisals.

SCHOOLS

- Have schools assume before/after care.
- Facilitate parental participation.
- Share business/management training courses with the community.
- Help schools clarify the resources they need to succeed.

CITIZENSHIP

- Establish policy for time-off for community service ("time-tithing").
- Make volunteerism a performance objective.
- Establish sabbaticals for volunteer work.
- Communicate a new employee contract.

---

organizations. Issues including changes in technology, competitive structure, changing customer base, demographics, and others have very different implications on a growing biotech company than they would on an industrial manufacturer or an urban hospital. Moreover, the "external" visioning that was the primary focus of the two processes described here does not adequately address individual company culture. For example, decision-making processes, values, and standard work hours will have significant implications for how trends concerning work, family, and community play out in work-family management.

DEFINING EXCELLENCE IN CORPORATE RESPONSE TO
WORK AND FAMILY

For any organization attempting to be more strategic in its approach to work and family, completing some type of visioning process should be of great value. On an even more fundamental level, however, it's important that companies have a sense of what they are striving for or what it really means to be a "family-friendly" employer. Broadly speaking, policy makers agree that companies should focus less attention in the future on programmatic responses, and more on the issue of culture and informal support of a balance between employees' work and nonwork lives. Work-family champions need to mainstream the issue in order to gain line management support so that the work and family issue is not seen as another employee benefit or human resources initiative. Another consistent trend involves addressing the needs of the total workforce, and not just those of women or parents. Despite progress in these and other areas in efforts to push work and family in a more positive and strategic direction, we do not yet have a common understanding of what defines excellence in this field.

To respond to this need and to continue the visioning work done by the group in the past, members of the roundtable began a project in 1995 to develop a set of Principles of Excellence for the work and family field. The primary purpose of this initiative was to develop a self-assessment tool that could be used by a wide range of employers. We also hope that the principles will be used to generate new and creative responses by both organizations and employees. The Principles of Excellence consist of two primary components: (1) a set of four broad principles and defining dimensions; and (2) a companion assessment tool to guide companies in evaluating how they are doing with respect to each principle. The first component, completed in early 1996, resulted in the publication of the principles and key dimensions shown in Figure 17.3. A roundtable subcommittee is currently leading the effort to develop the assessment tool, to be completed in 1997.

The four principles, in effect, reflect a "why-what-who" description of responsiveness to work and family needs. While they were not written to imply that a sequential approach is necessary, there is agreement that a commitment to the first principle on strategy is likely to drive responses to the other three. The first principle, concerning strategy, describes the rationale, or *why*, behind company involvement in work and family. The second principle, covering issues of programs, culture, communication, and evaluation, describes *what* companies actually do to respond to the need for employee work/home-life balance. And the final two principles, which discuss shared responsibility between employer, employee, and the external community, address the issue of *who* is responsible for meeting these needs. A discussion of each principle and specific company examples are the focus of the remainder of the chapter.

Figure 17.3
Principles of Excellence in Work and Family

---

1. **The employer recognizes strategic value of addressing work/personal life issues**

- Business is practiced with sensitivity to employee's work/personal life needs.
- Work/personal life solutions are aligned with business goals.
- The employer's commitment to addressing work/personal life issues is viewed as a long-term investment.
- Work/personal life strategies are flexible to meet changing organizational and employee needs.

2. **The work environment supports individual work and personal life effectiveness**

- The employer's informal culture supports healthy work/personal life balance.
- The employer provides meaningful work/personal life programs and policies.
- The employer is committed to ongoing education of key stakeholders – employees, management, and the community.
- The employer strives for continuous improvement through ongoing evaluation and assessment.

3. **The management of work and personal life effectiveness is a shared responsibility between employer *and employee***

- Managers and employees are empowered to develop solutions that address both business and personal objectives.
- Managers and employees are held accountable for their behavior in support of these objectives.

4. **The employer develops relationships to enhance external work and personal life resources**

- Partnerships are formed to maximize value of employer and community resources available to employees and community members.
- The employer serves as an active role model.
- The employer is open to working with the public sector to strengthen policy that benefits both employers and individuals.

Principle 1: The Employer Recognizes Strategic Value of Addressing Work/Personal Life Issues

The first standard for companies to meet is one that addresses the business rationale. This principle has probably presented the greatest challenge to work-family champions, who struggle to find hard data to rationalize a company's commitment to this issue. Making the business case for being responsive to work and family issues, however, should be viewed much more broadly than in dollars and cents associated with absenteeism or other measurements of lost productivity. There are endless examples of situations within companies that call for a response that benefits both business and employee needs. One financial institution credited the inclusion of its work-family manager in an important client meeting for saving the account, because of a demand made by the client to determine how responsive the organization was in the areas of diversity and work-family. Another organization, responding to the growing need of its West Coast and international customers for longer hours of service, found that a large percentage of employees were interested in working nontraditional hours in order to meet their family and personal life responsibilities.

The dimensions listed under this principle reinforce the issue of work and family needing to be viewed as a "two-way street" meeting issues, not only of employee accommodation, but also of the business. Contributions to the "bottom line" can be identified in terms of discrete outcomes, such as effects of work-family initiatives on turnover rates, but it is preferable to identify the broadest possible impacts. For example, what is the relationship of turnover to departmental goals, strategies, or stakeholder (employee, customer, supplier) concerns? Framing the appropriate questions is also a key to measuring business impacts. For example, "How will this policy help in implementing our globalization strategy?"[4]

Principle 2: The Work Environment Supports Individual Work and Personal Life Effectiveness

The second principle addresses what companies are doing in terms of four dimensions: programs and policies, culture, education, and assessment. The dimensions under this principle should be viewed as a group, since too many employers believe they have done what is needed by merely instituting a set of programmatic responses. However, the value of certain programs and policies to specific individuals and groups of employees should not be understated. One example is the case of lower-income employees. Many critics of family friendliness argue that company responsiveness has been targeted primarily to professional employees. The irony in this is that most research indicates that what professional employees value most is responsiveness in terms of flexibility and other cultural issues rather than programs and policies. New benefits and programs may be more valued, and contribute more to increased employee productivity, among the nonprofessional staff. For example, in focus groups with hotel workers, employees identified subsidized child care and access to a phone to call home as the two "benefits" that would most help them meet their work and family responsibilities.[5]

The need for culture change has long been recognized as the most significant challenge for companies striving to be family friendly. In a model introduced by the Families and Work Institute, Galinsky, Friedman, and Hernandez argued that organizations typically progress through three stages in terms of work-family responsiveness, with the third being one in which real culture change occurs.[6] Companies' ability to achieve this goal, however, has been slow in coming. Since programmatic solutions are more tangible and simpler to implement, many companies have focused their energies here. Best-practice models on concrete strategies and practices that have facilitated a movement to real culture change are also more difficult to come by than innovative policies and programs.

Research on culture change with respect to work and family supports the argument that progress on this front has been slow. In a survey of 100 work-family managers, 40% responded that supervisors did not have a good understanding of the work-family issues of employees and only 11% believed that supervisors respected employees' need to balance work and family "to a great or very great extent."[7]

An example from Baxter Healthcare illustrates the potential power of a concrete tool that encourages behavioral change. After conducting extensive focus groups and interviews with managers and employees, the firm's work-life team produced a document called *Elements of a Supportive Work Culture* (1995). The document lists, in bullet form, simple behaviors and practices that employees identified as supportive of the need for work and life balance. Examples include:

• Travel on Monday and Friday afternoons should be the norm preferred over weekend travel.
• 24-hour advance notice should be required for all overtime work.
• Scheduling weekend sales meetings is not appropriate.

The document provides encouragement for individual work groups to refine the list, including additional or different behaviors that are tailored to their specific work environment. Response at Baxter has been favorable, with both managers and employees acknowledging the value of a uniform tool that can be used to discuss work habits and tailored to the needs of a diverse organization.

The third dimension of this principle, addressing education and communication, has also been a challenge for many organizations. Many companies have found that the most appropriate form of education is not stand-alone "work and family training," but rather the incorporation of work and family issues into existing company training and education initiatives. In the area of communications, companies have found that while successful communication strategies employed for other types of employee benefits are applicable to work-family programs and policies, alternative strategies need to be used to communicate the notion of cultural support. Many companies have published some type of work and family mission or value statement that is endorsed by the CEO to reinforce the company's commitment. The best known example of this is Johnson & Johnson's "Credo," which was modified to include the following statement: "We must be mindful of ways to fulfill their family responsibilities."

Finally, this principle calls for a commitment to ongoing evaluation and assessment. On this dimension, companies need to make a commitment to continuous improvement. For reasons that probably have to do with lack of widespread support and loose linkages to business goals, decision makers have approached assessment differently from other human resource initiatives. Assessment often takes the form of listing programs and other initiatives that a company offers and comparing these to the efforts of companies viewed as leaders in the field. Very little methodical research has been done, so companies often rely on any numbers they can find, whether or not they are credible or applicable to their environment.

Decision makers may be afraid to do an adequate assessment out of fear of having resources taken away. Because many believe it is impossible to take away a "benefit" given to employees, we seem to be afraid to investigate whether or not it's meeting a need. However, if companies are devoting resources to an existing work-family benefit that could be better spent somewhere else, we need to make the tough decisions that will benefit the greater common good. For example, after several years of offering child care resource and referral, a needs assessment in one company found that employees expressed a significantly greater need for help with elder care than they did with child care. While it turned out that the company ended up offering both, it could have cut back on child care services to meet the changing needs of the employee population, especially if additional funds were not available.

Principle 3: The Management of Work and Personal Life Effectiveness Is a Shared Responsibility

The objective behind this principle is to emphasize the need for employee ownership of the management of the work and personal life balance. A prevalent theme in the work and family arena in the mid-1990's is the growing sense of entitlement among some employees, who have come to expect their employer to take the lead role in helping them balance their work and home lives. Many companies have addressed this issue by developing specific guidelines that emphasize shared responsibility. At Lotus, for example, a job-sharing guidebook was developed that outlined the responsibility of all parties involved when developing and implementing a job-sharing arrangement. AT&T has produced a similar booklet for telecommuters. On a broader level, some companies have issued work-family value statements that speak to the issue of shared responsibility. In RJR Nabisco's "Management Statement on Worklife," one of the four "guidelines" listed reads:

Balancing work with family and personal obligations is a shared responsibility involving the company, its managers and employees. Successfully balancing family and personal needs of the business requires a cooperative effort between the employee and his or her manager. Fundamentally, the company's role is to provide the tools and support that will help employees find solutions to their own problems—not to solve their problems for them.

The two concepts highlighted in the dimensions of this principle are empowerment and accountability, both of which are obviously management challenges that extend far beyond the issue of work and family. Companies appear to be making greater progress in the area of empowerment, providing managers and employees with considerable autonomy in developing reasonable solutions. The wording of many work-family policy statements typically includes language such as that from a John Hancock policy manual: "Flextime lets you and your manager work out a regular schedule that suits you both." There seem to be fewer success stories of companies developing practices that encourage greater accountability on the part of both managers and employees. While there are few examples of performance management systems that reflect the need for appropriate sensitivity to work-family balance, there are more and more anecdotes of companies addressing this concern informally. For example, the *Wall Street Journal* ran a column profiling Deloitte & Touche, which included the story of an employee who was advised to "cut her work hours to make time for a personal life" by a firm partner who was worried that the "rising star" would eventually burn out and quit.[8]

Principle 4: Employer Develops Relationships to Enhance External Work and Life Resources

Companies committed to work and family have always been surprisingly open to sharing their experiences with one another. More recently, we have witnessed the development of several collaborative efforts between companies and communities. When companies collaborate with each other, there is an obvious goal of taking advantage of economies of scale or pooling resources to meet a need that a single company could not achieve on its own. The consortium for backup child care, which was initiated in New York City and replicated in other locations, is a good example. While no one company had enough demand from its employees to provide emergency or backup child care on its own, 11 companies working together were able to make the per-company cost manageable.[9]

In contrast to corporate collaborations, partnerships between companies and communities have traditionally been driven from a philanthropic or "good corporate citizen" rationale. Even companies that have adopted a more strategic approach to community relations seem to do so because it makes business sense to be a good corporate citizen. In the area of work and family, partnering with communities can actually help to lessen the burden of companies unable to tackle such a broad social issue alone. Marriott's development of a community-based resource program for its low-wage employees is an example of community outreach that can have a significant payoff for companies. Recognizing that many of the traditional work-family benefits did not meet the needs of its lower-wage employees, Marriott developed a "Family Resource Line," which connects employees to a multilingual staff of social workers to help them solve problems including issues of child care, domestic violence, household finance, transportation, and housing. The service, which is managed by an external resource and referral provider, relies on community service agencies, including

Catholic Charities, to service the needs of its employees, who are located throughout the country. Preliminary surveys indicate that the company is getting more than a 400% return on its investment, in terms of reduced absenteeism, higher quality of work, and improved relationships with coworkers. One employee survey found that 29% of workers said that they would have quit their jobs if it had not been for the existence of the hotline.[10]

Of course, the potential to strengthen communities as a result of partnerships should not be overlooked and is therefore listed as a key dimension under this principle. The American Business Collaboration (ABC) for Quality Dependent Care is one model that illustrates the benefits for both companies and communities when successful partnerships are formed. Initiated in 1992 with a grant from IBM, the collaboration consists of regional partnerships of employers seeking to improve the quality of dependent care. More than 350 projects, ranging from family child care training to an in-home volunteer elder care service, have been funded by a consortium of 156 employers. As companies look to the future, we are likely to see increased partnerships between the private and public sectors as the parties in both recognize the potential value of working together to meet the work-family needs of employee and community members.

CONCLUSION

We have identified several of the driving forces that are likely to determine how the work and family issue will be played out in the coming years. The way in which employers will respond to clear trends, such as changing technology or the increased globalization of business, remains less certain. There seems to be consensus that the investment in work-family initiatives, at least to some extent, is good, not only for employees and families, but also for business. Policy makers disagree, however, on the extent to which companies should take on a major role in helping employees meet their personal life responsibilities. As employers provide more and more social supports, some fear that employees will become too dependent, a potentially problematic scenario as lifetime employment, or even minimal job security, is no longer a reality for most workers.[11] It's likely that the relationships among employers, community, government, and families will continue to evolve, subject to variations in corporate culture, social trends, demographics, and changes in the political scene in Washington. Part of our vision for the future is that the necessary forces will come together to create the systemic change needed. At that point, the terminology of "work and family" or "work/life" will connote an image of integration rather than conflict.

NOTES

1. The Work and Family Roundtable is a national membership organization of approximately 40 companies recognized for their leadership in the area of work and family.

It is one of two employer partnerships developed by the Center on Work and Family, a research and policy institute at Boston University.

2. P. Schwartz, *The Art of the Long View* (New York: Doubleday, 1991).

3. S.A. Lobel, B.K. Googins, & E.C. Bankert, "The Future of Work and Family: Critical Trends for Practice, Policy and Research" (manuscript submitted for publication, 1995).

4. S.A. Lobel, *Work/Life and Diversity: Assessing Linkages and Strategic Value*, Policy Paper Series (Boston: Boston University Center on Work and Family, 1996).

5. J. Swanberg, "Work/Family Issues of Low-Wage Workers" (unpublished raw data, 1995).

6. E. Galinsky, D.E. Friedman, & C.A. Hernandez, *The Corporate Reference Guide to Work-Family Programs* (New York: Families and Work Institute, 1991).

7. M. Catsouphes, P. Mirvis, & L. Litchfield, *Behind the Scenes: Corporate Environments and Work/Family Initiatives* (Boston: Boston University Center on Work and Family, 1995).

8. The discussion of Lotus, AT&T, RJR Nabisco, and John Hancock are based on internal company publications. The discussion of Deloitte & Touche is based on S. Shellenbarger, "A Crucible in Balancing Job and Family," *Wall Street Journal*, December 13, 1994, p. B1.

9. Marcy Levin-Epstein, "Back-up Child Care Center Debuts in New York City," *National Report on Work and Family*, September 28, 1994, p. 2.

10. See Chapter 11 of this volume.

11. L. Nash, "The Nanny Corporation," *Across the Board* (July-August 1994), pp. 17–22.

CHAPTER 18

Moving from Programs to Culture Change: The Next Stage for the Corporate Work-Family Agenda

Dana E. Friedman and Arlene A. Johnson

The sweeping changes in work, workers, families, institutions, and communities have given life to a new functional title in human resources, a new consulting area, a new foundation program area, a new academic focus—in short, a new field known as "work-family" or "work/life" issues. The reciprocal relationship of our personal and work lives is under closer scrutiny these days because the intersection of the work and personal spheres of our lives has been magnified by other changes in society and the economy. Companies now need to rely more on their employees' commitment—that is, to consider their employees' hearts, and no longer simply their hands—to boost quality and productivity. As growing numbers of workers seek meaning in their work, the best way to motivate people is to provide meaningful work, with some control over how they do it. Such conditions, if met, would let people have a family and personal life. A focus on the needs of people in the organization is expected to help the company as well as the employee. And it is clear that people's needs have changed, given changes in the family.

A variety of disciplines and sectors are represented among those who saw the connections between work and family issues and championed the cause. The linkages are far more complex than imagined, and the scope of concern has moved from child care to a broader array of work-family issues, and in some cases, "people" issues, reflected in the more inclusive term, "work/life."[1] One indication of this movement can be seen in the 1996 announcement that the Association of Corporate Child Care Consultants, Inc., will change its name to the Alliance of Work-Life Professionals.

This chapter will put the emergence of a corporate work-family agenda into historical and organizational context. First, we shall discuss the forces that have influenced both the prevalence and nature of a corporate response to family concerns over time. Next, we shall profile the efforts of some companies to create family-friendly policies and programs. The chapter proceeds with a stage theory describing the evolution of companies' work-family agendas and the juncture of issues that presently define the field. This discussion is intended to provide a framework for understanding the progress and likely direction of corporate initiatives in the work and family area.

HISTORICAL CONTEXT

Since the beginning of the Industrial Age, employers have taken notice of work and family issues only during periods of national emergencies. For example, during World War II, it was understood that women could not help in the war effort without child care for their children. After World War II, many women returned home, the workforce was replenished by returning servicemen, and industry's interest in child care lay dormant until the 1960's, when corporate social responsibility motivated some companies to build child care centers. Serious interest in a range of child care services, and eventually, support for a variety of family needs did not occur until the 1980's, when concerns about productivity and competing in a global economy gave way to a host of corporate changes.

In 1987, the U.S. Department of Labor released a report called "Workforce 2000."[2] It warned business about the significance of demographic shifts in the population and how these shifts would affect recruitment and retention efforts. The predictions for an increasingly diverse labor market comprised of more women, minorities, and aging workers gave business the most explicit rationale for addressing work and family concerns. At the same time, a growing number of companies began to be concerned about a "glass ceiling" that not only prevented well-trained women from entering senior management ranks, but also prevented companies from amortizing their investment in women's recruitment and training. Worksite research pointed to work-family conflict as a contributor to women's unequal and shorter career ladders.

From the latter 1980's through the present day, there has been widespread downsizing among large corporations and a nagging threat that work and family issues will be moved to the back burner. What has happened, though, is quite the contrary. Work-family programs are flourishing, and work-family issues are garnering greater visibility than ever before. A 1991 benchmarking study by the Families and Work Institute found that the strongest predictor of corporate family friendliness is change—particularly, downsizing, merger, or replacement of the CEO.[3] The reasons for the growth of work-family initiatives in the early 1990's, during this period of corporate upheaval, are varied. The first is company concern over the morale of employees surviving a downsizing, who must now handle more responsibility with less support. The provision of inexpensive dependent care initiatives and flexibility is seen as a way to ease the pain of layoffs and show support for the "survivors."

Another reason for recent growth of work-family initiatives relates to the critical mass of organizations that now offer family support programs—without economic ruin. By 1995, it was difficult to ignore the 20 or so years of research and experience in the area of work and family. Many large companies now have highly publicized work-family initiatives or initiatives that are underway. Hundreds of companies now employ designated "work-family managers," thereby adding a new job description within corporate human resources and creating a market for work-family conferences and on-line services. Many benefits consulting firms have developed a work-family practice area. Numerous state and city agencies have recently created work-family task forces or education campaigns. Passage of the Family and Medical Leave Act in 1993 thrust into the limelight the problems with how companies were dealing with pregnancy, parenting, adoption, and family illness. In June 1996, President Bill Clinton and Vice President Al Gore, along with their wives, addressed a national conference sponsored by Vice President Gore on the subject of work and family. An entire work-family industry has formed and continues to grow.

CURRENT EFFORTS OF COMPANIES TO ADDRESS FAMILY CONCERNS

The very first initiatives in the work-family arena were shaped by child care advocates. An elder care focus in the late 1980s resulted in terminology related to "dependent care." Soon after "work-family" became an accepted frame of reference, concerns about equity and backlash led to the term "work/life" to include single people and those not in "traditional" families.

For each segment of the work population in need of some kind of work-family support, companies typically hire a consultant, conduct a needs assessment, and develop a set of policies and programs that will address identified needs. Company actions cluster into five different types of initiatives: information and counseling, financial assistance, products and services, time-off policies, and organizational development activities. The prevalence of these policies and programs among large corporations is depicted in Table 18.1.

One can see from the array of program options offered that flexible time and leave of absence are the most popular. Some of the initiatives—part-time work and flextime—were in vogue before a work-and-family focus emerged. And while most of the policies enumerated are formal and written in a company's policy handbook, practice is determined case by case (i.e., at the discretion of the manager).

Many companies have redesigned their benefits packages in order to keep abreast of changes in the demographics of the workforce. For example, cafeteria plans acknowledge that employees' needs change in the course of their lifetimes. Another example is financial assistance for dependent care, which is available

Table 18.1
Prevalence of Work-Family Programs in Companies

Rank	Program Description	Percent of Companies Offering Program
1	Part-time Schedules	87.8%
2	Employee Assistance Programs	85.6
3	Personal Days	77.4
4	Flextime	77.1
5	Personal Leaves of Absence	70.4
6	Child Care Resource and Referral	54.5
7	Spouse Employment Assistance	51.9
8	DCAPs (Dependent Care Assistance Plans)	49.5
9	Job-Sharing Arrangements	47.9
10	Flexplace	35.1
11	Family, Child Care Leaves for Mothers*	28.0
12	Family Counseling in Relocation	26.9
13	Work-Family Seminars	25.7
14	Cafeteria Benefits	25.1
15	Wellness/Health Programs	23.4
16	Elder Care Consultation and Referral	21.1
17	Adoption Benefits	15.7
18	Child Care Centers	13.0
19	Work-Family Management Training	9.6
20	Work-Family Support Groups	5.3
21	Corporate Foundation Giving	5.3
22	Family Illness Days	4.8
23	Discounts for Child Care	4.8
24	Sick Child Care	4.3
25	Work-Family Coordinators	3.2
26	Work-Family Handbooks	2.7
27	Long-Term Care Insurance	2.1
28	Consortium Centers for Child Care	1.6
29	On-site Caregiver Fairs	1.6
30	Vouchers for Child Care	1.1

Note: Ranking does not include disability leaves for new mothers, which are available in 100% of the companies surveyed.

*Family and child care leave policies for mothers that are also available to fathers are found in 22.3% of the companies, and are extended to adoptive parents in 23.4% of the companies. Policies that include extended care for relatives are available in 16.0% of the companies. These variations are not counted separately in the table.

through company-sponsored voucher programs or Dependent Care Assistance Plans (DCAPs). DCAPs were stimulated by changes in the 1981 Economic Recovery Tax Act, which made dependent care a nontaxable benefit to employees. As a result, companies are able to offer financial assistance to employees by letting them pay with pretax dollars for the child care and elder care services they use. To this day, this is the most popular form of corporate support for dependent care because the government absorbs the cost.

The work-family field began with a preoccupation with on-site child care centers, but only a small proportion of employers pursued that option because there is significant cost in establishing and managing a center, not all employed parents can be served by a center, and many employees prefer home-based child care instead. Most notable about on-site child care are the slow, but continual, growth in the number of child care centers and the increased sophistication of the child care companies hired to manage them. In addition, a growing number of employers have created multiple centers as a result of the positive effects of neighborhood child care for the company.

Not surprisingly, referral networks designed to assist large numbers of employees with dependents are significantly more popular among employers than other forms of support, which tend to be more costly or serve fewer employees. In the early 1980's, large companies began setting up referral networks by contracting with local, community-based resource and referral agencies. When large, multisite companies became interested in setting up referral networks, national vendors of referral services contracted with local referral agencies or created centralized databases of services. As child care and elder care referrals have broadened to include counseling services on a range of employee needs and interests, some companies and some vendors have begun to merge their referral services with Employee Assistance Programs (EAPs). With changes in managed care for mental health, there are likely to be changes in EAPs.

Table 18.1 lists what might be considered core programs of a corporate work-family agenda. In addition, several emerging themes in corporate work-family activity are outlined, which demonstrate the broadening corporate interest in dependent care and the increased corporate focus on the community and on how work is done:

- *School-age child care*: Employers are recognizing that lack of, or inadequate, arrangements for school-age children not only contribute to employees' distraction, stress, and absence, but also are detrimental to society—which eventually pays the price in young people's delinquency, substance abuse, and learning problems. A growing number of programs help parents find quality care and enrichment for children after school and during school holidays.

- *Short-term and emergency child care*: Employee surveys show that emergency child care problems (e.g., when the child care provider is sick or when regular arrangements temporarily break down) are an ongoing concern for parents, as well as a source of unpredictable and costly absences for employers. Accordingly, businesses that would never have otherwise considered building a child care center have shown a surge of interest in emergency child care centers—even in midtown and urban locations.

- *Elder care*: Despite employers' oft-stated intention to address employees' elder care needs, the actual picture is one of slower-than-expected progress. A handful of firms have created on-site adult day care centers, which are used largely by community residents unrelated to employees. Employees participate in and appreciate referral programs and informational seminars, but employers are frustrated by a national delivery system of services designed for the aged and not the caregiver. As baby-boomers get older, the elder care needs of their parents will be both more visible and more prevalent. Those in leadership positions are likely to support an increased focus on elder care needs as they themselves experience dependent care problems with their aging parents and loved ones.

- *Assisting low-income workers*: With fewer financial resources and, therefore, fewer options, low-income workers are especially subject to work-family stress but do not benefit proportionately from the increase in work-family programs. The *National Study of the Changing Workforce* found that the lower a person's income, the less likely he or she is to have access to family-supportive benefits such as dependent care or flexible work arrangements. This is likely to become a major topic of company discussion and an opportunity for the creation of public-private partnerships to address these needs.

- *Dependent care development funds*: A small, but growing, number of companies are designating a sum of money for investment in the improvement of community service for dependent care in communities where their employees live. The money may be from the corporate foundation, but just as often it comes from human resources operating budgets. This concept is a natural next step for companies that offer dependent care resource and referral programs, whose effectiveness depends on the adequacy of services in the community.

- *Corporate collaboration*: Acknowledging that they can do more together than any one company can do separately, employers are coming together to share information and to create collaborative programs and services. The largest such collaboration—the American Business Collaborative—was launched in September 1992, when 137 organizations across the country joined to invest $25 million to improve the supply and quality of dependent care programs in 44 communities where their employees live. To date, the collaborative has supported more than 300 dependent care projects ranging from summer camps to transportation programs for employees' elderly dependents.

- *Community mobilization*: Employees are also becoming more active in community efforts to improve local services. For example, they may sit on city or state task forces with other stakeholders to identify problems and create workable solutions.

- *Flexible work arrangements*: Flexibility is not only the most desired, but also the most elusive, of work-family benefits. Despite the prevalence of policies for part-time and alternative work arrangements, managers and supervisors often look upon employees using these policies as uncommitted and unpromotable. This is considered a "mixed message" because the company offers employees a flexible work arrangement policy, but very few employees feel free to use it. It is now widely acknowledged that closing the gap between policy and practice requires addressing manager attitudes and repositioning flexibility, not as an employee accommodation, but as a management tool and a mainstream alternative for getting the work done. A growing number of companies see flexibility as both the ultimate test of family-friendliness and a powerful lever for integrating work-family concerns into job processes and everyday operations.

The past decade has produced literally hundreds of different kinds of family-supportive corporate programs, ranging from lactation support programs and providing beepers to expectant fathers working in remote work locations to concierge and on-site convenience services for busy families—to name only a few. Assessments of employee need have identified sources of work-family stress and programs for reducing them. But as the number of programs has grown, so, also, has the realization that a proliferation of programs does not, by itself, address basic work-family issues.

RECOGNIZING THE WORK ENVIRONMENT AS A WORK-FAMILY VARIABLE

One of the most significant changes in the course of recent corporate attention to family issues is the realization that no policy or program will help people who work in an unsupportive culture. Going forward into the latter half of the 1990's, effective employer work-family initiatives will increasingly focus on variables related to the work culture, work processes, and workplace relationships.

In the *National Study of the Changing Workforce*, a nationally representative study published in 1993, workers who had started a new job within the past two years were asked to name the factors they considered most important when taking on that job. The most popular answer was "open communications." The second most important factor was the effect of the job on family life. The nature of work, the quality of management, and the relationship with supervisors followed. Wages and salary were 16th on the list.[4] When asked in an open-ended question, "How do you define success at work?" more than half of the respondents said, "doing a good job" and "getting respect from supervisors." These answers support the idea that employees are motivated more by intrinsic factors than extrinsic benefits and services. An unpublished study of employee attitudes and work-life issues conducted at IBM in 1991 adds a new dimension to this observation: among the top performers in the company, work-family balance was the second most important factor in deciding whether they would stay with the company.

The nature of the job and the workplace environment are critical for balancing work and personal life. Independent corporate studies conducted by the Families and Work Institute repeatedly have shown that employees with more autonomy in their jobs and more social support from supervisors, coworkers, and the workplace culture report less work-family conflict, less stress, and more effective coping than other workers. Job autonomy and workplace support were also found to correlate positively with employees' degree of commitment to their work and with their interest in having the company succeed.[5] These findings were corroborated by an evaluation of Johnson & Johnson's comprehensive work-family initiative, in which support from supervisors and workplace culture proved to have a positive and independent impact on employees' perceptions of work-family balance. Employees who believe that their supervisors are supportive of, and responsive to, their family needs also admit to feeling better about themselves, about their jobs, and about their ability to keep work and family from negatively affecting one another. The findings were similar for employees who experience a supportive workplace culture.[6]

There is no question that work-family programs are necessary for helping people deal with work-family stress—and that they help to convey a supportive culture—but they are not sufficient in themselves to create a sense of work-family well-being or to foster discretionary effort on the part of employees. For those employees who have access to family-responsive policies, there appears to be a positive, measurable effect on employees' reading of the culture and on their commitment to the company. Users of work-family policies are also more likely to support reorganization efforts and total quality initiatives. A study at Fel-Pro, a midsized, Illinois-based manufacturing company, found that the company's extensive work-family initiative creates "a culture of mutual commitment between employer and employee . . . [and] provides a foundation on which to implement organization changes that require substantial employee involvement."[7]

The *National Study of the Changing Workforce* revealed that the strongest predictors of both family well-being and work-family conflict, as well as job satisfaction and discretionary effort, are related to the work environment, the nature of the job, and workplace relationships. The most important factor is control over one's job—that is, over the tasks performed and the hours worked. But more than half of the workforce reports having very little control over their work hours. The other factors that are most predictive of positive work and family outcomes are employee relationships with supervisors and coworkers, employee perceptions of a supportive culture, chances for advancement, and the absence of discrimination against employees. When these factors are positive, workers are likely to be more loyal, committed, and innovative; more satisfied with their jobs; likely to experience less burnout; and more willing to help the company succeed than workers who do not have these supports at work. Employees are also likely to report less work-family conflict, less stress, and better coping than employees in unresponsive companies.[8]

In the end it comes back to the workplace. Characteristics of jobs and workplaces affect not only workers' attitudes and behaviors at work, but also their general well-being and their abilities to balance work and family life. Work-family solutions will be most effective if they focus on the nature of jobs, relationships at work, and the organizational culture.[9]

STAGES IN THE EVOLUTION OF A CORPORATE WORK-FAMILY AGENDA

In an attempt to chronicle the evolution of work-family initiatives by companies, the Families and Work Institute conducted a series of surveys and interviews to learn about the progression of efforts across industry groups (see Table 18.2). Three discernible stages in the evolution of a corporate work-family agenda have been reported so far, and a fourth stage may be emerging.

As reported in 1991 in the *Corporate Reference Guide for Work-Family Programs*, these stages represent a snapshot in the dynamic and rapidly changing field of work and family. A current look at company initiatives in this area suggests that the stages have blended somewhat and that, especially in Stages 3 and 4, the evolution is more of a complex feedback loop than a linear progression. While the stages may not be as distinct as before, they are still helpful in marking the movement in corporate activity.

The sharpest distinction seems to exist among those companies between Stages 2 and 3. Moving from Stage 2 to Stage 3 may be more difficult than making the leap to Stage 1. It may be more accurate to describe two *planes* of activity, with companies in Stages 1 and 2 on one plane and companies in Stages 3 and 4 on another.

Stage 1

A company in Stage 1 is generally focused on child care and women's issues. A women's task force, or some newly created body comprised largely of women, often assumes responsibilities for identifying needs and recommending a course of action. After spending considerable time uncovering data that will make the case for a bottom-line return on investment, corporate champions are likely to find considerable resistance to work-family policies from senior management and skepticism from other parts of the organization. Once the case has been made successfully, companies in Stage 1 typically develop one or two child care initiatives. They assume the problem has been "solved," and management then looks forward to returning to "real" business issues.

Stage 2

Companies in this stage broaden the issues addressed and expand policies and programs accordingly. The CEO is more supportive of a work-family agenda and sanctions a task force called "work-family" (rather than "child care" or "women's issues"). Work-family initiatives become the part- or full-time responsibility of someone in a newly created position called "Work-Family Manager." A company at this stage often prints user-friendly employee handbooks describing the array of family supports offered.

Expansion of flexible work arrangements policies is the hallmark of a com-

Table 18.2
Evolving Focus of Work-Life Initiatives

	Stage 1	Stage 2	Stage 3	Stage 4
COMMITMENT	**Grassroots** • A champion exists, with little support from top management	**Human Resources** • More top-level support • Target managers to be more sensitive and aware	**Culture Change** • Critical top-level and middle management support	**Work Redesign** • Recognition that work-family issues are integral to key business decisions and design of work processes • Target front-line supervisors
PROCESS	**Identify the Problem** • Child care or women's task force begins inquiry • Needs assessment	**Centralize Responsibility** • Task force on work-family • Instituting work-family manager • Communicating policies	**Align and Mainstream Concepts** • Task force on work-life • Mission revised • Synergy with other strategic aims	**Embed in Work Processes** • Task force on people/human effectiveness • Work redesign and reengineering involves Human Resources
INITIATIVES	**Programmatic** • Defined as a woman's issue • Child care is primary focus • Usually some form of dependent care assistance	**Integrated** • Focus on the life cycle of employees • Packaging of policies and programs • Flexible work arrangements	**Strategic** • Eliminate mixed messages • Publicize role models • Performance reviews include work-family objectives	**Fundamental** • Alternative career paths • 360 degrees of feedback • Work teams have responsibility for individual scheduling
COMMUNITY FOCUS	**Shared Information** • Attend conferences • Learn about community marketplace • Identify experts	**Project-Based Collaboration** • Consortia	**System-Wide Collaboration** • Participation on planning/policy committees • American business collaborative efforts • Dedicated funds	**Contributions through People** • Volunteer efforts • Targeted philanthropic agenda

pany in Stage 2. Management training may accompany the roll out of flexible work options, as flexibility is not considered an entitlement; rather, it is an option permitted by the manager or supervisor.

Overall, in Stage 2, companies move away from a fragmentary approach to work and family policies; adopt an expanded, more integrated array of policies and programs; and give more attention to communicating these policy changes to their employees.

Stage 3

In Stage 3, companies recognize that an innovative set of policies and programs will be effective only if they exist within a supportive culture. Communication is a key component of a Stage 3 effort. The company expends much effort on identifying and removing mixed messages to its employees, and on aligning policy with practice. For example, a company's criteria for rewarding and recognizing employee achievement are a very powerful communication tool, but too often they convey a message that contradicts the stated purpose of the organization's work-family policy. If the criteria used for evaluating managers does not consider family and personal life, there is little accountability for supervisors in managing work-family conflict and few guidelines for employees about how to set personal priorities while also supporting business goals. A Stage 3 company recognizes that there must be fundamental changes in the way its employees are valued, promoted, and rewarded. Otherwise, the policies and programs will not only be ineffective, but there might be negative outcomes for those who use them.

In Stages 1 and 2, the thrust of the business rationale for work-life efforts is on increasing employees' productivity by reducing the distractions and problems caused by family responsibilities and work-family conflict. In Stage 3, the business rationale becomes less focused on recruitment or retention per se but rather on supporting employees' well-being, affirming the "whole person," and, thereby, enhancing commitment, creativity and individual contributions.

In keeping with the emphasis on creating an effective workplace by releasing the potential of all employees, work-family issues expand to embrace single employees, employees who don't have children as well as employees with elderly dependents. This is why many Stage 3 (and some Stage 2) companies change the terminology from "work-family" to "work-life" or "work-personal life" to include men and nontraditional families, such as gay couples, domestic partners, and grandparents raising grandchildren.

To create a Stage 3 awareness, company initiatives might include:

- An audit of all corporate communications to identify key cultural messages, paying special attention to career development and recruiting materials, performance review criteria, and company image conveyed in marketing literature (including the annual report).

- Revision of the company's mission statement to include a commitment to family and employees' well-being.

- Use of senior management communications to reinforce and sanction the idea that the company values employees' personal lives. For example, relate anecdotes or personal statements in speeches and presentations—the more often, the better.

- Senior management as role models in the community and in business. This may require coaching senior managers in how they can better "walk the talk."

- Showcasing in in-house communications, the company's "best practices" in flexibility and manager support.

- Design of marketing and sales materials that align with employee diversity efforts and the company's work-family values.

- Trained ombudsmen to help employees identify available resources in the organization that deal with work-family issues and to negotiate with managers and work teams.

Stage 3 emphasizes linkages and synergy between work-family efforts and other functions and strategic initiatives within the organization. In making these strategic alliances, the work-family label will occasionally fall away and be replaced by compatible terminology from organization effectiveness, quality improvement, or management development gurus. Without these strategic linkages, work-family issues are not likely to be understood as essential to the business. Such initiatives include:

- Audits of all ongoing functions and initiatives that address work-family goals (both implicitly or explicitly) and identify priorities for creating new collaborations and synergy.

- Work-family messages incorporated into core management training.

- Revised career development materials and performance criteria to reflect work-family concerns.

- Work-family questions included on the climate survey, 360 feedback and all employee-sensing instruments.

- Rewards to managers not only for task management, but also for their "people skills" and support of employees' personal lives.

Clearly, Stage 3 focuses on valuing employees and relationships in the organization. The only way to introduce flexibility into the organization without career penalties is to trust employees—and to trust supervisors to use good judgment in balancing the varied needs of individuals with the ongoing need to get the work done. Research finds that a climate of trust and support is key to employees' sense of well-being and balance as well as to inspiring employees' commitment and effort. Creating a climate of trust among employees and between managers and employees might involve:

- A spirit of local experimentation, or "pilots," for meeting the varied needs of work teams and individuals. In the spirit of any learning experience, making employees feel that it's safe to experiment and to learn from mistakes as well as be successful.

- Examining practices to see where individual autonomy and decision-making are needlessly restricted or penalized. Attendance and lateness policies can be liberalized to emphasize personal responsibility rather than focus on negative behavior.

- Principles of empowerment can be applied to individual time management. When evaluating people, outcomes should be emphasized rather than "face time" or time spent at the office.

- Training of employee teams for ways to help their "teammates" resolve work-family conflicts.

Stage 4

As a company becomes more and more aware of how its culture and communications are aligned with work-family goals, the logical next step is to focus on work processes themselves. Just as programs and policies are not effective unless they're carried out in a supportive culture, the real test of cultural values is in how the employees do the work and work together. At their most fundamental level, both the source of, and the solution to, work-family problems are linked to how the customer is served, how projects are planned and staffed, how work is scheduled, and how day-to-day problems are handled. A fourth stage is emerging, in which the focus shifts to work processes, and how companies are to bring a work-family perspective to daily operations and task management.

In Stage 4, there is an opportunity for companies to support creative flexibility, to identify and correct inconsistencies, and to "partner" with their employees in reengineering efforts. As a company moves into Stage 4, it starts asking some of the following questions:

- What assumptions do our work processes make about people's availability and time?

- What work-life issues arise from our method of service delivery? Can we make changes within our infrastructure that would enhance our service delivery as well as our employees' lives?

- Are there inefficiencies in how we direct our employees to plan and conduct their work? Could we be more respectful and considerate of our employees' time and still meet customer needs?

- Is the job staffed appropriately? Are our work expectations and timelines realistic? Who pays the price if they're unrealistic—the employee, the customer, or the company itself?

- When problems arise, what is our approach to solving them? Does this approach entail employee work-life considerations?

- What changes would help employee teams work together more effectively?

Moving Across the Stages

Companies at the Stage 1 and 2 levels have taken giant steps in understanding how family issues affect the workplace and what supports they can offer to reduce the negative impact of work-family conflict. However, for most Stage 1 and 2 companies, work-family issues are viewed as individual accommodations to be meted out by managers. As a result, large groups of individuals who do not want to ask for favors or accommodations in a time of high job insecurity, do not make their concerns known. As a result, the subject of meeting family needs remains marginal, largely disconnected from broader organizational goals.

The notion of work-family support as an accommodation leads to some of the problems with current practice. Employee accommodations, after all, are exceptions not mainstream practice. They are reserved for only the most "deserving" or for highly valued employees. Companies perceive work-family supports as "favors," primarily benefiting the recipients and not the organization that offers them. And since they are somewhat of an exception to the rule, companies expect payback or quid pro quo. Hence, flexible work arrangements are perceived as rewards for good performance.

However, when viewed as a business *strategy*, and not as employee accommodations, work-family efforts take on a different quality because a strategy benefits the organization. Instead of being reserved for special occasions or available only on demand, work-family policy will be used whenever the occasion merits and wherever gain can be realized. Far from being rationed, a strategy is promoted precisely because the more it is understood and the more it is used, the more the organization will benefit. When a company moves into Stages 3 and 4, it creates the opportunity for flexibility and other work-family efforts to become organizational strategies rather than individual employee accommodations.

While Stage 3 and 4 companies emphasize the strategic utility of work-family efforts, they also see their employees' needs more holistically than in Stages 1 and 2 where the intent of corporate work-family policies and practices is to make employees more available for work, absent less often, less distracted, and less conflicted by family demands. By design, these policies exact more hours from employees and greater productivity for the company.

This has led to some ironic definitions of what is "family friendly." There are companies on *Working Mother* magazine's list of best companies that, in addition to having exemplary work-family policies, give awards to "outstanding employees" because they stayed up all night or spent all weekend working. In the end, what is created is an awkward value structure that gives priority to the organization over the individual, but never realizes that the organization's needs are not being met because the individual's needs have been ignored or sacrificed. The relationship between the organization and the individual is depicted as one-directional. Addressing work and family issues, therefore, is defined simply as removing any distractions or inconveniences that might get in the way of the employee's job performance.

From the employee's perspective, work and family are parts of a whole. Unlike Stages 1 and 2, companies in Stages 3 and 4 are moving toward a more ecological view of what goes on in the lives of today's workers. Since employees' commitments and expectations have changed along with changes in the employer-employee contract, companies need to better focus on employee motivation and expectations, as well as on what it will take to inspire an individual's full contribution. Stages 3 and 4 acknowledge the fundamental reciprocity between families, the broader society, and business results. Companies at these stages begin to ask questions such as: "If work hours are strictly defined, will people feel trusted and will they take more initiative?" "If rewards and recognition are linked strongly to the number of hours worked, where do quality, creativity, and flexibility fit in?" "If a woman on maternity leave is encouraged to come back to work sooner than she or her baby are ready, will she be productive at work?"

A company will begin to ask these questions when it has accepted work-and-family issues as a strategic concern of the business, rather than as a problem to be solved or program to be implemented. It takes an enlightened leader, a compelling business case, and healthy relationships between employees and managers for movement to occur.

In individual companies, the evolution of work-family efforts as described here is a highly individualized problem-solving and discovery process. While research can alert decision makers to the major issues and options, and while competitive benchmarking can provide the incentive for broadening work-family efforts, in the end it is the business needs of companies that drive the change. These are the kinds of questions that prompt movement from Stages 1–2 to Stages 3–4, first in the minds of a handful of change makers, and gradually throughout the organization.

- Why, even after the introduction of an array of work-family programs, do employees indicate they are dissatisfied with their quality of life?

- Why are so few employees taking advantage of the policies offered?

- How does employee stress and dissatisfaction affect the organization's effectiveness?

- What kind of management is needed to respond to changing markets and globalization?

- How can the company engage employee commitment for the challenges of organizational change?

Though there are very few companies at this time that would profess mastery of Stages 3–4, most of the leadership companies now claim this as their vision for the direction of work-family efforts.

CONCLUSION

Work-family issues can provide a powerful lens for understanding organizations, but the opportunity is often obscured by mixed messages that exist between policies and the corporate culture. These inconsistencies sideline family issues at the workplace. Despite impressive growth in the number and types of work-family programs in companies today, most still think that work-family issues are diversions from the real strategic aims of the organization or, at best, some simple add-ons that can boost morale for survivors of a downsizing.

It is more important than ever for business leaders to accept the importance of work-family issues in today's corporate culture, and to consider them in their strategic planning. As companies deal with the changes brought on by globalization and technology, management must think of family needs as more than something to be appeased or accommodated. Sadly, current efforts to reengineer do not incorporate a work-family perspective and employees' work-family concerns are rarely used as levers for change.

The terminology and perspective of work-family initiatives that are focused only on programmatic efforts are inadequate at the present time. Increasingly, the focus must be on aligning work-family issues with the corporate culture and work processes within the organization. This effort is *not* about tinkering at the margins of the organization and doing something "nice" for the employees. This is *not* about restructuring and moving the boxes around. Instead, this is about *real change* that challenges long-held beliefs about ways of doing business that are out of synch with the needs of workers and the demands of competition.

Programs and services are part of an effective employer response to work-family issues, but relying on programs alone results in "solutions" that only provide marginal help, or quick, short-term fixes to their employees' family needs. Real solutions must respect the complexity of the relationship between work and family and consider the sources of conflict lying deep within the organizational infrastructure. Research and company experience are beginning to reveal that *effective* solutions call for fundamental changes in how employees are valued, assessed, managed, trained, and promoted. The focus must be on trying to understand the work environment, cultural norms, managerial practices, and work processes—that is, the factors that have been shown to be the strongest predictors of work-family conflict and stress, as well as negative work behaviors. Perhaps it is time to redefine the problem so that we can arrive at different solutions.

It is becoming clear that separating work-family issues from strategic business concerns helps neither the individual *nor* the organization. At the heart of the work-family perspective is a notion of reciprocity that speaks to the need for a more ecological view of workers and the workplace. Employees cannot be segmented into their roles as "workers" and "parents" for specific hours of the day. Rather, employees are whole human beings, whose desires for fulfillment at home and at work are inextricably linked—and must be understood if the employer is to benefit from their full contribution. Workplaces are not islands. They are affected profoundly, not only by the larger economy and workforce demographics, but also by the diverse families that shape the lives of workers and by the communities from which workers are drawn and to which they return every day.

It is this reciprocity of interests that makes work-family efforts a legitimate investment for companies. As employers incorporate an ecological, work-family perspective, they become more significant players in the broader community— to create economic value and to foster family and community well-being.

NOTES

1. While the terms *work-family* and *work/life* are today often used interchangeably, this chapter uses the term *work-family* to emphasize the particular implications for the family.

2. W.B. Johnston & A.H. Packer, *Workforce 2000: Work and Workers for the 21st Century* (Indianapolis: Hudson Institute, 1987).

3. E. Galinsky, D.E. Friedman, & C.A. Hernandez, *The Corporate Reference Guide to Work-Family Programs* (New York: Families and Work Institute, 1991).

4. E. Galinsky, J.T. Bond, & D.E. Friedman, *The Changing Workforce: Highlights of the National Study* (New York: Families and Work Institute, 1993), p. 17.

5. Ibid., p. 101.

6. Families and Work Institute, *An Evaluation of Johnson & Johnson's Work-Family Initiative* (New York: Families and Work Institute, 1993).

7. Susan J. Lambert et al., *Added Benefits: The Link between Family-Responsive Policies and Work Performance at Fel-Pro Inc* (Chicago: University of Chicago, School of Social Service Administration, 1993).

8. Galinsky et al., pp. 101–102.

9. Ibid., p. 101.

CHAPTER 19

The Impact of Corporate Culture on Work-Family Integration

Lotte Bailyn

I start this chapter with a fable.[1] It is the story of a company that only employed short people. For a long time it was very successful, but then times changed and the pool of talented short people became diminished, so it also started to hire tall people. This was a bit of a problem, however, since the door to the company was built for short people and the new, tall employees couldn't get in. What should they do? "Easy," the company said, "We'll teach them." So they started holding training sessions for the tall people, teaching them how to stoop down so that they could get into the door. And they urged the managers of these new employees to be understanding, in case the more awkward entrance of their new employees made them a little late. The company was well meaning, and it allocated time and money to this effort. No other solution occurred to anyone.

This image frames the chapter. I use it to address three questions. First, though in the fable it is obvious what it is about the door that makes life difficult for tall people, it is less clear in the work-family area. What is it about organizations that makes life so difficult for committed employees with serious outside involvements? What are the barriers? That is the first question.

Second, why is it so difficult to come to the conclusion that we must rebuild the door? The fable makes this solution obvious—which is why I use it. But in real organizational life, this is far from obvious. On the contrary, our main effort has gone into providing policies designed to ease the physical burden that the door places on tall employees and training them and their managers in the techniques of stooping.

Finally, I want to look at the role of the door in the whole building and to place work-family concerns in the context of the larger efforts at organizational transformation that are underway today in American business.

Figure 19.1
Time and Managerial Control in Three Work Sites

	WORK SITE			
	PDT	**CAC**	**SSD**	
			Sales	**Service**
Time	long	rigid	long	uncertainty
Control	statusing	surveillance	targets	beeper

Note: PDT—product development team; CAC—customer administration center; SSD—sales/
service district.

The data on which I base many of my observations stem from a research project in which my colleagues and I have been engaged for the last few years.[2] This project, supported by the Ford Foundation, has attempted to identify the cultural barriers that make it so difficult to rebuild the work-family door. We worked at three sites in the Xerox Corporation. They were all quite different from each other, and they dealt with work-family issues in different ways.

One is an engineering group—part of a product development team—that was developing a new product under a very tight schedule, part of the effort of the company to reduce its time to market. This was a heavily male environment where work-family issues were not uppermost in people's minds. There was a good deal of ad hoc flexibility for occasional personal needs, but the presumption was that these would be kept to a minimum and that work needs would always have first priority.[3]

The customer administration center that we studied was quite different. The task here was relatively routine and consisted of sitting at a computer in order to deal with customer issues on billing, scheduling, and so on. The workforce was primarily female, and work-family issues were very salient. Work hours were kept to a fixed period, but there was very little flexibility within those bounds.[4]

The third site was a sales and service district. The goal here was to produce revenue (via the sales team) and to ensure customer satisfaction by means of timely installations and efficient service (via the service staff). The two groups were quite different. The sales staff was approximately evenly divided between men and women. They had to respond to ever-increasing sales targets, which were set centrally and monitored monthly. Service workers were primarily blue-collar men. They were on 24-hour call via beepers, and committed to a 2-hour response time.[5]

I use these examples to explore cultural barriers to work-family integration and to understand how they play themselves out in these different settings. I start by analyzing the culture surrounding time and managerial control in each of these sites (see Figure 19.1).

One obvious barrier to a less stressful work-family integration is the way that time is used and understood in organizations. Putting in time—being visibly at work, often for long hours—is seen as a sign of commitment, of loyalty, of competence and high potential, and in many cases as an indicator, in and of itself, of productive output. In the product development team, managers clearly assumed that employee time belonged to the company: they would hold meetings early in the morning, late at night, or over weekends, and they felt they could legitimately expect their engineers to put in as many hours as they thought the work required. Indeed, if engineers finished their deliverables within a normal time span, it was not assumed that they had been efficient and creative—on the contrary, it was assumed that they had not been given enough work to do.

Obviously, such a culture made men and women with "hard stops" (as it was known at this site)—that is, those who had to leave at certain times because of family obligations—appear as less committed, perhaps even less competent. And yet, one of the key findings of this study was that there were some people, often those with external constraints on their time, who worked in ways that actually were more productive and more important for getting a complex product out the door.[6] But their efforts were not recognized. As one astute engineer observed: "If there are two people of equal performance, the promotion will go to the one who has put in the overtime. But that means it took that person longer to get the same level of performance, so the other guy is the better one. It makes no sense."

Long hours were also a problem for the sales group, where commitment is measured by the amount of time "on the street"—only by putting in the time, it was felt, could the targets be met. But this is not the only way that cultural assumptions about time can constrain people's ability to integrate work with family. At the customer administration center, time was also seen as a sign of commitment, but here it took the form, not of long hours, but of never being late or absent. Indeed, these were carefully measured—again a barrier for those with caring responsibilities to which they had to respond. For service employees, the time issue that made their family lives difficult was its uncertainty. They never knew when they might be called to work unexpectedly or when they would be on a service call that required them to work well into what they had expected to be their free time. In all cases, the assumptions concerning time, deeply embedded in the work culture of each site, created difficulties for employees' private lives.[7]

This emphasis on visible time resides in the way managers define control—which is a second cultural barrier to work-family integration. The conviction that managers must closely monitor the way their subordinates are working makes any kind of accommodation to personal needs more difficult. The careful count of absences and lateness at the customer administration center is one manifestation of this control. So is the fact that despite a full array of available family policies, the only one deemed compatible with business needs was a shift of up to an hour at the beginning and end of the day. This belief in the necessity to supervise the way employees do their jobs, meant, for one manager, that she had to be around for all the hours that her employees worked—which, needless to say, did not make her very supportive of the requests by her subordinates for any great variety in working hours.

In the engineering site, too, control was an issue, though here it took a different form. Statusing—reporting on the status of work to one's supervisor and preparing for reviews by higher management—was the vehicle for control at this more professional site. Managers were always interrupting their engineers to discover whether they were on schedule, what problems they might encounter, and how they might deal with them. These then were reviewed in meetings and incorporated into elaborately prepared reports that went up the managerial ladder, all of which contributed to the long hours at this site.

Control in sales was through the process of setting targets and tying compensation to meeting them. In service, in contrast, control was enforced through hours worked, supported by federal legislation governing overtime. In both cases, accounting was highly individual and precluded possibilities for collaboration that might have eased the pressures on these employees.

But perhaps the greatest cultural barrier—the most important feature of the work-family door—is the definition of "work-family" itself. The issue is framed as ensuring that certain people with particular family needs (primarily mothers of young children) need some help in meeting the needs of work as currently defined (need help to get through the existing door). Underlying this belief is the view that having children is a private choice, has nothing to do with business or society, and therefore is a strictly individual concern. At its worst, this set of assumptions gets translated into the view that women who have children should stay at home to care for them, and if they are so greedy for material goods that they have to go to work, then they should not have them—a view expressed by some of the older men in our study. More benignly, but anchored in the same underlying position, is the statement of one female engineering manager that it was her choice to have three children, so if she had problems with a particular job, she had no reason to complain.

This deeply held set of beliefs is part of our business and national culture. Work is work and family is family—and basically, the two do not mix. Moreover, women are primarily in charge of family, and men of work. This gendered separation of the world of paid employment from that of private care is at the heart of how work-family issues are framed. "Work-family" is defined as an issue of family rather than of work, and is seen as relevant primarily to women, particularly those with children. Successful workers are those who keep a strict separation between work and family, and whose family concerns never intrude into the workplace. One woman manager told us with pride that her work colleagues did not even know that she had children. Given this set of beliefs, any accommodation that needs to be made is done by the individual, in private, with occasional help from a manager.[8]

I do not deny the value of these individual accommodations and the usefulness of the family policies that allow them to be made. On the contrary, given the current state, they are critical—life would be considerably worse if they did not exist. After all, if tall people are going to work in our companies, we need to help them get through the door. My point, rather, is that these family-friendly accommodations have an ironic, unintended consequence: they keep us from rebuilding the door. They reinforce the complete separation of family from work, and reaffirm the myths that work-family concerns are women's concerns, to be dealt with at the margins in individualistic, not systemic, ways. Thus, they keep us from understanding the strategic nature of these issues, and divert us from looking at the conditions of work that make such accommodations necessary in the first place.

I have come to think of these dynamics as self-reinforcing ironies. The very practices that, in the short run, are meant to help employees' work-family concerns actually support the work systems that undermine them in the first place. Let me give you a few examples from our research of how this works.

Engineers in the product development team, whose work hours included evening, night, and weekend work (one woman—a mother of three—came in at 2:00 A.M. once each week, since this was the only way she knew how to get the uninterrupted time she needed to meet her individual work goals), were fully aware of the toll this work schedule was taking on their personal lives. But they told themselves that this was only a temporary measure necessitated by a particular crisis situation at work. Framing the situation as temporary—contrary to the evidence, I should add—resulted in denying the necessity to look at the reasons why the work in this unit was in a perpetual state of crisis.[9] This framing, therefore, inadvertently reinforced the underlying condition that brought about the need for long hours. It prevented people from serious reconsideration of their way of working, which also made it difficult for this unit to meet the corporate goal of shortening time to market.

In the customer administration center, the rigid adherence to limited flextime as the only possible way to meet work-family concerns actually increased the degree of absence and tardiness, which was of significant concern in this unit. People had to deal with personal issues, and when they were denied the ability to find a schedule that allowed them to do this in ways compatible with meeting their work goals, their only choice was to deal with them on an ad hoc basis.

In the sales/service district, the highly individualistic, competitive culture meant that sales and service did not share the information each needed to meet their business goals of revenues and customer satisfaction or to deal with their personal issues around the conditions of their work. One service technician, for example, found that he had spent hours servicing a machine that sales was about to replace; and sales representatives had no way of tapping into the customer knowledge available to the service workers. This lack of critical information contributed to the stress and uncertainty of these jobs.

In some small way, our work at these sites made an inroad into changing these underlying dynamics. At the customer administration center, our work led the division manager to experiment with opening up all available work-family policies to every employee as long as the work groups met their stated work goals. The result was that men as well as women changed their schedules, and absences dropped by 30%. Moreover, this change had an effect on the culture of control at that site. Now, work groups had to decide jointly about their schedules, which moved work-family issues from a purely individual, to a more collective, level. This change has meant a shift of control from the manager to the work group—a change in the direction of creating the self-managed teams that have been the goal at this site.[10]

At the engineering site, we worked with a group of software engineers in a series of experimental interventions, which set aside particular times for engineers to work on their individual deliverables as well as set times for interactions.[11] This kept the degree of interruptions down, and allowed the group to achieve, despite expectations to the contrary, an on-time launch of the product. It also has led to a reconsideration of which interactions are critical for the work and which are not, and made the engineers and their managers appreciate the difference between necessary interactions and unnecessary interruptions, which resulted in much less statusing by managers and many fewer top management reviews. In both of these sites, we started with issues concerning time. But the end result was to change managerial behavior and to shift the cultural expectations about control.

Finally, at the sales/service district the situation was somewhat different. In this case, time per se was not the focus of the intervention. Rather, we collaborated with management to establish a cross-functional team focused on one particular product group. Despite initial negative stereotypes of each other, the team members learned to appreciate their interdependence and to share information more knowledgeably. This allowed them to make a sale to a customer who had been about to switch to another company, and permitted the group to meet their targeted expectations for the first time in a number of years. It also meant that both groups were more able to begin to plan their own time and to have more assurance that their plans could be adhered to.[12]

I do not want to suggest that these issues have now been solved at these sites. On the contrary, the old ways are still operative, and there are many self-reinforcing ironies that still exist in the system. Changes such as these are difficult to bring about and take a long time, and I cannot say that they have been institutionalized. The results at the customer administration center are the most lasting, and there are aspects of the changes that persist at the other sites. The examples do show, however, that a different way of thinking about work-family issues can have positive results, not only for employees' family and personal concerns, but also for business goals.

The trouble is that the beliefs (I would call them myths) that ''work-family'' is an individual issue, concerns mainly women (especially those with children), refers only to family, and is basically separate from work—these beliefs are very strong. And we are not aware that our current practices perpetuate these myths and thus make it difficult to see that rebuilding the door may be the only real solution to these problems.

Let me, therefore, tell you some of the other findings from our work at this company—because I think they are quite general in American industry. Ironically, the sensitive manager who provides individual accommodations to selected employees inadvertently perpetuates these myths and the status quo in which they are embedded. The very act of providing individual and ad hoc flexibilities—"jiggling" the system, as it was called at one of our sites—creates dynamics that undermine any attempt to rebuild the door. This happens, I think, through two mechanisms. The first is the understanding exhibited by the manager, and the second is the gratitude engendered in the employee.[13]

Let me explain what I mean. A manager can be very understanding of the need of an employee (particularly a woman with children) to be unable to stay at a meeting that lasts beyond 5:00 P.M. But if he nonetheless continues to hold this meeting, he contributes to the view that those with family constraints on time are less important employees and probably, also, less competent. Only by not holding meetings at such a time could such a situation be dealt with equitably, and that would require a rethinking of the use of meetings in the work of the unit—namely, a rebuilding of the door.

Such individual accommodations, further, lead to gratitude on the part of employees—obviously if they did not have such understanding managers, their lives would be considerably worse. But gratitude makes it even harder to consider asking for work changes (for instance, in meeting times) and thus reinforces the marginality of these issues and the disinclination to bring them to the fore.[14] It also makes less likely any reconsideration of existing work practices.

Consider, also, the role of Human Resource (HR) departments. They have provided the necessary policies and programs and the guidelines on how to use them. All must be approved by an employee's manager and are subject to business need—in whatever way it is currently defined. Training films to help managers deal with these situations emphasize the individual accommodations that can be made. This approach—though critically important at the present time—nonetheless perpetuates the existing framing of the work-family issue as individual and as unrelated to the work of the unit. In no way does this emphasis help redefine business needs in directions that meet both organizational and employee goals; nor does it challenge the pervasive presumption that in order to succeed, you have to make your family invisible. Further, by trying to protect upper management from having to engage these issues, HR departments contribute to the complete separation of work-family issues from strategic thinking about work.

These are the kind of self-reinforcing ironies that perpetuate the current system and make it more difficult to think about rebuilding the door. In order to overcome this inertia we need to think of work-family issues not as individual but as systemic—as part of the overall organization and culture of work. This means that these are concerns, not only of women, but of all employees. Nor can they be based on a narrow definition of need—either of employee need (as, for example, the care of children) or of business need (defined as doing things the way they have always been done). It means a shift from considering the structure of work as given to an emphasis on reconfiguring work—around the task, rather than around time, and including the personal requirements of employees as an integral part of the equation.

In some ways, the current attempt at transforming American business organizations—what is generally called reengineering—comes close to this goal, but with one important difference. It ignores completely the personal situation in which today's employees find themselves. And this brings me to the last question I want to address—and the last, most general, irony.

The top part of Figure 19.2 (A) depicts the reengineering effort. These are the pressures that are leading companies to rethink their work processes in order to be able to "do more with less" and thus become more competitive. The effect on the individual (B) is supported anecdotally—the stress that individuals feel in the current climate is palpable whenever one deals with an organization that is going through this process. What is completely below the line—out of awareness—is the role that family, community, and personal needs are playing in this process (C). And this is where the ultimate irony lies. For the forces stemming from employees' private lives do have an effect on what the company is trying to do: the pressure they exert on employees' concentration and peace of mind actually decreases the productivity and the quality of work, and they affect cost containment through unplanned absences. Further, the efforts at cost containment are themselves increasing the pressures on employees and their families. So a vicious cycle is established. The beneath-the-line, unrecognized needs are actually undermining the goals of the reengineering effort. This results in a deterioration of the competitive situation, which leads to even more stringent efforts at reengineering, which further increases the pressure on employees. It is a system ready to explode. What keeps it in check—so far—are the efforts by companies to deal separately, and disconnected from the rest of the transformation process, with family concerns. And this, as I have tried to indicate, only serves to reinforce the conditions that cause these problems.[15]

This is the larger situation as I see it. The only solution, in my opinion, is to bring the "family" needs above the line and include them up front in the reconsideration of the way work is organized. This is what we have tried to do in our project, on a small scale, in local sites. There, we have had some success. Though diffusing such thinking throughout an organization may not be easy, it is clear from these examples that looking at work through a work-family lens releases creative energy that not only eases employees' lives, but makes the work more effective. After the success of the cross-functional team in the sales/service district, for example, we were told that management had previously tried such a team, and it had failed. What, they asked us, is the difference? The

Figure 19.2
Creating a Vicious Cycle

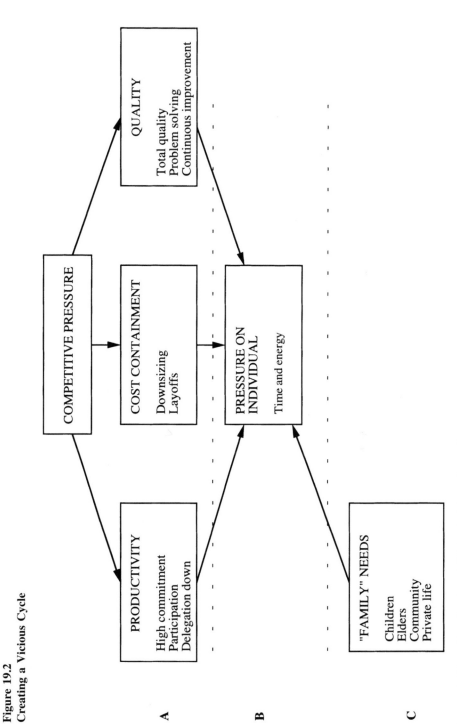

Source: L. Bailyn, *Breaking the Mold* (New York: Free Press, 1993), p. 113.

difference, we replied, is the strategic linking of employees' personal lives with key business goals.[16]

One of the managers we were working with in our project, after we had explained what we were doing in some detail, indicated that it was revolutionary. He realized that to seriously consider the personal concerns of all employees as fully legitimate would require redesigning many habitual ways of working: the way we schedule, allocate, and evaluate work, as well as the way we define what we consider to be valuable work in the first place. Such comprehensive change in work practices is what I mean by rebuilding the door. Though not easy, I think it will be necessary in order to derail the vicious cycle in which I now see us, where everything—family and community, as well as productivity—is in danger of being undermined.

NOTES

1. I am indebted to Deborah Kolb for alerting me to this formulation.

2. This project was supported by the Ford Foundation under grant #910-1036. The research team consisted of myself, Deborah Kolb, Joyce Fletcher, Maureen Harvey, Susan Eaton, Robin Johnson, and Leslie Perlow, with Rhona Rapoport as the consultant. See L. Bailyn et al., *Re-linking Work and Family: A Catalyst for Organizational Change* (Sloan School of Management Working Paper #3892-96, 1996) and R. Rapoport & L. Bailyn et al., *Relinking Life and Work: Toward a Better Future* (New York: Ford Foundation, 1996). The project was a full team effort, and everyone contributed to the ideas in this chapter. See also L. Bailyn, *Breaking the Mold: Women, Men and Time in the New Corporate World* (New York: Free Press, 1993) for a precursor to this project.

3. See J. Fletcher, "Toward a Theory of Relational Practice in Organizations: A Feminist Reconstruction of 'Real' Work" (doctoral dissertation, Boston University, 1994), and L. Perlow, "The Time Famine: An Unintended Consequence of the Way Time Is Used at Work" (doctoral dissertation, MIT, 1995), for detailed reports about this site.

4. See R. Johnson, "Where's the Power in Empowerment? Definition, Difference and Dilemmas of Empowerment in the Context of Work-Family Management" (doctoral dissertation, Harvard University, 1994), for a description of this site.

5. The work at this site was done primarily by Maureen Harvey and Susan Eaton. See Bailyn et al., *Re-Linking Work and Family*, for more details.

6. Fletcher, "Toward a Theory of Relational Practice."

7. See Perlow, "The Time Famine," for a general discussion of time in the workplace.

8. Bailyn, *Breaking the Mold*; J. Fletcher & L. Bailyn, "Challenging the Last Boundary: Re-Connecting Work and Family," in M.B. Arthur & D.M. Rousseau (eds.), *The Boundaryless Career: A New Employment Principle for a New Organizational Era* (Oxford: Oxford University Press, 1996); J. Fletcher & R. Rapoport, "Work-Family Issues as a Catalyst for Organizational Change," in S. Lewis & J. Lewis (eds.), *The Work-Family Challenge: Rethinking Employment* (London: Sage, 1996).

9. I am indebted to Leslie Perlow for this formulation.

10. Johnson, "Where's the Power in Empowerment?"

11. Perlow, "The Time Famine."

12. This work, done mainly by Susan Eaton and Maureen Harvey, is described in detail in Bailyn et al., *Re-Linking Work and Family*.

13. Johnson, "Where's the Power in Empowerment?"

14. Dana Friedman, of the Families and Work Institute, refers to this as "the grateful dead."

15. This is a classic "shifting the burden" archetype: see P.M. Senge, *The Fifth Discipline: The Art and Practice of the Learning Organization* (New York: Doubleday/ Currency, 1990).

16. Rapoport and Bailyn et al., *Relinking Life and Work*.

CHAPTER 20

Shared Responsibility for Managing Work and Family Relationships: A Community Perspective

Bradley K. Googins

Work-and-family has become a widely understood concept in the United States over the past decade, due in large part to the emergence of a corporate role in responding to the needs of a new generation of working parents. Private sector leadership, in creating what are often referred to as "family-friendly" corporations, has broken down long-held traditional values that argued for the separation of work and family as independent domains.[1] While this corporate involvement has been driven by self-interest in ensuring a highly productive workforce, it continues to evolve, both as a concept and as a corporate program and strategy.

During the early stages of corporate work and family development, the focus was primarily on a few specific issues such as child care and dual career stress.[2] Over time, the work-and-family umbrella embraced a considerably wider spectrum of issues ranging from the care of elders to latchkey children, and more recently, to a comprehensive set of benefits that begin to resemble a social welfare system. As the benefits focus of work-and-family increased, a parallel stage of corporate culture change began to address the environment of the firm within which work-and-family operated, and issues such as flexibility and alternative work schedules began to receive increased attention.[3] During this period of intense activity, the very term "work-and-family" became a household word, due in part to the media's constant attention to work and family issues.

It is the major premise of this chapter that the set of activities that launched the work-and-family field over the past decade constitute but the first phase of an evolving concept of work-and-family, a phase that can best be considered one of raising awareness within the corporation, and the development of benefits as a hallmark of the corporate response to work-and-family. During this phase, work-and-family moved from becoming a nonissue to a discussible one, from remaining invisible within the corporate environment to becoming one of the fastest growing components of corporate benefits.

However, as work-and-family has become more institutionalized within the corporation, a more robust stakeholder analysis reveals a considerably broadened concept of work-and-family, one that moves beyond the confines of the firm to include the larger community environment. What has begun to emerge more recently on the periphery of the work-and-family movement is a growing real-ization of the limits of corporate involvement, the inadequacy of a corporate-driven model, and a faint vision of a more comprehensive approach to the needs of work, family, and community. As the contours of the next phase of work-and-family emerge, they suggest a more active involvement of the community sector through a focus on community-based institutions and a reframing of cor-porate work-family initiatives within a public policy framework. The inclusion of the community within the work-and-family model leads to an exciting set of challenges during this next stage of development within work-and-family.

THE FRAGMENTATION OF WORK-AND-FAMILY: A STAKEHOLDER ANALYSIS

Kanter's treatise on the separate worlds of work and family was largely re-sponsible for the conceptual underpinnings of work-and-family as it has become framed within today's world. The myth of separate worlds of work and family had served as a formidable barrier in preventing the issues of families from becoming recognized as legitimate within the workplace. The revolution con-cerning work-and-family that began in the mid-1970's ushered in an era in which issues, such as child care and elder care, that had been relegated largely to the family were now squarely on the corporate agenda. Conflict between work roles and family roles became exacerbated, and a new work and family role system began to emerge.[4] However, as the awareness of the interdependence of the work and family spheres increased, work and family roles and responsibil-ities became more fragmented among the various stakeholders.

The broadening of both the scope and the locus of work and family roles and responsibilities beyond the family has been focused almost exclusively on the corporation and the private sector. Families and workplaces are often seen as active participants, if not partners. However, there are additional stakeholders, some of whom have not yet been perceived as stakeholders or claimed owner-ship of these issues. These stakeholders can be found, neither in the family nor in the workplace, but in the community, broadly defined, that surrounds both the family and the workplace. It is the contention of this chapter that the com-munity is the forgotten stakeholder; that, in effect, the community constitutes a critical partner along with the family and the workplace. It will further contend that the future of work and family is tied to an active community role, and that in order for work-and-family to achieve its full potential within the social and economic system of the United States, it will have to reconfigure the current conceptual model on which work-and-family is built, and include the community as an active third sphere.

By examining the spheres or domains of the workplace, the family, and the community, it becomes clear that each of these spheres perceives work-and-family through a different lens. While all of these lenses are legitimate perspectives on the larger picture of work-and-family, and tend to intersect with each other in the work-and-family model, they are nevertheless different from one another.

The Corporation as Stakeholder

The work-and-family issue is defined and operationalized as a business issue through the corporate lens. The corporation, in an attempt to achieve its profit-driven goals, sees the set of issues falling under the work-and-family rubric as related to the achievement (or barriers toward achievement) of its goals. As with any other corporate activity, a particular work-and-family benefit, or even the package of benefits or policies is viewed through a productivity screen related to return on investment (ROI).

The emergence of the concept of the "family-friendly corporation" signaled the beginning of an active corporate role.[5] Why the corporation should be friendly to the family other than as an attempt to be courteous can be examined from a number of perspectives. While the rationale of involvement can be tied to the business case, there are other driving forces that help explain the adoption of these roles within the corporation. A corporate decision to respond to work and family issues is not necessarily based on a single objective measure of productivity or on ROI. Rather, it is based on productivity, wrapped around other measures, and corporate values that are held in high esteem within the organization such as employee morale, commitment, loyalty, and so on.[6]

The initial corporate experience concerning work-and-family was that of being confronted with a new set of corporate demographics, particularly the difficulty of working women with dependent care responsibilities in carrying out both work and home roles simultaneously. Thus the corporate response was cast primarily to offset the negative impacts of women's nonwork roles (and, increasingly, men's) on their work roles. The concept of the family-friendly corporation marks the recognition of the connection between employees' personal and family roles and their performance and productivity at work. Although data supporting this linkage remains thin and not well developed, the growth in family-focused benefits and work-family initiatives within most large corporations speaks to the acceptance of work-and-family as a business issue.[7]

Corporations also look at this issue through an external lens. In today's competitive environment, work-and-family becomes a strategy for ensuring a competitive advantage in attracting and retaining employees, and for developing a positive public image. Over the past several years, corporations have used the development of family-focused benefits to develop a corporate image of family-friendliness. By some measure, this has taken on the air of becoming politically correct in ensuring inclusion on the family-friendly bandwagon. The quest for inclusion in the *Working Mother* magazine list of the top companies for working women is one example of how the corporation at the very least seeks to project an image of being a family-friendly corporation. To an extent, this public relations strategy is congruent with the overall business strategy of linking work-and-family to the business case; but that is a subject for another day.[8]

The Family as a Stakeholder

Families are, as one might expect, a primary stakeholder, positioned at the heart of work-and-family. Through their lens, the primary challenge is the balancing of job roles and responsibilities with those of the home while ensuring a high degree of family well-being. Because of strong cultural and ideological values, the family has been perceived, within American lore, as an independent and self-resilient entity, not to be interfered with by either an excessively intrusive government or a paternalistic workplace. Left to their own out of virtue, families now are confronted with a new set of roles and responsibilities at work and home that were unimaginable to those early pioneers, who left to carve out an existence with nature. They are constantly negotiating and reacting to complex and quickly changing environments on both the home and work fronts. By most accounts, the family continues to experience a considerable degree of stress, despite a growing recognition of work-family stress, and new responses by family-friendly corporations.[9]

The past decade in particular has accentuated such stress for families at work and home. Unparalleled technological change and global competition have revolutionized, not just the workplace, but the very nature of work, careers, and working lives. Simultaneously, families have been confronted with social and economic forces at home that have created an even greater strain on achieving family well-being. The growing sense of insecurity at home and at work contributes towards an uncertain and less structured environment surrounding family life. Consequently, most families experience the work-and-family challenge in isolation, with relatively few supports, and with limited assistance from resources outside the family.

The Community as a Stakeholder

Communities are perhaps the least involved conceptually in the work-and-family domain, and have not yet become active stakeholders. Through their lens, work-and-family has been dominated by both families and corporations, and they have remained primarily on the sidelines. The community can be viewed as comprising both the informal and formal systems that support family life, from schools to family service agencies and hospitals to friends, bowling leagues, and civic organizations. Today, much of that informal system has eroded. Those who traditionally carried out these roles within the community are more frequently unavailable in the workplace today, and have little time to provide such supports. Neighborhood life is virtually empty during working hours, and cannot support children, the ill, or the infirm.

As the traditional informal supports, such as neighbors sitting on stoops and barn raisings, have virtually disappeared in modern life, formal institutions have been created through both government and nonprofit arenas to fill that vacuum. However, an increased government role runs counter to the long-standing ideology of a minimalist government in the United States, not to mention the prevailing movement to cut back even further what role government is currently carrying out. In addition, as Drucker and others have observed, government as an agency to run social services has also proven to be almost totally incompetent.[10]

If, however, communities, both formal and informal, constitute an essential component for mediating and supporting working families, then the fault lines that have developed over the past decades signal ominous news for families struggling to relieve stress brought on by uncompromising work and family roles and responsibilities. As presently constituted, communities remain, not only a silent partner in the work and family arena, but one that has neither been appreciated nor exploited in a broader conception of work and family. Consequently, communities have neither the supporting ideology and motivation, nor the mechanisms, by which work and family can be integrated within their domain.

TOWARD AN INTEGRATED MODEL OF WORK, FAMILY, AND COMMUNITY

When work-and-family is removed from a parochial setting and examined through a broader lens of work, family, and community, a more systemic model begins to emerge. Although the leadership for work-and-family has been most recently exercised by exemplary corporations in the private sector, few would be prepared to argue that the care of children and frail elders, for example, is the primary concern of the corporate sector. Likewise, few would argue that the community or the government should play no role in supporting families. This conception of public/private roles dominated our society three generations earlier, when education was the primary responsibility of the family. The advent of public education as it is known today was brought about as a response to the changing circumstances of a newly industrialized society in which families could no longer offer home schooling and carry out their roles in this new work environment.

In the revolution of work and home life that has emerged over the past decade, a more contemporary set of challenges is brought to the shifting roles of public

Figure 20.1
Current Corporate-Focused Model

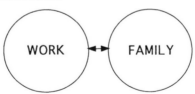

and private sectors. Families who had borne the principal responsibilities for competing work and home demands began to find existing strategies and arrangements increasingly dysfunctional as women, the traditional caregivers, entered the paid workforce. As these issues spilled over into the workplace in terms of absenteeism, tardiness, increased stress, and difficulties in attracting and maintaining high-performing employees, the corporation began to respond to protect and preserve its productivity goals through a family-friendly strategy that spoke to its self-interest. This led to the adoption of new corporate roles and brought on the day of the family-friendly corporation.

During this same time period, the community sector stayed largely on the sidelines, and neither the government nor the nonprofit sector assumed any role of note in work-and-family, or were looked to for carrying out these roles. However, as corporations began to increase their visibility and roles in this arena, the limitations of their involvement are beginning to become clearer, and the downsides of a corporate-driven family-friendly model increasingly look to the community sector for resolution.

All of this discussion serves as prologue in suggesting that the evolution of work-and-family has reached a new stage of development in which the existing corporate-driven model needs to be reexamined in light of the changing environments that surround both families and workplaces. (See Figure 20.1.) What has begun a decade earlier as a corporate response to employees with increasing levels of work and family stress has led to a creative and highly energized organizational response of family-focused benefits and policies. However expansive this model might become, and even with the addition of benefit after benefit, the corporation cannot, and should not, be the sole proprietor of work-and-family concerns. A more realistic analysis of the stakeholders surrounding work-and-family suggest an alternative model that would significantly broaden the community sector. (See Figure 20.2.)

The current corporate focused model faces a number of inherent deficiencies.

1. Work-and-family issues such as child care are not corporate issues per se. Rather, they are essentially public policy issues that have found their way into the corporate arena as the result of a minimalist government model in the United States.

Figure 20.2
Corporate-Community-Family Model

2. Any attempt to place the sole, or even the major, responsibility for work-and-family on one sphere, such as the corporation, will fail. Such a narrow conception of stakeholders recognizes neither the essential roles that each of the current stakeholders plays, nor the critical nature of their interdependence.

3. The current attempts to address work-and-family issues within a corporate model is limited to a relatively narrow band of employees and their family. The vast majority of citizens remain unsupported by family resources such as those found in the small number of family-friendly corporations.

4. Without an organized constituency, there can be little change in the current model. At present, there are few organized groups that can speak to work-and-family issues, and even fewer with the political or economic power necessary to achieve desired changes.

In contrasting the two models, several significant differences exist. First, there are three equal partners in the new corporate-community-family model. This not only deviates from the highly involved and enmeshed corporate model, but links the three major stakeholders together in a mutually reinforcing set of roles and responsibilities. In a word, the new model creates a genuine partnership among families, corporations, and communities.

Second, the community, the government, and the nonprofit sector play critical roles within this model. Whereas the community had been at best a silent partner, and virtually uninvolved with the work and family agenda, it now steps to stage-center.

Third, the relationship among the three is mutual. No longer will workplaces offer work and family benefits simply to help their employees manage their family roles, or to ensure a minimal level of interference with corporate goals. Each partner both gives and gets in this relationship, thus creating a series of mutually beneficial roles and responsibilities.

Success in bringing in the community sector to a work-and-family framework, however, faces a number of major obstacles. If there is reluctance for the cor-

poration to become involved with family issues, there is an even greater ideological and cultural set of beliefs present in American society that government
in particular should play a minimalist role in family matters. This ideology, as
operationalized in both national and local policies, is quite distinctive from that
of other industrialized nations, in which government plays a very active role in
responding to work and family needs.[11] American democracy at its core continues to be driven by values that place a premium on individual self-reliance and
self-sufficiency.

Until the recent surge of the family-friendly corporation, the community has
been the primary support and backup for family growth and development. Work-
and-family issues such as child care and tending to ill family members have
traditionally been met by an extensive network of formal and informal supports.
These resources provided both the supports and the flexibility for families to
balance work and home responsibilities. However changes in the social fabric
of American society began to weaken the fabric of the community sector. As
family mobility created greater distances between family and kin, and as the
informal community gatekeepers entered the workforce, the community system
of informal supports gradually began to disappear, rendering the family more
isolated and unsupported, unable to assume the demands of work and continue
to provide the care giving necessary for family well-being. It is unlikely that
the informal system of community supports will be established in light of today's changing culture. It is even less likely that the government will increase
its role in providing such supports.

However bleak the prospect of reestablishing community as an essential component of work and family, it is the contention of this chapter that community
has to be brought into the work and family arena as an active partner. Unless
the community, including both government and nonprofit organizations, assumes
a more proactive role and refocuses its institutions, there is little likelihood that
either the family or the workplace can adequately respond to the set of issues
facing working families and achieve a higher level of family well-being.

IMPLICATIONS OF A COMMUNITY-FOCUSED WORK-AND-FAMILY MODEL

Creating new alternatives that can fill the gap of those traditional informal
support mechanisms will be no small feat. Because our national ideology and
lore have so grounded our perception and images of family life within these
informal mechanisms, creating new mechanisms that fit the demands of contemporary family life will not be easy. While trying to support and encourage the
continuance of these informal systems, a new, community-based model will
necessitate new attitudes and require behaviors through those formal systems to
become more responsive to families. Thus, schools, for example, will have to
better understand the demands of working parents and how the former can adapt
and change to meet these new family needs. Scheduling of appointments, and

more flexible hours of institutions such as city hall, health agencies, and family service programs can become considerably more family focused. Asking all community-based institutions to focus on families in much the same way that family-friendly corporations have done at the workplace would provide a much-needed relief to those families who currently are literally home and on their own when it comes to feeling support from their communities.

Reframing work-and-family as a community issue in effect changes the calculus for work-and-family, broadening the boundaries and forcing the field to confront the larger system issues such as family policy and citizenship. As community becomes a partner with corporations and the family, it reorients the very conception of work and family as an issue cutting across workplaces, communities, and families, and forces a new public/private response to the broad range of work-and-family issues. If work-and-family is a legitimate issue for all citizens, then a model of family benefits based solely on a corporate model cannot be the basis for creating such responses. Work-and-family is legitimately a public policy concern. New partnerships can be created with almost no existing community institution. Why can't communities, like corporations, develop visible programs and benefits for working families that would draw off specific partnerships both with institutions such as schools, libraries, health clinics, and with corporations, unions, and not for profit groups such as Lions and YMCA?

The inclusion of a community focus opens up the work-and-family agenda to consider a number of new approaches, populations, and strategies not now possible under the more narrowly defined corporate model.

- *Working poor*: A significant minority of employees are working at or just above a sustainable level of income for supporting families. Many of these families have complex work-and-family lives, quite different from those who work in large corporations, where generous benefit plans are in place and where work-and-family initiatives create additional support. The working poor do not generally work in family-friendly corporations and are not well represented in work-and-family initiatives.

- *Welfare as work-and-family*: Work-and-family can also be viewed within a community context when considering the current issues that surround the heated debate on welfare. Getting citizens off the dole and back to work, to use the current rhetoric, has generally been a discussion focusing on entitlements, extended dependency of single mothers on government support, and the dysfunctional aspects of a welfare system that seems to have led to a surge in illegitimate births, fatherless homes, and a perpetuation of poverty.

However, an alternative framework for the welfare issues could be cast within a work-and-family framework. For that part of our population currently receiving public assistance, their work-and-family issues are generally the absence of a job, the need for job training, and a community environment not conducive to family well-being. By shifting the focus from a values-driven discussion that examines the deficits of a broken system to one of developing a new strategy for addressing the work-and-family issues of a vulnerable population unprepared and unable to participate in the mainstream of family and work life, much of the angry rancor and rhetoric surrounding the current debate may well be diffused and channeled into more productive approaches.

- *Revised role of government*: Currently, public policies on work-and-family are barely visible in the United States. The recent passage of the Family and Medical Leave Act is the rare exception, and that was instituted over considerable dissension among private sector corporations. At the state level, a few states had instituted local versions of family and medical leave prior to the national legislation, but even at the state and local level, public policy has remained relatively mute on work and family issues.

By including the community in the work and family equation, the role of government on both the local and national level becomes discussable. If government has a legitimate role in assisting working families, as it does in other countries, then a more rational examination of trade-offs can be contemplated between public, private, and family roles and responsibilities. Current policy is almost exclusively driven by a corporate work-and-family model. By bringing a public sector voice into the picture, a community-based model would be able to develop that would both work with the current, corporate, family-friendly model and more accurately reflect the needs of all citizens.

- *Family-focused institutions*: Community institutions such as schools, social service agencies, and municipal government are critical for ensuring family well-being. However, most of these institutions have not acknowledged or adapted to the changing needs of working parents. Creating family friendly institutions which can respond more creatively to these families would go a long way in reducing the stress of working families.

- *Family impact statement*: Not unlike the monitoring of the physical environment, a family impact statement would monitor community institutions and infrastructure to assess family well-being and the social and economic environments critical for families in balancing work-and-family demands. Such a statement would include criteria for monitoring policies and institutions that would examine the program or policy impact on its family focus. Does this policy have positive impacts on family growth and well being? Has this institution (such as a school) developed visible policies and practices that encourage family participation and involvement?

SUMMARY AND CONCLUSIONS: MOVING TOWARD A FAMILY-FRIENDLY SOCIETY

All of these examples are given to examine the inclusion of a community component to work-and-family as a means of overcoming some of the inherent limitations to a corporate-driven work-and-family model. They point to the potential benefits for work-and-family if community is to be included. The corporation cannot, and should not, continue to be looked toward as the primary sector responsible for responding to these issues. If work-and-family is a legitimate issue for all citizens, then corporate citizenship cannot be the basis for creating such responses. Work-and-family is a public policy issue and, as such, deserves to have a stronger public policy presence. The fact that the corporation has taken leadership around this issue clouds over the fact that the issues of work-and-family are universal, not confined to a particular segment of society. A family-friendly society is much preferred to a family-friendly corporation.

Perhaps more importantly, the incorporation of community recognizes that no one sector can, or should, bear the major responsibility for these issues. A more effective model brings all the stakeholders into a partnership that can best deliberate, negotiate, and implement an environment and a set of policies that maximize both family and workplace well-being. The new partnership recognizes the interdependency of families, workplaces, and communities. This does not simply mark a new stage in the development of work and family, but carves out a new paradigm that builds upon shared roles and responsibilities tied to mutual benefits.

The corporation of today, faced with global competition and a world of change on every level, recognizes that its future lies in the creation of new and creative partnerships.[12] What has worked well in the past is no longer adequate for meeting the needs and challenges of today. So, too, if the world of work-and-family is going to realize its vision, it as well will have to work toward a future where it is tied to a partnership of workplaces, families, and communities. By broadening the current conception of work-and-family, new opportunities are introduced and energetic new stakeholders become involved. What has become a ''stalled revolution,'' in the words of Arlie Hochschild, will now have the promise of new ways of achieving the goals of a work and family agenda.[13]

This revitalized model introduces opportunities for work-and-family to draw upon the creative energies at the community level, and to ensure more responsive community institutions to the complex needs of the work-and-family issues of its citizens. The real set of work-and-family issues within this model, such as life satisfaction, quality of life, and balance, are more likely to be achieved through a mutually satisfying set of negotiated roles among families, workplaces, and communities. By moving toward a family-friendly society and away from a family-friendly corporation, the potential of work-and-family for both corporations and families will be realized.

NOTES

1. R.M. Kanter, *Work and Family in the United States: A Critical Review and Agenda for Research and Policy* (New York: Russell Sage Foundation, 1977).

2. On child care, see D. Friedman, *Corporate Financial Assistance for Child Care* (New York: Conference Board, 1985). On dual-career stress, see F.S. Hall & D.T. Hall, *The Two Career Couple* (Reading, MA: Addison-Wesley, 1979).

3. On the environment, see L. Bailyn, "Changing the Conditions of Work: Responding to Increasing Work Force Diversity and New Family Patterns," in T. Kochan & M. Useem (eds.), *Transforming Organizations* (Oxford: Oxford University Press, 1992), pp. 188–206. On innovations in work flexibility, see Catalyst, *Flexible Work Arrangements: Establishing Options for Managers and Individuals* (New York: Catalyst, 1989).

4. On the exacerbation of conflict, see J.H. Greenhaus & N.J. Beutell, "Sources of Conflict between Work and Family Roles," *Academy of Management Review* 10 (1985): 76–88. On the new system, see J. Pleck, "The Work-Family Role System," *Social Problems* 24 (1977): 417–427.

5. S. Lewis & C. Cooper, *Beyond Family-Friendly Policies* (London: Demos, 1995).

6. J. Gonyea & B. Googins, "Beyond the Productivity Trap," *Human Resource Management* 31(3) (1992): 209–226.

7. See F. Miliken, J. Dutton, & J. Beyer, "Understanding Organizational Adaptation to Change: The Case of Work-Family Issues," *Human Resources Planning* 13 (1990): 91–107.

8. B. Googins, "Family Friendly: Rhetoric or Reality?" *Solutions*, June 1995, p. 20.

9. J. Greenhaus, "The Intersection of Work and Family Roles: Individual Interpersonal and Organizational Issues," in E. Goldsmith (ed.), *Work and Family: Theory, Research and Applications* (Beverly Hills, CA: Sage, 1989), pp. 23–44.

10. P. Drucker, "The Age of Social Transformation," *Atlantic Monthly*, November 1994, pp. 53–80.

11. B. Greve, *Social Policy in Europe: Latest Evolution and Perspective for the Future* (Danish National Institute of Social Research, 1992).

12. M. Porter, "The Competitive Advantage," *Harvard Business Review* 73(3) (1995): 86–95.

13. A. Hochschild, *The Second Shift* (New York: Avon, 1990).

CHAPTER 21

The Integration of Work and Family Life: Barriers and Solutions

*Jeffrey H. Greenhaus
and Saroj Parasuraman*

What *is* the work-family problem? After 20 chapters, the answer should be clear. There is no work-family problem, or at least there is no *single* work-family problem. Rather, the interaction between work and family produces a variety of issues, problems, challenges, and dilemmas for different stakeholders. What is perceived as *the* work-family problem depends upon the lens through which the situation is viewed. However, despite its different faces, we agree with Priest's assessment that the ultimate work-family dilemma represents "a difficulty in performing at a high level at work, while maintaining a strong commitment to one's family at the same time."[1]

In this concluding chapter, we attempt to integrate the perspectives presented in the book by focusing on solutions to this ultimate work-family dilemma. Before specifying these solutions, however, it is important to appreciate the barriers and obstacles to the achievement of work-family integration that are experienced by different segments of society.

BARRIERS TO THE INTEGRATION OF WORK-FAMILY LIFE

Despite the heightened awareness of work-family problems, the intense pressures on society to respond to these problems, and the proliferation of work-family programs in the corporate sector, we have confronted a "stalled revolution" in our attempt to achieve work-family integration.[2] This sluggish progress can be attributed to a number of barriers and obstacles constructed, however unwittingly, by a variety of social institutions.

A number of significant barriers to the integration of work and family lives reside within the cultures of the employers themselves. In fact, cultural barriers are perceived to be so crucial that the work-family movement has moved toward culture change within organizations as a dominant thrust of its efforts (see Chapters 7, 17, and 18). It has often been suggested that organizations have historically been designed for married men whose wives are full-time homemakers. Long hours, evening and weekend work, extensive travel, and frequent relocations have comprised the prevailing model of career advancement, which requires an unswerving willingness on the part of employees to put organizational needs ahead of personal or family needs. Who are better able to adhere to this model of career success than married men with stay-at-home wives who are fully prepared to support their husbands' careers?[3]

This view of the primacy of work, in conjunction with an autocratic managerial style, has created an organizational culture that equates time and physical presence at the workplace with productivity and commitment, and that develops external control mechanisms to assure employee compliance with work requirements. This type of culture is inimical to work-family integration because it does not provide employees with sufficient flexibility and authority to manage the tensions that arise at the intersection of their work and family lives.

Another central component of most organizations' cultures is the definition of work and family as a problem of (and created by) the family, born of individuals' (especially women's) decisions to combine work with parenthood (see Chapter 19). Hence, the problem is seen as one of the employee's making, as a failure of the employee to prevent his or her family life from intruding into the world of work, rather than as a systemic problem created by the structure of work. In addition, since many organizations devalue employees' family lives, families are seen as nuisances whose intrusions into the workplace need to be minimized rather than as a source of well-being that can actually improve employees' effectiveness at work (see Chapter 3).

It is no wonder that organizations, especially those in the early stages of family responsiveness (see Chapter 18), are more likely to make individual accommodations to valued employees on a case-by-case basis than to reexamine and restructure the way they organize their work. These individual accommodations become, in Bailyn's terms, self-reinforcing ironies that sustain the underlying culture that produces the problems in the first place (see Chapter 19).

In addition to the barriers created by the structures and cultures of work organizations, the minimal supports provided by the larger community have produced or exacerbated work-family problems. Lewis observed that national governments differ greatly in the extent to which they help their citizens manage the tensions of their work and family lives, and emphasizes the fact that "work and family systems operate within, influence, and are influenced by wider social systems, which incorporate cultural norms, state institutions, and public policies" (Chapter 9). Ideologies that vary across national cultures affect the prominence of the role played by social policy in addressing work-family issues.

Lewis noted that cultural ideologies that emphasize individual responsibility for the well-being of the family, that adhere to a male breadwinner model with women playing a full-time mothering role, and that sanction a sexual division of labor at work and at home are unlikely to encourage a proactive role for government and public policy.

Although Lewis was writing primarily about cultural variations in Europe, there are clear implications for other parts of the world (see Chapter 10 on the impact of culture on work-family issues in India). In the United States, an ideology of individualism and minimalist government intervention has resulted in relatively few publicly mandated work-family supports compared to other parts of the industrialized world. The limited presence of such initiatives as publicly supported child care and, until recently, statutory leave to care for family members, has placed more pressure on employers to provide services that, in other countries, are required or underwritten by the government. Moreover, as O'Hare has observed, the diversity of cultural backgrounds in the workforce presents a special challenge to counselors, who must realize that their clients' work and family lives may be conditioned by the particular society in which they were raised (Chapter 6).

Finally, local communities have not provided substantial help to their residents in balancing their work and family responsibilities. Many of communities' formal institutions—such as schools, libraries, and family service agencies—still operate within the outmoded model of single-earner families and are not particularly family friendly. And such informal sources of social support as family and friends are either dispersed geographically or are unavailable because of their own work demands (see Chapter 20).

In sum, there are a variety of obstacles to the achievement of work-family integration. Most of these barriers are related to cultural norms and ideologies of work organizations and of the larger society in which employees and employers operate.

SOLUTIONS TO WORK-FAMILY PROBLEMS

The chapters in this volume have provided many insights into the solution of work-family problems. Some of these solutions must come from the corporate sector, whereas other solutions must arise from the government, local communities, and employees and their families. Ultimately, the most effective solutions must involve partnerships among these segments of society.

Corporate Actions

First and foremost, the corporate world must expand its conception of why it needs to be concerned about work-family issues. The "business case" that has evolved to this point has focused primarily on recruitment and retention (see Chapters 15 and 18). Because an increasing number of employees are confronting intense work-family pressures, the argument goes, we must be responsive to their family needs if we are to attract and retain the most capable human resources.

This business case has merit and has helped to justify corporate attention and expenditures on work-family initiatives. But, as amply demonstrated in this book, it does not go far enough in seeing the potential connections between family and work. Several authors have observed that corporations will require extraordinarily committed and creative employees to permit them to survive and prosper in a turbulent and highly competitive marketplace (see Chapters 2 and 18). In order to promote this energy and commitment, employers must demonstrate concern with the whole person, with employees' "hearts, and no longer simply their hands" as described by Friedman and Johnson (Chapter 18). Organizations also must understand that employees will be more creative, more committed to the organization, and more productive if they are able to manage their work and family lives effectively than if they are in a constant state of conflict and stress.

However, this expanded business case can only succeed if the organization is willing to reexamine and change its culture to be more supportive of employees' work *and* personal lives. Creating culture change will be challenging as individuals and institutions struggle to understand and solve problems that they did not confront in earlier times. Nevertheless, persuasive cases have been made in this volume regarding the specific directions in which such cultures must move.

First, organizations must recognize that work-family issues involve work as much as family, and that many of the root causes of work-family stress stem from the way organizations and work are structured. Since the resolution of employees' work-family dilemmas can improve the long-term effectiveness of the organization, corporate initiatives must not be seen as benefits or as individual accommodations but rather as a management strategy to attain business objectives.

Moreover, organizations must pay more than lip service to the view that balancing work and family is not a woman's issue but rather a human issue. It is widely known that men participate less extensively than women in work-family programs (see Chapter 16), and that this sex difference in participation exists even in socially progressive societies (see Chapter 9). As long as they are seen as a woman's issue, organizations (especially male-dominated organizations) will marginalize work and family efforts and not permit them to enter the mainstream of organizational life.

The complex interconnections between work and family clearly have important implications for work effectiveness in organizations, and demonstrate the need for action on many fronts. For one thing, organizations will have to sever the perceived link between time and location of work, on the one hand, and employee productivity and commitment, on the other. Until employees' contributions are assessed in terms of specific work accomplishments, additional flexibility will be elusive. This focus on accomplishments will require increased communication to assure that there is mutual agreement on performance expectations, and it will demand more effective performance evaluation systems than are currently available in most organizations. Riley and McCloskey rightly indicate that an emphasis on accomplishments is essential for the management of telecommuters, who regularly conduct their work outside of the organization's physical boundaries (Chapter 13). Yet a focus on accomplishments rather than time is crucial for all employees who need to balance their work and family commitments regardless of the location of their work.

Moreover, employees must be granted more control over the content of their work. Control permits employees to satisfy some of their more significant needs for success and independence (see Chapter 3), enabling them to feel better about themselves, their employers, and their lives. In addition, some of the major impediments to the solution of work-family problems lie in the structure of the task. Bailyn (Chapter 18) and Christensen (Chapter 3) have each illustrated how empowered groups can redesign their work in ways that not only lead to greater effectiveness, but also are less likely to interfere substantially with their family responsibilities. In most business reengineering efforts, employees' personal lives are not explicitly taken into account (see Chapters 18 and 19). Bailyn concludes that "the only solution . . . is to bring the 'family' needs above the line and include them up front in the reconsideration of the way work is organized" (Chapter 19).

We are describing a culture where it is legitimate to discuss work-family issues openly, and where individuals and groups have sufficient control over their work to meet both organizational and family/personal needs. This culture not only requires substantial job redesign but is likely to involve the redesign of career systems as well. Connor, Hicks, and McGuire's discussion of competency-based career paths in a professional services firm (Chapter 15) illustrates how career path flexibility can enable employees to contribute to the organization *and* meet their work and personal needs as well.

Moreover, one of the most important obstacles to the utilization of flexible work arrangements is the employee's fear of career derailment. Employees considering telecommuting, part-time schedules, family leave, and alternative career paths are often concerned that they will be forgotten or, worse, stigmatized as uncommitted to their careers. This is one reason why men have been particularly reluctant to assume more flexible work arrangements even when they are available (Chapter 16). In the new culture, employers will not write off employees who are utilizing these opportunities for flexibility. Employee contributions will be assessed, their career needs will be discussed in light of the organization's needs, and actions to foster continued career growth will be taken. This will require considerable planning and communication on the part of the employer and the employee.

In effect, we are describing a framework for a new social contract at the workplace. Several authors in this volume have expressed serious reservations about the current version of the social contract, with its focus on employability and its limited commitment to employees. Christensen proposes a new social contract based on trust, independence, and choice (Chapter 3). Friedman and Johnson echo the importance of trust and identify the conditions necessary for a climate of trust to emerge (Chapter 2). Not surprisingly, autonomy and empowerment are on their list of requisite conditions.

This new social contract requires that organizations "rebuild the door," to use Bailyn's compelling metaphor (Chapter 19). Tall people who are forced to stoop to enter the building will likely remain stooped to navigate the premises, for buildings with small doors may have low ceilings as well. And people who spend their days with hunched shoulders will hardly be able to make substantial contributions to an organization.

To achieve significant cultural change and greater family supportiveness, organizations need to understand what constitutes excellence in the work-family arena. Fortunately, efforts toward this end are underway. Bankert and Lobel describe four "principles of excellence" developed by the Roundtable of Boston University's Center on Work and Family to help organizations assess their progress in this area (Chapter 17). Similarly, Christensen provides "standards of excellence" for six areas relevant to work/life supportiveness (Chapter 3). What is so significant about these approaches is their focus on excellence rather than on minimally acceptable behavior, because it is only through striving for higher levels of accomplishment that organizations can develop a vision of what they would like to achieve.

In discussing the importance of culture change and the restructure of work, we are not deemphasizing the significance of the more "traditional" work-family initiatives. Friedman and Johnson's "core" work-family programs include many initiatives that do not necessarily involve the redesign of jobs or organizational structures (Chapter 18). These initiatives will always will be crucial staples of a corporate work-family agenda, and Klein's analysis identifies the challenges of providing these types of initiatives to an economically and ethnically diverse workforce (Chapter 11). Nor should we forget Gutek's message regarding the usefulness of work-family initiatives that focus on the employee as a harried consumer of goods and services (Chapter 8).

Public Policy, Community, and Work-Family Initiatives

The current approach to work-family issues in the United States is driven by the corporate sector, whose development of work-family initiatives has arisen in part from self-interest and in part by default. Googins has raised some serious questions about the adequacy of this corporate-focused model, and views it as merely the first stage in an evolving conception of work and family (Chapter 20). It is difficult to disagree with Googins's assessment of the corporate model as overly limiting. Even if the corporate world adopts many of the recommendations contained in this book (an unlikely occurrence), there will still be substantial gaps in the working population's opportunity to utilize work-family initiatives. There will always be an unevenness in the extent to which private sector employers possess the awareness, resources, and inclination to become more supportive of their employees' family needs. Moreover, since organizations providing work-family initiatives are largely motivated by the business case, they may withdraw these initiatives if they believe that an economic case can no longer be made or when they are facing financial hardship.

Besides, as Googins observed, work and family balance is legitimately a public policy concern. Work-family difficulties are experienced by so many people at different socioeconomic levels, and with different employment relationships (part time, contingent, self-employed), that it is unrealistic to expect the corporate world to solve all of the problems by itself. The other major stakeholders in the work-family arena—the government, the nonprofit sector, and local communities—must do more, as must the corporate sector, of course. In short, "A family-friendly society is much preferred to a family-friendly corporation" (Chapter 20). Yet the roles to be played by these stakeholders are still unknown. They need to be discussed, debated, and ultimately, resolved.

We have seen that cultural norms within a society determine the level of involvement that its government will assume in addressing work-family issues. The prevailing norm of individualism in the United States makes it unlikely that the government will play a dominant role in the work-family arena, at least from a legislative perspective. This is not to say that legislation responding to work-family problems should not be passed and revised when necessary. Indeed, minor extensions to the Family and Medical Leave Act are currently being proposed by the administration. However, as Drake has noted, the legal system, with its focus on minimal standards and its emphasis on "thou shalt not's," will not solve work-family problems by itself (Chapter 12).

Perhaps the most useful role for the government to assume is to place the work-family issue in the public eye, assure that the issue gets the attention and debate it requires, and assist other segments of society to plan and implement work-family initiatives. For example, the federal government could form a Work-Family Coordinating Council composed of representatives from the corporate world, unions, academia, research and advocacy organizations, and community institutions. This council could begin to define the direction in which the work-family agenda should move and specify the roles of the major stakeholders in the movement. The council could also organize conferences on research and practice to share recently discovered knowledge and issue an annual "state of the union" assessment of progress in the work-family arena.

Perhaps most importantly, the coordinating council could encourage and fund (through public and private moneys) partnership pilot programs that establish and solidify relationships among the major stakeholders. These projects could involve partnerships between corporations and unions, between corporations and community institutions, and among different institutions within the corporate and community sectors.

Actions by Individuals and Families

Regardless of the level of corporate, government, and community involvement, individual employees have an endless number of decisions to make, including what job to accept, what career path to pursue, and what amount of time to devote to work. At home, many of these same individuals and their families must decide on a desired lifestyle and standard of living, the level of priority given to each partner's career, and a host of issues regarding the expenditure of time in life's many roles. All of these decisions can have substantial effects on the relationship between their work and family lives.

The role of the individual and the family in the work-family arena should not, and has not, been neglected. One of the principles of excellence put forth by Bankert and Lobel contains the assertion that "The management of work/personal life effectiveness is a shared responsibility" (Chapter 17). Their emphasis on employee ownership of this process is consistent with Christensen's concept of self-management, which requires employees to understand their values, manage their lives according to these values, and manage their time effectively (Chapter 3). Miller demonstrates the importance of self-insight and the ability to prioritize life roles in juggling work, family, and personal concerns (Chapter 5), and Phillips highlights the role of the consultant in helping employees define and resolve their work-family problems (Chapter 4).

The concepts of shared responsibility and self-management are compatible with the recent emphasis on individual responsibility for career management.[4] Career management has been viewed as the problem-solving process by which individuals can make informed decisions about their work lives, and as we have seen throughout this book, career and family issues are inextricably connected.[5] Therefore, individuals need to develop competencies to help them learn more about themselves and their environment, to set personally meaningful objectives, and to develop and implement plans to achieve these objectives.

Effective career management, especially in today's world, also involves linking family needs to career decision making so that work and family roles are in balance. Families face critical decisions regarding the establishment of an equitable division of labor within the home. Although dual-earner men participate more extensively in household and child care activities than in the past, there is still a sizable gender gap to be overcome. Many husbands and fathers will have to change their attitudes and behavior if women are to achieve a balance between their work and family responsibilities that is consistent with their underlying values. In addition, the development of a more egalitarian attitude and a greater sensitivity to work-family concerns should enhance men's ability to deal effectively with employees from diverse cultures and lifestyles. Finally, family members, men and women alike, will need to develop more effective communication skills so that they can provide each other with the type and amount of social support that they require.

CONCLUSIONS

All facets of society must contribute to the solution of work-family problems. Individuals and families must proactively expand their repertoire of coping resources through cooperative efforts with neighbors, friends, and coworkers who have experienced similar dilemmas. Employers need to modify their cultures and their practices to assure that their employees can perform at a high level of effectiveness while remaining strongly committed to their families. The government must assert the importance of families to the health and well-being of society in a policy statement that corresponds to the public pronouncements made by candidates seeking election to public office. The government must also play a more active role in framing the issues, communicating their urgency to other stakeholders, and facilitating the establishment of collaborative partnerships to address the problems. And local community institutions must examine their relevance and revise their goals and practices to be more compatible with the needs of their residents.

It is impossible to predict how extensively and at what pace these changes will occur, or even whether they will occur at all. If they do not take place, we can predict that employers will encounter deteriorating workforce effectiveness, and that employees and their families will experience even higher levels of frustration and stress than they currently experience. How can society prevent such dysfunctions from materializing?

Perhaps the answer lies in the concept of the "common good" expressed so eloquently by Wohl (Chapter 2). We, as a society, need to take a panoramic view of the work-family landscape and identify shared values around which all segments of society—private and public, individual and institutional—can rally. Whether the common good exists around the needs of children, as Wohl believes, or, more generally, around the notion of achieving a balanced, healthy life—with the ability to work and to love—the vision must be sufficiently compelling to arouse our emotions, activate our will, and enable us to risk change so that we can accomplish together what none of us can accomplish separately.

NOTES

1. See the quote by Priest in Chapter 2.
2. See a recent discussion of A. Hochschild's *The Second Shift* (New York: Avon, 1990) by J. Smolowe, "The Stalled Revolution," *Time*, May 6, 1966, p. 63.
3. It should not be surprising, then, that single-earner fathers earn greater compensation than dual-earner fathers, as Brett's research (Chapter 14) indicates.
4. R.H. Waterman, J.A. Waterman, & B.A. Collard, "Toward a Career-Resilient Workforce," *Harvard Business Review* 72 (July-August 1994): 87–95.
5. On career management as a problem-solving process, see J.H. Greenhaus & G.A. Callanan, *Career Management*, 2nd ed. (Forth Worth, TX: Dryden Press, 1994).

Selected Bibliography

SELECTED READINGS ON WORK-FAMILY ISSUES

Bailyn, L. *Breaking the Mold: Women, Men, and Time in the New Corporate World.* New York: Free Press, 1993.

Barnett, R.C., & Rivers, C. *She Works, He Works.* San Francisco: Harper, 1996.

Bowen, G.L., & Pittman, J.F. *The Work and Family Interface: Toward a Contextual Effects Perspective.* Minneapolis: National Council on Family Relations, 1995.

Brett, J.M., Stroh, L.K., & Reilly, A.H. *Impact of Social Shifts and Corporate Change on Employee Relocation.* Washington, DC: Employee Relations Council, 1990.

Crosby, F.J. (ed.). *Spouse, Parent, Worker: Gender and Multiple Roles.* New Haven, CT: Yale University Press, 1987.

Eckenrode, J., & Gore, S. *Stress between Work and Family.* New York: Plenum Press, 1990.

Ferber, M.A., & Farrell, B. *Work and Family: Policies for a Changing Workforce.* Washington, DC: National Academy Press, 1991.

Galinsky, E., Bond, J.T., & Friedman, D.E. *The Changing Workforce: Highlights of the National Study.* New York: Families and Work Institute, 1993.

Galinsky, E., Friedman, D.E., & Hernandez, C.A. *The Corporate Reference Guide to Work-Family Programs.* New York: Families and Work Institute, 1991.

Gerson, K. *No Man's Land: Men's Changing Commitments to Family and Work.* New York: Basic, 1993.

Gilbert, L.A. *Two Careers/One Family.* Newbury Park, CA: Sage, 1993.

Gupta, N., & Jenkins, G.D. "Dual-Career Couples: Stress, Stressors, Strain, and Strategies." In T. Beehr & R.S. Bhagat (eds.), *Human Stress and Cognition in Organizations.* New York: John Wiley, 1985, pp. 141–175.

Gutek, B.A., Repetti, R.L., & Silver, D.L. "Nonwork Roles and Stress at Work." In C.L. Cooper & R. Payne (eds.), *Causes, Coping, and Consequences of Stress at Work.* New York: John Wiley, 1988, pp. 141–174.

Hogg, L., & Harker, C. *The Family-Friendly Employer: Examples from Europe.* London: Daycare Trust, 1992.

Jackson, S.E. & Associates. *Diversity in the Workplace: Human Resources Initiatives.* New York: Guilford Press, 1993.

Kofodimos, J.R. *Balancing Act.* San Francisco: Jossey-Bass, 1993.

Kumar, U. "Indian Women and Work: A Paradigm for Research." *Psychological Studies* 31 (2) (1986): 147–160.

Lewis, S., Izraeli, D.N., & Hootsmans, H. (eds.). *Dual-Earner Families: International Perspectives.* London: Sage.

Lewis, S., & Lewis, J. *The Work-Family Challenge: Rethinking Employment.* London: Sage, 1996.

Magid, R.Y. *When Mothers and Fathers Work: Creative Strategies for Balancing Career and Family.* New York: AMACOM, 1987.

Making Work Flexible: Policy to Practice. New York: Catalyst, 1996.

Milliken, F., Dutton, J., & Beyer, J. "Understanding Organizational Adaptation to Change: The Case of Work-Family Issues." *Human Resources Planning* 13 (1990): 91–107.

Powell, G.N. *Women and Men in Management* (2d ed.). Newbury Park, CA: Sage, 1993.

Pritchett, P. *New Work Habits for a Radically Changing World.* Dallas: Pritchett & Associates, Inc., 1994.

Sekaran, U. *Dual-Career Families.* Newbury Park, CA: Sage, 1986.

Sekaran, U., & Leong, F. *Woman Power.* Newbury Park, CA: Sage, 1993.

Stoltz-Loike, M. *Dual-Career Couples: New Perspectives in Counseling.* Virginia: ACA, 1992.

Walker, L.S., Rozee-Koker, P., & Wallston, B.S. "Social Policy and the Dual-Career Family: Bringing the Social Context into Counseling." *The Counseling Psychologist* 15 (1987): 97–121.

Zedeck, S. *Work, Families, and Organizations.* San Francisco: Jossey-Bass, 1992.

SELECTED PUBLICATIONS OF THE WORK AND FAMILY RESEARCH GROUP, DEPARTMENT OF MANAGEMENT, COLLEGE OF BUSINESS AND ADMINISTRATION, DREXEL UNIVERSITY

Granrose, C.S., Parasuraman, S., & Greenhaus, J.H. "A Proposed Model of Support Provided by Two-Earner Couples." *Human Relations* 45 (1992): 1367–1393.

Greenhaus, J.H. "The Intersection of Work and Family Roles: Individual, Interpersonal, and Organizational Issues." In E. Goldsmith (ed.), *Work and Family: Theory, Research, and Applications.* Beverly Hills, CA: Sage, 1989, pp. 23–44.

Greenhaus, J.H., & Beutell, N.J. "Sources of Conflict between Work and Family Roles." *Academy of Management Review* 10 (1985): 76–88.

Greenhaus, J.H., & Callanan, G.A. *Career Management* (2d ed.). Fort Worth: The Dryden Press, 1994.

Greenhaus, J.H., & Parasuraman, S. "A Work-Nonwork Interactive Perspective of Stress and Its Consequences." *Journal of Organizational Behavior Management* 8(2) (1986): 37–60.

Greenhaus, J.H., & Parasuraman, S. "Work-Family Conflict and Social Support." In

M.J. Davidson & R.J. Burke (eds.), *Women in Management: Current Research Issues*. London: Paul Chapman, 1994, pp. 213–229.

Parasuraman, S., & Greenhaus, J.H. "Personal Portrait: The Lifestyle of the Woman Manager." In E.A. Fagenson (ed.), *Women in Management: Trends, Issues, and Challenges in Managerial Diversity* (Vol. 4). Newbury Park, CA: Sage, 1993.

Parasuraman, S., & Greenhaus, J.H. "Determinants of Support Provided and Received by Partners in Two-Career Relationships." In L.A. Heslop (ed.), *The Ties That Bind*. Canadian Consortium of Management Schools, 1994, pp. 121–145.

Parasuraman, S., Greenhaus, J.H., & Granrose, C. "Role Stressors, Social Support, and Well-Being in Two-Career Couples." *Journal of Organizational Behavior* 13 (1992): 339–356.

Parasuraman, S., Greenhaus, J.H., Rabinowitz, S., Bedeian, A.G., & Mossholder, K.W. "Work and Family Variables as Mediators of the Relationship between Wives' Employment and Husbands' Well-Being." *Academy of Management Journal* 32 (1989): 185–201.

Parasuraman, S., Purohit, Y.S., Godshalk, V.M., & Beutell, N.J. "Work and Family Variables, Entrepreneurial Career Success, and Psychological Well-Being." *Journal of Vocational Behavior* 48 (1996): 275–300.

Index

About the Editors

SAROJ PARASURAMAN received her Ph.D. in organizational behavior from the State University of New York at Buffalo, and is currently Professor of Management at Drexel University. Her research interests include work-related stress, job attitudes, turnover, and career development of women and minorities. In recent years, her research has focused on work-family relationships especially as they relate to dual-career couples, and the role of social support processes in the work-family stress process. Parasuraman's research has been widely published in the leading academic journals such as the *Academy of Management Journal, Journal of Vocational Behavior, Journal of Organizational Behavior, Work and Occupations, Group and Organization Studies, Journal of Management, Journal of Organizational Behavior Management, Organizational Behavior and Human Decision Processes, MIS Quarterly, Journal of Systems Management,* and *International Journal of Man-Machine Studies.* Her publications include several book chapters and numerous scholarly papers presented at national and international conferences. Parasuraman is a member of the Academy of Management, and serves on the Editorial Review Board of the *Journal of Vocational Behavior.*

JEFFREY H. GREENHAUS received his Ph.D. in industrial-organizational psychology from New York University and is currently the William A. Mackie Professor of Commerce and Engineering and a Professor of Management at Drexel University. His research interests include work-family relationships, career management, and the management of diversity. His research findings have been published widely in the leading scholarly journals, and he is coauthor (with Gerard Callanan) of *Career Management,* now in its second edition. He is currently completing (with Stewart Friedman and Saroj Parasuraman) *Crossing*

Great Divides: Business Professionals' Lives in Transition, which examines the impact of family life on career achievements and the influence of career experiences on personal and family well-being. Greenhaus has served on the editorial boards of the *Journal of Applied Psychology, Journal of Vocational Behavior, International Journal of Career Management*, and *Lifestyle: Family and the Economy*, and was Associate Editor of the *Journal of Vocational Behavior* from 1993 to 1995.

About the Contributors

LOTTE BAILYN is the T. Wilson Professor of Management at MIT's Sloan School of Management, and, for 1995–1997, the Matina S. Horner Distinguished Visiting Professor at the Radcliffe Public Policy Institute. Her research deals with the interrelation between managerial practice and employee lives. Her work centers on technical and managerial professionals ("knowledge workers"), and has dealt with such workplace innovations as telecommuting, flexible scheduling, and family benefits. She is author of *Living with Technology: Issues at Mid-Career* (1980), coauthor of *Working with Careers* (1984), and, most recently, author of *Breaking the Mold: Women, Men, and Time in the New Corporate World* (1993). She has a B.A. from Swarthmore College in mathematics and a Ph.D. in social psychology from Harvard University.

ELLEN C. BANKERT is the Associate Director for Corporate Programs at the Center on Work and Family at Boston University. Her primary responsibility is managing the center's Work and Family Roundtable, a national membership organization of 35 corporations recognized for their leadership in the work/family field. Her other responsibilities in the corporate programs area include the New England Work and Family Association, the Leadership Institute, and corporate-sponsored research and special projects. Prior to the formation of the center in 1990, Ms. Bankert was the Assistant Director of the Human Resources Policy Institute at Boston University. She received an M.B.A. from Boston University and a B.A. in economics from St. Lawrence University.

JEANNE M. BRETT is the DeWitt W. Buchanan, Jr., Professor of Dispute Resolution and Organizations at the J.L. Kellogg Graduate School of Management, Northwestern University. She divides her research time between the study

of negotiation and dispute resolution, especially in cross-cultural settings, and
the study of the career experiences of male and female managers, with particular
emphasis on how family affects career. Dr. Brett received a Ph.D. in industrial/
organizational psychology from the University of Illinois and an A.M. degree
in industrial and labor relations from the same institution. She has published
widely on topics such as employee relocation, psychological involvement in
work and family, salary progression of female managers, and salary progression
of male managers with employed wives.

PERRY M. CHRISTENSEN is currently the Director of Human Resource Strategy and Planning at Merck & Co. Inc., with corporate responsibilities for human
resource strategy and policy, succession planning, and work/life initiatives. Prior
to his assuming current responsibilities, Perry held positions in a wide variety
of human resource functions at Merck. He has lived and worked for eight years
outside of the United States, including three years in Norway, where he was
responsible for all human resource activities for the Scandinavian region, and
three years in Montreal, with responsibilities for all the company divisions
within the Canadian market. Perry received an M.S. in Organizational Behavior
from Brigham Young University in 1982. He is a member of the Conference
Board's Work and Family Research Advisory Council and Boston University's
Work and Family Roundtable. He is also the cochair for the Wharton/Merck
Work-Life Roundtable, and his collaboration and research with the Wharton
School on work-life issues has been profiled in the *Wall Street Journal, Finan-
cial Times*, the *New York Times*, and numerous trade journals.

MONIQUE CONNOR is a Senior Manager in the Chairman's Office of Price
Waterhouse LLP, where she works closely with the Vice Chair on human resource strategies and initiatives for the firm. Her current projects include issues
related to flexible work arrangements, diversity in general and women's issues
in particular, career models, creation of learning organizations, and other strategic intellectual capital issues. Prior to receiving her M.B.A. degree from Stanford University in 1995, Connor, who is also a Certified Public Accountant,
served in the Financial Services Industry Practice of Price Waterhouse as a tax
adviser to clients in the investment company industry. She received her B.S.
from the Wharton School of the University of Pennsylvania.

EILEEN DRAKE is a Partner in the Portland law firm of Stoel Rives LLP,
where she concentrates in all areas of labor and employment law. She has also
been an associate with Clark, Klein & Beaumont in Detroit, and she spent three
years with Tektronix, Inc., as Legal Counsel for Employment Matters and then
as Director, Employee Relations. She has been an adjunct professor of law at
Lewis and Clark College, is a frequent lecturer on employment law issues, has
published in legal and management journals, and is a member of the editorial

review board of the *Oregon Labor Letter*. Drake received a B.A. from Mundelein College and a J.D. from the University of Michigan.

DANA E. FRIEDMAN is Cofounder and Copresident of the Families and Work Institute, a national, nonprofit organization that conducts research on business, government, and community efforts to help people balance their work and family lives. She was previously affiliated with the Conference Board and the Carnegie Corporation of New York. She has published widely and is the author of "Child Care for Employees' Kids" (*Harvard Business Review*) and "Elder Care: The Employee Benefit of the 1990's?" (*Across the Board*). She also writes "The Juggling Act," a monthly column in *Working Mother* magazine. Friedman has a B.S. in Child Development from Cornell University, an M.S. degree in Early Childhood Education from the University of Maryland, and a Ph.D. in Social Policy from Harvard University.

BRADLEY K. GOOGINS is the Founder and Director of the Boston University Center on Work and Family and Associate Professor at the Graduate School of Social Work. The center is engaged in a variety of research projects and policy initiatives that speak to work-life issues. It has created the Work and Family Roundtable of 40 leading corporations in the work-life arena, and, through partnerships with other organizations, has been active in developing international initiatives addressing a global set of work and family issues. Googins has published extensively on work-family issues, employee assistance programs, and workplace substance abuse, including: *Balancing Job and Homelife: Changes over Time in a Corporation* (1994), *Work/Family Conflicts: Private Lives— Public Responses* (1991), and *Linking the Worlds of Family and Work: Family Dependent Care and Workers' Performance* (1990). He received a Ph.D. in Social Policy and Research from the Heller School at Brandeis University and M.S.W. and B.A. degrees from Boston College.

BARBARA A. GUTEK is Professor and Head of the Department of Management and Policy at the University of Arizona. She received a Ph.D. from the University of Michigan and is author or editor of 11 books and over 80 articles on topics such as women and work, job satisfaction, the computerization of work, survey research methods, and service organizations. A recipient of research grants from the National Institutes of Mental Health and the National Science Foundation, Gutek is a fellow of the American Psychological Association and the American Psychological Society, chaired the Women in Management Division of the Academy of Management, is president-elect of the Society for the Psychological Study of Social Issues, and has served on the editorial review boards of numerous journals. In 1994, she received two awards from the American Psychological Association (the Division 35 Heritage award and the "Distinguished Leader for Women in Psychology" award) as well as the Sage

Scholarship award, presented by the Women in Management Division of the Academy of Management.

KAREN HOOKS, C.P.A., Ph.D., is the Price Waterhouse LLP Practice Issues Research Professor at Florida Atlantic University. For more than 15 years, she has been involved in research regarding human resources, women's upward mobility, and work-family balance in the accounting profession. Hooks's research has been published in leading academic and professional journals such as *Accounting, Organizations, and Society, Auditing: A Journal of Practice and Theory, Behavioral Research in Accounting, Research in Accounting Ethics, Accounting Horizons*, the *Journal of Accounting*, and the *CPA Journal*. She has held numerous national leadership roles in the American Institute of CPAs, American Accounting Association, and American Woman's Society of CPAs. In addition, she serves in editorial and editorial board positions for numerous journals.

ARLENE A. JOHNSON is Vice President of the Families and Work Institute, a nonprofit research and planning organization committed to developing new approaches for balancing work and family roles. She provides needs assessments, managerial training, and consultation for the institute's corporate clients, and also conducts policy research on a broad range of issues related to the changing demographics of the workforce. Previously affiliated with the Conference Board, she was Program Director for workforce research and editor of the *Work-Family Roundtable*. Her publications include titles such as, "Strategies for Promoting a Work-Family Agenda" and "The Emerging Role of the Work-Family Manager." Ms. Johnson graduated magna cum laude from Mount Holyoke College; she then earned an M.Div. from Union Theological Seminary and an M.B.A. from Rutgers Graduate School of Management.

DONNA KLEIN is the Director of Work-Life Programs at Marriott International, Washington, DC, where she is responsible for the planning, development, implementation, and management of corporatewide work-life initiatives to address the needs of Marriott's diverse workforce. Under her direction, Marriott has created a comprehensive list of work-life programs, and she has widened the focus programs of that support from the professional and managerial population to comprehensive services for the lower-income population in the service industry, serving as national spokesperson in the arena of work-life initiatives for the lower-income worker. Active at the national level, she is a founding member of FlexGroup, a corporate partnership organization for workforce flexibility, and President of the Board of Directors of Central Atlanta Hospitality Child Care, a nonprofit organization. In 1994, Klein was appointed to the National Academy of Science Child Care Workshop Project to help define the federal research agenda for child care.

MEERA KOMARRAJU earned two Ph.D. degrees, one in applied social psychology from the University of Cincinnati and the other in organizational behavior from Osmania University, India. She is currently an adjunct faculty member with the Department of Management at Southern Illinois University, Carbondale. Her research and teaching span three countries—India (Osmania University), Malaysia (University Sains Malaysia), and the United States (University of Cincinnati and Southern Illinois University)—and includes executive training and consulting. Komarraju's research interests are in the areas of work-family relationships, cross-cultural studies, and more recently, quality-related issues in rural health care services. She has published in the *Journal of Applied Behavioral Science, Managerial Psychology, Indian Journal of Applied Psychology*, and *Psychology Research Bulletin*, among others, and has presented scholarly papers at various regional and national meetings and conferences.

MARCIA BRUMIT KROPF is a Vice President and codirector of the Research and Advisory Services Department at Catalyst, where she has directed a wide range of research projects, including proprietary environmental assessment studies, in a number of companies and professional firms. Recipient of a Ph.D. in educational communications from New York University, Kropf currently serves as the principal researcher for Catalyst's study, *The Reorganizing of Work: Effective Strategies for a Changing Workforce*. She led the project team responsible for creating Catalyst's 1996 guide to implementing flexible work arrangements (*Making Work Flexible: Policy to Practice*), and is the primary author of *Child Care in Corporate America: Quality Indicators and Model Programs* and *Flexible Work Arrangements II: Succeeding with Part-Time Options*. She has made numerous presentations and speeches at professional meetings and conferences, and has been interviewed frequently by publications such as the *New York Times*, the *Washington Post, Working Mother*, and *Fortune*.

SUZAN LEWIS received her Ph.D. in organizational psychology from the School of Management, University of Manchester Institute of Science and Technology (United Kingdom), and is currently Reader in Psychology at Manchester Metropolitan University. Her research interests are in the interrelated areas of work, family, community, and organizational change. She has published widely on these topics in academic and professional journals and books and has presented her research at numerous national and international conferences in Europe and North America. Dr. Lewis is coauthor (with Cary Cooper) of *Career Couples* (1989) and *Managing the New Workforce: The Challenge of Dual Income Families* (1994), coeditor (with Dafna Izraeli and Helen Hootsmans) of *Dual Earner Families: International Perspectives* (1992), and coeditor, with Jeremy Lewis, of *The Work Family Challenge: Rethinking Employment* (1996). She is coordinator of a European Commission–funded Roundtable on workplace practice for the reconciliation of work and family.

SHARON A. LOBEL (Ph.D., Harvard University) is an Associate Professor of Management at Seattle University. Lobel's research focuses on the many aspects of managing diversity and work-life in organizations. She is a Research Fellow at the Work and Family Roundtable, established by the Center on Work and Family at Boston University. As a member of the Wharton-Merck Work-Life Roundtable, she has been active in efforts to develop training materials for business schools and corporations on work-life concerns. She is a member of the Research Advisory Panel at Catalyst for a study of the implementation of flexible work arrangements. She is an Associate Editor of *Human Resources Management* and a member of the editorial board of *Academy of Management Journal*. Her publications have appeared in these journals as well as *Academy of Management Review, Journal of Cross-Cultural Psychology, Organizational Dynamics*, and elsewhere. Lobel's forthcoming publications include a coedited book, *Managing Diversity: Human Resource Strategies for Transforming the Workplace.*

DONNA WEAVER McCLOSKEY is a doctoral candidate specializing in decision sciences (management information systems) at Drexel University, and is currently a Senior Lecturer at Widener University. Her research interests include international information systems, technology acceptance, and the impact of technology on changing work roles. Donna's research currently focuses on the work and personal outcomes of telecommuting. Her work has been presented at regional, national, and international conferences and published in numerous conference proceedings.

TERRY McGUIRE is Director of Compensation Strategies for Price Waterhouse LLP. In this role, he is responsible for working with each of the firm's service lines to develop reward systems that support their human resources and business objectives. He has held a number of positions during his 17-year career with Price Waterhouse including service as the firms's Director of Diversity Programs, Director of Finance and Administration for the Detroit Group, and as a Tax Senior Manager in Detroit. McGuire holds a degree in business administration from the University of Michigan and is a Certified Public Accountant. He is a member of the American Institute of Certified Public Accountants, where he serves on the Minority Initiatives Committee, the National Association of Black Accountants, the American Compensation Association, and the Society for Human Resources Management. McGuire was also a charter member of the Conference Board's Council on Workforce Diversity.

SUSAN MILLER is a working mother juggling the demands of family, community, and career. Her involvement in the local community includes serving as an active member of the Junior League and a volunteer for the United Jewish Appeal. Ms. Miller is currently Vice President of Shopping Services for Bloomingdale's, where she manages all of the special services offered to customers, including the bridal registry, the interior design studios, corporate services, and personal shoppers. Prior to joining Bloomingdale's in 1993, Miller held positions at Avon Products, Booz-Allen & Hamilton, and the former General Foods Corp. She earned her M.B.A. from the Stanford Graduate School of Business and has a joint undergraduate degree (B.A. and B.S.) from the University of Pennsylvania Wharton School.

MARIANNE O'HARE, Director of Counseling and Psychological Services at Drew University for the past 10 years, has also been in private practice and teaching. A licensed psychologist with a cognitive-behavioral theoretical orientation, O'Hare's expertise is in posttraumatic stress disorder and coping. She received a Ph.D. in Counseling Psychology from Seton Hall University, and her research interests include stress and coping, transition and adjustment, decision making, women and work, and work-family relationships. She has presented papers at several major professional conferences, written book chapters, and published articles in such journals as the *Journal of Counseling Psychology, Journal of Vocational Behavior, Journal of Counseling and Development*, and *Journal of College Student Personnel*. O'Hare is a member of the American Psychological Association (APA) and APA Divisions 17 (Counseling Psychology) and 35 (Psychology of Women), the New Jersey Psychological Association, and the American Counseling Association.

TYLER PHILLIPS, founder of the Partnership Group (TPG), Inc., is its Chief Executive Officer and leader of its executive management team. While he is responsible for all functional areas, he focuses his energies on the services provided to employers. Prior to founding TPG in 1982, Tyler served as an executive with the General Electric Company for 14 years and for 2 years as the administrative director of a Delaware Valley human resources training firm. He is a recognized and published expert on productivity and has taught on a part-time basis at several colleges. His expertise on the subject of employer-supported dependent care makes him a frequent speaker at national and local conferences. Tyler is a member of the Society for Human Resource Management, NAEYC, and the American Society on Aging—Business Forum on Aging Governing Council, and a founding member of the Delaware Valley Child Care Council. Tyler has a B.S. in economics and an M.B.A. in management.

GARY N. POWELL received his Ph.D. in organizational behavior from the University of Massachusetts-Amherst and is currently Professor of Management at the University of Connecticut. His research primarily addresses issues related to diversity in the workplace, especially gender-related issues. He is author of *Women and Men in Management*, now in its second edition, and *Gender and Diversity in the Workplace: Learning Activities and Exercises*, has published over 60 articles and presented over 70 papers at professional conferences, and has served on the editorial boards of *Academy of Management Review* and *Acad-*

emy of Management Executive. Powell has served as Chairperson of the Women in Management Division of the Academy of Management and has won the Sage Distinguished Service Award for his contributions to the division. He has also served on the Board of Governors, and as CoChair of the Status of Minorities Task Force for the academy, and is a past president of the Eastern Academy of Management. A former project engineer and systems analyst with General Electric, he has provided management training and development for many companies and conducted numerous other workshops.

FRANCINE RILEY has been responsible for diversity at GTE Corporation since 1993 and was appointed Practice Leader—Organization Effectiveness in July 1995. In addition to her previous responsibilities for workforce diversity and work and family initiatives, Riley now focuses on alternative work design strategies, cross-business work climate and culture integration, and developing workforce cultural competencies to support GTE's global expansion efforts. Before joining GTE, she was a Professor in the Rutgers University Graduate School of Education. She has been a keynote speaker at many conferences, professional organizations, and civic groups on workforce diversity issues, and serves on the boards of the New York State Council for Economic Education and the American Association for Collegiate Schools of Business. Active in numerous professional and cultural organizations, she is listed in *Who's Who in Human Resources*. Riley has a B.S. from Tufts University and an Ed.M. in Psychology and Ed.D. in Educational Psychology from Rutgers.

FAITH WOHL is Director of the Office of Workplace Initiatives at the U.S. General Services Administration, the office that oversees the federal government's national system of child care centers for federal workers and its telecommuting initiative, as well as other programs designed to make the federal workplace more effective and family friendly. Prior to her appointment to the William Clinton administration, she had a career in the business world for more than 35 years. A major part of Wohl's career was the 20 years spent at the DuPont Company in Wilmington, DE, where, as Director of Community Affairs, she first become involved in work and family issues in the mid-1980s. As the first Director of a new organization within Human Resources, she pioneered many of DuPont's work and family benefits, policies, and programs. A frequent speaker and writer on work and family topics, she has been profiled in *Business Week*, the *Wall Street Journal, Working Woman Magazine*, and *New Woman Magazine*. Wohl has been widely quoted in national magazines and newspapers, has appeared on leading radio and television programs, and has testified before Congress on workplace issues and child care needs.

ISBN 1-56720-038-9